THEIR WORD
IS LAW

THEIR WORD IS LAW

Bestselling Lawyer-Novelists
Talk About Their Craft

Stephen M. Murphy

BERKLEY BOOKS, NEW YORK

B

A Berkley Book
Published by The Berkley Publishing Group
A division of Penguin Putnam Inc.
375 Hudson Street
New York, New York 10014

Collection copyright © 2002 by Stephen M. Murphy
John Grisham interview copyright © 2002 by Owen Prell
Book design by Tiffany Kukec
Cover design by Pyrographx

PRINTING HISTORY
Berkley trade paperback edition / July 2002

Visit our website at
www.penguinputnam.com

Library of Congress Cataloging-in-Publication Data

Murphy, Stephen M.
Their word is law / Stephen M. Murphy with a foreword by Steve Martini.
p. cm.
ISBN 0-425-18478-1
1. Legal stories—History and criticism.   2. Legal stories—Authorship. 3. Law in
literature.   4. Novelists, American—20th century—Interviews.   I. Title.

PN3448.L4 M87   2002
813'.5409355—dc21
2001056097

PRINTED IN THE UNITED STATES OF AMERICA

10   9   8   7   6   5   4   3   2   1

To Patty, who has generously given me her love, support, and patience for over two decades, and has blessed me with four wonderful children.

CONTENTS

FOREWORD

Lawyers have always been storytellers. What is a trial but the story of conflict between two parties? Law schools teach budding trial lawyers to use the elements of good storytelling to persuade juries. First, you must have a theme, they are told. The theme should be simply stated. In an auto accident case, something like, "One careless moment can cause a lifetime of pain." The lawyer should reinforce that theme throughout the trial from jury selection through closing argument. Jurors may not remember the details of a case but they will keep in mind the theme.

Other storytelling techniques are used in the opening statement. The lawyer must tell the jury what he believes the evidence will show. To be effective, this preview of the trial should hook the jury right away, just as the first chapter of a novel should make the reader want to keep turning the pages. An effective opening statement not only will make the jury want to know more about the case, but should also persuade the jury to the lawyer's position. But this must be done carefully, not by arguing the position, which is reserved for the closing, but by structuring information in a subtle yet convincing way. Certain facts must be presented in any trial (and in any novel). But in what order do you present them? What "spin" do you put on those facts? The trial lawyer should not discuss everything in the opening statement. There has to be some information the jury is not told. The lawyer must whet, not satiate, the jury's appetite.

The jury must also care about the client just as readers must care about a writer's protagonist. To care, a jury must know certain details about the client's background. What kind of person is the client? What life experiences has he or she had that will move the jury to empathize with the client? The lawyer can bring out this information from different witnesses, emphasizing those facts that will reinforce the theme. If the jury buys the theme and empathizes with the client, then the lawyer is more likely to get a favorable verdict.

Given the parallels between trials and storytelling, it should not be surprising that so many lawyers have turned to fiction writing. What is surprising is the breadth and quality of the writing. In *Their Word Is Law,* Stephen Murphy has compiled an impressive collection of interviews of lawyers, like myself, who have made the transition from law to literature. Some, like John Grisham and Scott Turow, have become household names. Others, like Richard Dooling and Louis Begley, have received literary acclaim without becoming mainstays on the bestseller lists.

Literary legend Louis Auchincloss eschews the term *lawyer-author.* He is an author, period. "I draw a very strong distinction between novelists and lawyers," he tells Murphy. "I don't interconnect the terms at all." He is quite right, of course. Some of us have used our legal background as an entrée to writing. The law and lawyers inform our work. Our titles tend to be legal phrases—*Compelling Evidence* or *Burden of Proof.* Our publishers put gavels and scales of justice on the dust jackets.

The current popularity of legal fiction can be traced to Scott Turow's *Presumed Innocent.* Published in 1987, the story of a prosecutor charged with murdering his former lover enthralled millions of readers. Turow took what on the surface was a standard murder mystery and put a lawyer right in the middle, as not only the accused but the narrator as well. What a brilliant stroke! Although I had written one novel before *Presumed Innocent* came out, I have to admit that I was greatly influenced by this engrossing story. Reading through these interviews, I realize I certainly was not alone.

Ironically, Turow, the moving force behind the popularity of lawyer-authors, was an author before he became a lawyer. A graduate of the Stanford Creative Writing Masters Program, he wrote one novel and published short stories in literary journals before going to law school. The same is true of other lawyer-authors: Jay Brandon earned a master's degree in writing from Johns Hopkins; Richard North Patterson studied creative writing under Jesse Hill Ford; and George Higgins wrote fourteen novels, most before going to law school, before getting published.

Whether "authors" or "lawyer-authors," we share a common bond: we were interviewed by Stephen Murphy. Although most successful authors are interviewed many times during publicity campaigns, rarely do we encounter an interviewer who asks probing, detailed, and incisive questions. It is rarer still to find an interviewer who has so carefully read your book! Mr. Murphy is that kind of interviewer. A prominent civil trial lawyer, he obviously did his homework before each interview. His questions get to the heart of the story and the characters. And he doesn't shy away from tough questions.

He has a knack for zeroing in on implausible plot turns. In prosecutor Christine McGuire's novel, *Until Death Do Us Part,* the first two victims' bodies are found in public places while the third is found at a school. The police do not bother to question any employees of the school, where (of course) it turns out the murderer works. When Murphy asked McGuire how that was possible, she responded, "Only a lawyer would ask that question." Perhaps, but not all lawyers. Only a lawyer who had carefully read the book.

His reading of Richard North Patterson's *Degree of Guilt* was so careful that he predicted the plot of Patterson's next book. "I know you're going to write another novel," Murphy said, "and I would guess it's going to be a love affair between Christopher Paget and Teresa Peralta. Is that where you're going?" Patterson's answer was similar to McGuire's: "You're not a lawyer for nothing."

Mr. Murphy's legal expertise also allows him to spot procedural mistakes in a lawsuit. Famed trial lawyer John Martel, winner of one hundred trials in a row, wrote about a personal injury case in his first novel, *Partners.* He must have cringed when Murphy wondered how a defendant could file a demurrer after an appearance. "Demurrer after an appearance—did I do that?" Martel told Murphy, laughing. "Steve, you're the first person to catch that and there should have been a motion to strike. That's amazing. I have no alibi or defense; it's wrong."

Although all of the authors interviewed share a legal background, they are still a diverse group. There is the famed "L" trio of female authors—Lisa Scottoline, Lia Matera, and Linda Fairstein—who have created a new breed of lawyer protagonists. There is a gay author, Michael Nava, whose background as a poet is reflected in his fiction. Gus Lee writes about growing up as the only son of Chinese immigrants in a black San Francisco neighborhood. And Alfredo Véa recounts in lyrical prose—both English and Spanish—the perils of life as a Hispanic migrant worker.

There is diversity also in protagonists and settings. Jeremiah Healy and Stephen Greenleaf keep alive the traditional detective, creating protagonists who are worthy successors to Philip Marlowe and Sam Spade. The settings, or, as lawyers would say, venues, are far-reaching: from California to Arkansas, Boston to Memphis, with stops in Sierra Leone, Hawaii, and Nazi-occupied Poland.

Their Word Is Law has something for every type of reader. Whether you enjoy traditional mysteries or literary fiction, you will be enlightened by the words of these authors. Stephen Murphy probes each author about his or her techniques, influences, and styles. His questions bring out details that illuminate not only the author's work, but also the author's life and influences. In only a few thousand words, Murphy manages to paint a picture of each subject as a lawyer, author, and human being. After reading these interviews, you will be struck by an urgent desire to read the authors' books. I know I was.

—Steve Martini

ACKNOWLEDGMENTS

This book owes its existence to a number of generous people. First and foremost, I thank Steve Martini for taking the time to read the manuscript and forwarding it to his fine agent, Esther Newberg. Without his help, and especially his foreword, the book probably would not have been published.

Thanks also to Jerry Spolter, the world's greatest mediator, who introduced me to Steve Martini, his law school classmate.

The staff at *San Francisco Attorney,* the magazine of the Bar Association of San Francisco, has been especially accommodating by continuing to publish the interviews despite regularly missed deadlines. A special thanks to Jim Hargarten, editor in chief, for his interest in legal fiction and for finding the space for my interviews.

The transcription of these interviews would not have been possible without the help of excellent assistants. For their patience and attention to detail, I thank Jody Mailloux, Mary Linn, and Jeff Meade.

Preparing for and taking these interviews necessarily took time away from my legal practice. Fortunately, I have worked with outstanding legal talent who have picked up the slack. For their invaluable help, I thank my mentor, Bob Bianco, and my associate Nikki Hall.

Lastly, my thanks go to the authors themselves, who were invariably pleasant, accommodating, and generous with their time. They are a credit to the legal and writing professions alike. A special thanks to those who went out of their way to continue the interview over lunch or drinks, including Jeremiah Healy, John Martel, Skip Walker, Gus Lee, Bob Tanenbaum, and fellow Holy Cross Crusader Barry Reed.

INTRODUCTION

These interviews began by chance. In late 1988 Scott Turow was scheduled to come to San Francisco as the featured speaker at the annual Barristers Club Judges' Dinner. I had just finished reading *Presumed Innocent* and, like many others, I loved it. I thought it would be interesting to meet Turow and talk to him about his book. On a whim, I called him at the Sonnenschein firm in Chicago, where he was (and still is) a partner. To increase my stature, I explained that I was a member of the board of directors of the Barristers Club (pretending this was somehow an official call, which it wasn't), and we'd like to publish an interview in our bar association magazine in conjunction with his talk. To my surprise, he readily agreed.

We met in his hotel room a couple of hours before the dinner. Since I considered him a giant in the literary world (nearly a decade earlier I had read *One L*), I was surprised at how physically slight he actually is. He greeted me warmly and introduced me to his wife, who quickly left us alone in the room. Although I had been a civil trial lawyer for six years, and had taken several hundred depositions, I was as nervous as a first-year lawyer. I turned on the tape recorder and stammered through the first few questions.

Turow and I talked for an hour and a half. At the end, I popped the minicassette containing the interview out of the recorder and secured it in my pocket as if it were a priceless gem. I felt like I had a real treasure. Next to lawyers, I have always held writers in the highest esteem. But a lawyer who is also a writer, now that was something. In my impressionable mind, anyone who had the ability to argue a case before a jury and also write compelling fiction was a true Renaissance person.

The Turow interview was supposed to be a one-shot deal, but then things snowballed. Other lawyers heard about the interview and suggested that I talk to a local lawyer who had written his first novel. After a quick phone call I soon found myself sitting across from John Martel in his office in the Russ Building, one of San Francisco's oldest office buildings. Martel had established himself as a preeminent trial lawyer before writing *Partners.* But he was open, candid, and friendly. I found myself enjoying this.

I read in the local legal newspaper that John Mortimer was speaking at a luncheon sponsored by a legal group in San Francisco. I had long been a fan of his Rumpole books and decided I had to interview him. I called the lawyer who had arranged Mortimer's trip and cajoled him into arranging an interview. The next week I interviewed Mortimer over coffee in his room at the Donatello Hotel. Strewn on the table were dozens of yellow legal-sized sheets with hand-writing scribbled all over them. "I'm working on the sequel to *Paradise Postponed,*" he explained. I was charmed by his British accent. During the interview he punctuated his answers with hearty laughs. He talked so fast that I had to fight to get the next question in.

The snowball soon became an avalanche. These first three interviews were published as the cover story in *San Francisco Attorney* magazine under the title "Lawyers Who Write." Everywhere I went, it seemed, lawyers had suggestions on whom I should interview next. I hadn't planned on there being a "next," but I couldn't resist. Soon the editors of the magazine were counting on me to turn in an interview every other issue. Although I was a fairly new partner in my firm, and carrying a very high caseload of personal injury and employment cases, I somehow found time to read each author's latest novel, conduct the interview, and edit the transcript.

Due to obvious logistical problems, many of the interviews were conducted by phone. All were tape-recorded and transcribed by my secretary. I soon realized that to make the interviews readable and interesting, I would have to edit them heavily. Most people, even highly articulate writers and lawyers, do not speak in proper grammatical sentences. Some have speech tics such as "like," "you know," "I guess," and the most common one, "sort of." I edited all of these out. To ensure accuracy, I allowed each author the opportunity to proofread the edited transcript and suggest changes. I made no guarantee that I would accept the changes, but that rarely turned out to be an issue. In fact, I was surprised that most of the authors made few changes, and typically the changes were grammatical rather than substantive.

My law practice got in the way of an interview only one time. In 1991 I had arranged to interview a new lawyer-author who had made a big splash with his second novel. John Grisham was virtually unknown when *The Firm* was released. I was scheduled to interview him by phone from his home in Oxford, Mississippi, when I got called out to trial. One of my coeditors for *San Francisco Attorney* magazine, Owen Prell, agreed to step in and conduct the interview. We all know what happened next, how big Grisham has become. Owen did a terrific job, but I never let him have a chance to conduct another one. I can remember little about the case that took me away from that interview, but I'll never forget the author who got away.

The impetus to turn these interviews into a book came a few years ago when young lawyers, unaware of my early efforts, started suggesting I interview authors I had already interviewed. Many lawyers would tell me, perhaps not with complete candor, that my interviews were the only thing they read in the magazine. So a book seemed the logical next step.

I have been constantly amazed at the growth of legal fiction as well as the number of lawyers who have published novels. In the early 1990s I thought I knew of all the lawyer-authors. But on occasion I'd spend a free lunch hour browsing in the new fiction section of local bookstores, and pick out one or two new ones every time. Soon I realized I would never exhaust the supply.

I chose my subjects with no definite plan in mind. Often I would read a book I particularly liked, and I'd track down the publisher to arrange an interview with the author. Sometimes a review would pique my interest. And lawyers continued to call me with recommendations.

I did, however, try to maintain some balance. I interviewed the famous and the not so famous, lawyers who write and writers who practice law. I know I've missed many excellent writers. No slight intended; I will catch up to them sooner or later, my law practice permitting.

In the meantime, I hope you get as much enjoyment reading these interviews as I did conducting them.

LOUIS AUCHINCLOSS

For nearly half a century, Louis Auchincloss has written stylish fiction about the foibles of the upper class. Auchincloss is a writer who happened to practice law, unlike some more popular authors who have used their legal careers as a stepping-stone to get published. Although his novels and stories often touch on the practice of law, their themes are universal, dealing with morals and ethics and the difficult choices people must make, transcending the class boundaries of his usually wealthy characters.

His novel *The Education of Oscar Fairfax* traces the formal education of a well-bred Easterner through prestigious St. Augustine's School and Yale College. Oscar eventually earns his law degree and joins his father's firm in its Paris branch, where he toys with the idea of writing a book on the artists and writers of the *belle* epoque. As narrator, Oscar reveals his ambivalence about artistic and literary criticism:

> *It bothers me how often the great art of others is denigrated by the artists who have been my own lifetime favorites. James undervalued the Russian novelists; their works to him were "fluid puddings." Edith Wharton found James's novels of the "major phase" almost unreadable. . . . What is evident, at least to me, is that it is the creation of art, rather than its reception, that saves the artist's soul. What then saves that of the simple viewer or reader, like myself, who does nothing but receive?*

As Oscar struggles for meaning in his own life, he confronts the ethics of a writer friend who writes a scathing fictional portrait of an older man, befriends the son of a hairdresser in the resort town of Bar Harbor, Maine, and steers his son toward a life in the law. During the course of his life (education), he comes to terms with adultery, homosexuality, legal ethics, and other profound issues.

At eighty-four years of age, Louis Auchincloss still writes regularly, adding to his prodigious output of over fifty books. He attended Groton School and Yale College, earning his law degree from the University of Virginia in 1941. After serving in the navy for four years, he practiced trust and estates law in various corporate New York firms, retiring in 1986.

This interview took place in 1996.

FICTION: *The Indifferent Children* (1947) ▪ *The Injustice Collectors* (1950) ▪ *Sybil* (1952) ▪ *A Law for the Lion* (1953) ▪ *The Romantic Egoists* (1954) ▪ *The Great World and Timothy Colt* (1956) ▪ *Venus in Sparta* (1958) ▪ *Pursuit of the Prodigal* (1959) ▪ *The House of Five Talents* (1960) ▪ *Portrait in Brownstone* (1962) ▪ *Powers of Attorney* (1963) ▪ *The Rector of Justin* (1964) ▪ *The Embezzler* (1965) ▪ *Tales of Manhattan* (1967) ▪ *A World of Profit* (1968) ▪ *Second Chance: Tales of Two Generations* (1970) ▪ *I Come as a Thief* (1972) ▪ *The Partners* (1974) ▪ *The Winthrop Covenant* (1976) ▪ *The Dark Lady* (1977) ▪ *The Country Cousin* (1978) ▪ *The House of the Prophet* (1980) ▪ *The Cat and the King* (1981) ▪ *Watchfires* (1982) ▪ *Narcissa and Other Fables* (1983) ▪ *Exit Lady Masham* (1983) ▪ *The Book Class* (1984) ▪ *Honorable Men* (1985) ▪ *Diary of a Yuppie* (1986) ▪ *Skinny Island: More Tales of Manhattan* (1987) ▪ *The Golden Calves* (1988) ▪ *Fellow Passengers: A Novel in Portraits* (1989) ▪ *The Lady of Situations* (1990) ▪ *False Gods* (1992) ▪ *Three Lives* (1993) ▪ *Tales of Yesteryear* (1994) ▪ *The Collected Stories of Louis Auchincloss* (1994) ▪ *The Education of Oscar Fairfax* (1995) ▪ *The Atonement and Other Stories* (1997) ▪ *The Anniversary and Other Stories* (1999) ▪ *Her Infinite Variety* (2000).

NONFICTION: *Reflections of a Jacobite* (1961) ▪ *Pioneers and Caretakers: A Study of Nine Women Novelists* (1965) ▪ *Motiveless Malignity* (1969) ▪ *Edith Wharton: A Woman in Her Time* (1971) ▪ *Richelieu* (1972) ▪ *A Writer's Capital* (1974) ▪ *Reading Henry James* (1975) ▪ *Life, Law, and Letters: Essays and Sketches* (1979) ▪ *Persons of Consequence: Queen Victoria and Her Circle* (1979) ▪ *False Dawn: Women in the Age of the Sun King* (1984) ▪ *The Vanderbilt Era: Profiles of a Gilded Age* (1989) ▪ *Love Without Wings: Some Friendships in Literature and Politics* (1991) ▪ *The Style's the Man: Reflections on Proust, Fitzgerald,*

Wharten, Vidal, and Others (1994) ▪ *La Gloire: The Roman Empire of Corneille and Racine* (1996) ▪ *The Man Behind the Book: Literary Profiles* (1996) ▪ *Woodrow Wilson* (2000) ▪ *Theodore Roosevelt* (2002)

MURPHY: *You've been writing fiction for nearly half a century now. For much of that time, of course, you also practiced law. You really were one of the first lawyer-authors. What do you think about all the lawyers who are writing fiction these days?*

AUCHINCLOSS: I really haven't kept up with them. I did for a while, when lawyers first started writing fiction, but then I stopped. I began to draw a distinction in my mind as to the lawyers who wrote fiction who were really simply capitalizing on the exciting moments and events of their profession in order to make a few big bucks in fiction, and those who were genuinely writers. The most notable of the latter is, I think, Louis Begley, who could be claimed as an author. In fact, you can't really call him an author-lawyer because you really wouldn't have any particular reason to believe, reading his fiction, that he was a lawyer.

MURPHY: *Have you read any of the more popular lawyer authors, like Grisham, Turow, Martini?*

AUCHINCLOSS: No. I haven't read any of them.

MURPHY: *Your fiction is much different from that of the lawyer-authors I mentioned. . . .*

AUCHINCLOSS: That's right, because I draw a very strong distinction between novelists and lawyers. I don't interconnect the terms at all. One of the reasons I have avoided reading just the books you speak of is that they seem really to have been written by lawyer–hyphen–authors. The author would not really have been published had he not been a lawyer, and vice versa. It was kind of a new genre and not one that I particularly admired or respected.

MURPHY: *Suspense is really not an element in your stories, and rarely is there a murder. Have you ever given any thought to perhaps adopting a pseudonym, as you did with your first novel, and writing a stylish legal thriller?*

AUCHINCLOSS: No, I'm not in the least interested in that. Fiction is a very serious business to me. Although I like to make money out of it—I like to make money out of anything—that hasn't been the primary thing.

MURPHY: *Given the body of your literary works, it is obvious that fiction is important to you. Why is fiction so important?*
AUCHINCLOSS: Because it is; it has been the most important thing in my life.

MURPHY: *Do you think fiction plays any role in changing the hearts and minds of readers?*
AUCHINCLOSS: No, and I don't care. I think the artist does it entirely for himself, because he has to do it, and for no other reason.

MURPHY: *You were quoted in a* Paris Review *interview as saying that "the style is the man." Is style the most important aspect of your fiction?*
AUCHINCLOSS: No, I don't think that. Style is simply, as I say, the man. Style is you—is yourself. You might say that "yourself" might be the most important part of your fiction, and therefore your statement would become true. But the remark was originally made by a French scientist, Buffon, in the eighteenth century, and I think it's very true; the style is the man.

MURPHY: *When you approach your writing, do you approach it from the perspective of exposing a character or telling a morality tale? How do you approach your stories?*
AUCHINCLOSS: I don't know. They come to me and then I want to do that particular thing. In my *Rector of Justin,* I had a desire to do something on the subject of the great headmasters of private schools of a particular period in history. When I wrote *The Embezzler,* I had been long interested in the crime of Richard Whitney and the particular impact it had on my parents' generation in the late 1930s. I saw drama and excitement in that. At other times, these stories simply come to me. When I wrote *The House of the Prophet,* I wanted to do

a study of the kind of man that Walter Lippmann was and the kind of dilemmas that he had in his life. But sometimes it's just simply a situation—a story or novel that can grow out of a particular situation, a very small thing that comes up in my mind. It sometimes seems very small, but you know if it's a seed; and if it's a seed, then it's yours, and you feel it.

MURPHY: *You said earlier that you did not really care whether your stories reached the hearts and minds of your readers. . . .*

AUCHINCLOSS: No, no, no—they have to satisfy me and if they do that, that's all. I don't really care very much if they sell or not sell if I've got the thing right; if it's right, then I'm very pleased, I like it.

MURPHY: *You say when you've "got it right." I know a lot of writers just say that's a feeling they have but can't articulate what makes it right.*

AUCHINCLOSS: You know it. You see it there. It's as if you'd finished a statue. You look at it and there it is. It's right. And that gives a great feeling of satisfaction. And it's fairly rare. I don't often have that feeling that I've gotten it just right.

MURPHY: *There was a review of your collected short stories published last year in* Legal Times *that made the statement that you write straightforward morality tales. Do you view your stories or books as morality tales?*

AUCHINCLOSS: No, I really don't. Morals play a role in them, just the way they play a role in every part of life, but I don't particularly think of them as morality tales. The mere fact that standards of morality are less stringent than they used to be doesn't mean that morality isn't there every single second. You can't pick up a newspaper, you can't read anything from Watergate to Whitewater without seeing that morals are an obsession. You might even say that the less stringent moral standards become, the more the public is interested in them.

MURPHY: *It's interesting that you say that. Your recent book* The Education of Oscar Fairfax *seemed to me to be divided in its chapter headings by different moral tales.*

AUCHINCLOSS: Well, as the man searches through life, he is strongly motivated by the desire to leave the world a little better than he found it. And he makes plundering efforts, and it takes him the whole book to find out how he can do the hardest thing in the world—how he can give a little bit of help to another human being.

MURPHY: *You do touch on various aspects of morality, such as writers' ethics. . . .*

AUCHINCLOSS: You can't get away from them. I don't see how you can get away from moral issues in anything at all. There's a great deal of talk about amorality and immorality today but that's just different ways of looking at morality.

MURPHY: *The chapter regarding Danny Winslow, the Yale writer, has an interesting quote I want to read to you. It says: "It's true that some writers can rely on their imagination alone, but others can't. Every character of Charlotte Brontë's is directly traceable to a living model." Were you making any commentary in that passage concerning whether it is ethically correct to model fictional characters after living characters?*

AUCHINCLOSS: No. I don't think so. I think there are certain cases where it is obviously a bad—and sometimes a wicked—thing to do to expose and libel a human being in a work of fiction and cause great pain and trouble. But ordinarily speaking, the mere use of bits and pieces of characters is very harmless. People hardly ever recognize themselves anyway and when they do they usually get it wrong. So I've learned not to worry about that. But there are examples of where it could obviously be ethically wrong. For example, the author of *Primary Colors:* If it turns out that the episodes about the alleged Mr. and Mrs. Clinton are untrue, it would have been a very cruel and bad thing for him to have put them in the book. [He or she.] And if they are true, well, then it would be justified only on political grounds and the public should know that.

MURPHY: *Have you, in your writing, tended to form your characters based on actual people?*

AUCHINCLOSS: I do and I don't. The most famous case was *The Rector of Justin,* which was notoriously supposed to have likened the character on Dr. Endicott Peabody, the famous old headmaster of Groton School. In actual fact, the character was closely modeled physically on Judge Learned Hand, a man whom I immensely admired. And the only person to pick that up was a famous poet who wrote me about it, saying, "I can see Hand in that character." The odd thing was that because Judge Hand was a famous judge and the character was a headmaster, that's all you have to do to put people off. Because I said once in a speech, you could write a novel about President Abraham Lincoln, put the Gettysburg Address in his mouth, make him a dentist, and no one will pick him out!

Of course, for the character in *The House of the Prophet,* I borrowed a great deal—and made no secret of the fact that I borrowed a great deal—from Walter Lippmann, whose lawyer I was and whom I admired immensely. In fact, that book was actually published by a press that was bringing out three of Lippmann's books. They brought out then a fourth as being part of Walter Lippmann's literature. So in that case, I varied very, very much from Walter's life and so on. But I picked a great many things from Walter. I couldn't ever have written that book without Walter Lippmann. Just as I couldn't have written *The Embezzler* without knowing Richard Whitney's crime, although I didn't use his personality. And I couldn't have written *The Rector of Justin* without Judge Hand and Endicott Peabody, because I had the career of one and the personality of the other. In those respects, I use people.

And then often in minor characters I've used people. In my novel *Portrait in Brownstone,* which was about my mother's family, I used very closely characters from the past, but they were all dead. I showed the manuscript to my mother and said, "If you object to this, I won't publish it." And she said, "No, they're all dead. Nobody cares."

MURPHY: *Have you ever had any trouble or controversy about using real people?*
AUCHINCLOSS: Never. Never a threat of a lawsuit. Never once. The only threat I ever had—in more than fifty books—of a lawsuit was a man

whose house in New York was used on the jacket by a photographer with whom I had nothing to do. He claimed his privacy had been invaded. But it was sort of a joke case. He didn't get anywhere at all. We laughed it off. After all, the skyline of New York belongs to everybody. And so—I never have. Once, very early in my legal career—in fact one of my first novels—I did a picture of a character of a man who recognized himself and was deeply hurt, and I decided I'd never do that again.

MURPHY: *That is the issue that comes up in* Oscar Fairfax. . . .

AUCHINCLOSS: Oh, yes, but that was a completely unscrupulous character. Plenty of them—who absolutely use people and feel totally justified and don't even bother to consider it. But I do. I don't want to hurt somebody.

MURPHY: *You also have a chapter that deals with lawyers' ethics involving Oscar's son, Gordon, and there's another interesting quote in there that says, "Gordon is already known for what some lawyers regard as an excessive scrupulosity, for not being quite 'one of the boys' in the downtown world."*

AUCHINCLOSS: I'm pleased by my example. I worked on the example, which was a little too complicated for fiction. I like to keep things quite simple. I was very pleased that I got letters from lawyers saying that they really couldn't decide what was the right thing or the wrong thing to do. I wanted to get a real borderline case.

MURPHY: *Have you found in your legal practice much material for dealing with ethics of this sort?*

AUCHINCLOSS: There is a great deal, but I didn't find it in my practice much. I don't remember ever being tempted to do anything against the canons of the ethics of the profession. But I had a rather quiet trust-estate practice so those things don't come up. But I constantly heard and saw and learned about very grave ethical wrongs. I was on different committees of the city bar association, including the executive committee in association with the bar of the State of New York, when I came up against very striking examples of lawyer malfeasance.

MURPHY: The Education of Oscar Fairfax *really seems to be about not just the education but the life of Oscar Fairfax.*
AUCHINCLOSS: Right. It's really a kind of autobiography.

MURPHY: *There's a passage toward the end of the book that refers to literary critics. The narrator says how it bothers him how often the great art of others is denigrated by artists who have been his own lifetime favorites and then Henry James and Edith Wharton are mentioned. I know those are two of your favorites. Was* The Education of Oscar Fairfax *perhaps your most autobiographical novel?*
AUCHINCLOSS: It's not autobiographical of my life; it doesn't have anything to do with my life. He's a different generation; he's considerably older, he's closer to my father's generation than mine. And his different experiences in Paris and so on have nothing to do with my life. He has an enthusiasm for the writings of Henry James but that's widely shared.

MURPHY: *Oscar Fairfax resembles many of your protagonists: He's from the upper class, he's struggling with his own sense of morality and life. Is there some distinguishing feature about him that made you want to write a whole book about him?*
AUCHINCLOSS: I think his distinguishing feature is really the point of the whole book—his desire to do something, to get into the lives of other people one way or the other. You could say that he—in a way—has got the soul of a novelist. He suggests that himself at one point.

MURPHY: *Right. And he also becomes a benefactor to the son of a hairdresser to try to control his life.*
AUCHINCLOSS: Oh, yes. He's again and again a benefactor, or would-be benefactor, and as he moves into people's lives they don't always work out the way he hoped they would.

MURPHY: The Education of Oscar Fairfax *is sprinkled with French and Latin phrases, a number of artistic and literary references.*

AUCHINCLOSS: Perhaps it's a bit overdone. I'm watching that in something I'm writing now. It's like mannerisms; they sometimes get out of hand and have to be pruned.

MURPHY: *It did seem to happen quite a bit in the book. Is that a reflection of your experience, or were you just emphasizing that aspect of the way people talk?*

AUCHINCLOSS: No, I think it's just that I'm so interested in literary references and things that I've been reading and so on that they creep into it. I think that's to be watched, cut down there a bit. They're quite heavy in that book.

MURPHY: *There are some scenes dealing with homosexuality with reference to one of the senior masters at St. Augustine's School, and a few scenes regarding adultery. These seem to be issues, particularly adultery, that you have dealt with frequently in your fiction.*

AUCHINCLOSS: Yes. I sometimes wonder what we novelists would do without adultery. It's amazing how much it gets in; you can hardly conceive of John Updike being able to write without adultery. Perhaps we overdo it. There are certain things that are so innately dramatic that when you want to focus or dramatize a particular scene, it's sometimes hard to do. For example, in French fiction of the nineteenth century the role of the duel is out of all proportion to the role of the duel in actual French life. But there's something about a duel that is so exciting and thrilling, and all the things that lead up to it. As a result, the French writers just couldn't resist it. Of course, it was a factor in life, but I think you'd get a false perspective in French fiction of the amount of it. I think adultery is that way today; of course, with the divorce rate going up to almost fifty percent, it does provide so much of the staple of life that it's bound to come into fiction.

Homosexuality is the same way. It used to be sort of in the closet but now it's all over the place. It's constantly talked about. New York papers are absolutely always filled with gay rights and lesbian rights and so on. That begins to assume, perhaps, even a larger percentage of life, but it's part of the staple of life.

MURPHY: *Homosexuality is probably something you wouldn't have written about fifty years ago. Has it become easier to write about it now?*

AUCHINCLOSS: Obviously, much easier to write about. As I look back upon my first novel, *The Indifferent Children,* it seems to me that the character Beverly Streblinus was obviously a repressed homosexual. He has all the symptoms of it. I had studied people like him rather carefully, but I think I naively missed it. They were not overt homosexuals or practicing homosexuals. But with the increased awareness we have today, I can psychoanalyze some of my own characters and find those things in them.

MURPHY: *You've been compared, because of your subject matter, with John Cheever and John O'Hara. Yet critics have said you've lived that life, they've only aspired to it.*

AUCHINCLOSS: John O'Hara would not have appreciated that. He disliked me. He was actually married to a cousin of mine, a second cousin.

MURPHY: *Did he dislike you personally, or was it because of your writing?*

AUCHINCLOSS: Every way—disliked my writing, disliked me. He made it very clear, the way John O'Hara does.

MURPHY: *It was probably a little bit of jealousy there?*

AUCHINCLOSS: No. He was angered by a quite harmless review I wrote once. He just took a terrific offense. He had a very great ego and he took terrible offense to it and was always angry. I was sorry, because I admired his writing very much and I had not regarded that review as offensive at all. It angered him. But I didn't mind that because it was a fair review. But O'Hara was a very unreasonable man. And a very big writer, I think.

MURPHY: *Did you ever meet Cheever?*

AUCHINCLOSS: I met Cheever exactly once. He was already dying of cancer and I had a chat with him. Although he wanted to meet me at that time, I have reason to believe from his daughter that he didn't think very much of my fiction.

MURPHY: *Your stories and books all deal with the upper class, which of course you're familiar with. What fascinates you about this class, this style of life?*

AUCHINCLOSS: I write about things that I know about. And my life has been connected both in the law and everything else pretty much with the managerial class, the people who run things, and that's what I write about. They used to be the only subject of fiction. It's only in the twentieth century that they dropped out a bit. But look at the number of books that are still written about them. I don't know why I get so peculiarly branded with that, considering there are so many other authors who also write about that. But I do—there's no question it sticks to me very hard.

MURPHY: *It may be because you write about the managerial class with such authority, that it makes an impression on people.*

AUCHINCLOSS: Yeah, that will be forgiven me when I'm dead. I have a whole book of reviews of Edith Wharton in her lifetime—quite an interesting book. She ran into that all the time but nobody says that now. They don't mind if you're dead. William Shakespeare spent half his time writing about kings and queens.

MURPHY: *Over the fifty years that you've been writing, have you seen any change in the way the public perceives the class that you write about: the people who went to Groton or, like Oscar Fairfax, to St. Augustine's and became the managers of the world?*

AUCHINCLOSS: I don't think of them as a class. My partners in law, my classmates in Groton, and my friends in the navy during World War II—I don't see as a class at all. The fact that I'm branded with that is probably an indication of a fault in my writing. I'll give you this example: Nobody thinks of *War and Peace* as a class book like that and yet every single character in *War and Peace* is a member of the very highest and most exclusive Russian society. But it's as if Norman Mailer had written *The Naked and the Dead* and had all his characters graduates of Groton School or St. Paul's, and yet nobody throws that against Tolstoy because Tolstoy saw the world in every human being. He has written not only about Russia, he has written about the world, he's written about war. So if you have that large mind and that vision, it doesn't make any difference what you describe. The whole world is in each character. That's true of Shakespeare and it's true of Tolstoy and it's obviously not true of Louis Auchincloss. So that's where you can talk about a class. You can say that thing about my fiction. That's a fault in my fiction which you couldn't bring against Tolstoy, although he has taken an even smaller social group to write about.

DAVID BALDACCI

David Baldacci's first novel, *Absolute Power,* became an international best-seller and was made into a hit movie starring Clint Eastwood. The book begins explosively: a beautiful young woman, wife of a prominent businessman, engages in sexual foreplay with the drunken president of the United States. When the president becomes violent and the woman fights back, the Secret Service burst through the door and shoot the woman dead. Watching the entire scene through a two-way mirror in a bedroom closet is a good-natured burglar, whose easy haul was interrupted by the unexpected entrance of the presidential entourage.

Baldacci's second novel, *Total Control,* also became an instant bestseller. A plane carrying nearly two hundred passengers, including the chairman of the Federal Reserve Bank, explodes in midair. On the passenger list is Jason Archer, an employee of a high-tech company. Although first feared dead, he later surfaces along with evidence that indicates he may have engaged in industrial espionage and blown up the plane. The book traces his wife's agonizing search for her husband as she tries to decide whether her husband is a victim or a killer.

A graduate of the University of Virginia School of Law, Baldacci practiced corporate law in Washington, D.C., for a decade before retiring in the mid 1990s to write full-time.

The first interview took place in 1996 and the second in 1997.

FICTION: *Absolute Power* (1996) ▪ *Total Control* (1997) ▪ *The Winner* (1998) ▪ *The Simple Truth* (1999) ▪ *Saving Faith* (2000) ▪ *Wish You Well* (2000) ▪ *Last Man Standing* (2001)

MURPHY: *Many reviews of* Absolute Power *have commented on the exciting beginning with the president and his mistress, Christy Sullivan, the battle in the bedroom, and then her getting shot. What was the genesis for this plot idea?*
BALDACCI: Growing up in the sixties I heard a lot of the stories about John F. Kennedy and his mistresses. Those stories didn't really interest me all that much. What did interest me was that the president, this very powerful person, was in a vulnerable situation during those types of activities if anything tragic or catastrophic happened. Yet the president had all the president's men and women around him. How far would they go to cover up something like that to protect themselves? I figured they'd probably go pretty far, particularly the way I structured the opening scene so that nobody really was directly responsible for Christy's death in a criminal way. The Secret Service killed her, but in doing so they did their job. That's what they're paid to do and what by statute they are supposed to do in protecting the president. I didn't have the president kill her because I thought the Secret Service would have gone to the authorities. That's why I had the Secret Service kill her in the course of their duty, because I didn't think it would be plausible to have them cover it up otherwise. It was structured so that nobody really wanted to claim responsibility; everybody had an incentive to cover it up and survive.

MURPHY: *The book does start explosively. When you first plotted the book, did you start with this event?*
BALDACCI: I really wanted to start with this event, because with my first novel I wanted to go chronologically forward. I didn't want to deal with a lot of flashbacks starting at point B instead of point A. It was important for this first horrific event to occur because it set in motion all the other action in the book. Everything really follows from that initial situation. Also, I did it that way because, with agents and publishers, you've got ten or twenty pages to make your point. If you can capture their attention, you have a good shot of them read-

ing the rest of the book. So I really wanted to come out the chute flying with this book.

MURPHY: *It's interesting you say that, because when I read the first three chapters I thought that any agent would want the book.*
BALDACCI: Well, I've gotten more than my share of rejections. But what I tried to do is learn the market. If your goal is to write for yourself and not worry about publishing, that's fine, you can do whatever you want to do. If your goal is to write and become published, then, whether you like it or not, you really have to understand your market. I try to be very realistic about that. I know the number of manuscripts that agents get and certainly I know that better than I knew before. But it's physically impossible for them to read every single page of every single manuscript. Sometimes you have to structure your storytelling around those parameters.

MURPHY: *You got a lot of ink when the book was originally sold because of the high price of two million dollars. Was Aaron Priest the first agent you approached?*
BALDACCI: I sent the book to about a half dozen agents. I had gotten names, including Aaron Priest, from contacts I had in Los Angeles. I had at least gotten my name out there as a screenwriter. Even though I hadn't sold anything, a number of people in Los Angeles liked my writing. I sent the manuscripts simultaneously to all of them with a cover letter saying I was doing that and giving them some background on me and on the story. Of the six or seven I sent it to, five of them called back and said they read it and they wanted to represent me, including Aaron's agency. So I went to New York and interviewed all of them, which was surreal for me. I'd never even gotten close to getting an agent before, so I went up and interviewed them, and Aaron and I hit it off. I didn't really have anything against the other agents—they were all good and seemed enthusiastic—but he and I just clicked for whatever reason.

MURPHY: *You said you've written screenplays. Was this before starting the novel?*

BALDACCI: Yeah. My writing career actually started when I went to law school back in 1983. I spent five years just trying to write, and to learn the craft. I never finished anything, I never even finished a short story. And then I spent three or four years writing short stories—about a dozen. I tried to sell them and never got anywhere, but I kept going. Then I started writing screenplays for three or four years. Actually, I almost sold one the summer before the book sold. I had an agent in Hollywood, I'd hooked up with a producer who really liked my script, an action-adventure thriller. Two producers out there, the guy who did the movie *Speed* and guy who did the movie *Blown Away,* read my script and loved it. So they split the town up and went around and competed against each other at the studios, trying to sell the script so they could make the movie. It was one of those things where everybody was saying, This is going to sell, it's a great script, big bucks behind it, and all that. Eventually it didn't sell for a lot of different reasons. But again it was sort of a silver lining. Even if the people didn't buy it, when I later came back and said, "I've got this book, do you know any literary agents I could send it to?" I got a lot of positive feedback and names of good agents.

MURPHY: *I find it curious that you had all that experience writing because the articles on you make it seem like you woke up one day and said, "I'm going to write this blockbuster novel," and two years later it came out and sold for two million dollars.*
BALDACCI: Yes, I'm a twelve-year overnight success.

MURPHY: *You use an interesting plot device in having a burglar, Luther Whitney, in the closet watching the entire series of events through a two-way mirror.*
BALDACCI: Right. He was sort of symbolically the voyeur in all of us. I set it up that way because I thought it was an interesting device to allow the reader to see everything from his eyes, and experience it as much emotionally as Luther was doing at the time. I thought it would be an effective foil to use. Once I decided that's what I wanted to do, it really lent itself to creating a very effective first couple of chapters as far as getting the action involved. You can get the whole

cast of players in front of you, like seeing it on a big movie screen, which was appealing to me for a number of reasons.

MURPHY: *There are several sex scenes in the book—at the beginning with Gloria Russell, the chief of staff, and the unconscious president, which is an eye-opening scene to say the least. And then you have some more down the road with her and Tim Collin, the Secret Service agent. One may say cynically that you put these in, particularly the beginning scene, solely for sales purposes. How would you respond to that?*

BALDACCI: I've gotten a lot of—I won't say flak—but I've gotten a lot of comments on that scene. I debated whether to keep it in or not. Ultimately I did because I wanted to show, as vividly and as graphically as I could, Gloria Russell's sexual involvement with the president. When Luther watches this entire scene, I wanted him to have reasons to change his mind about running away from this and confront the problem and ultimately bring these people to justice. I also did it to show, in just a couple of bold strokes, what sort of a person she was. One scene where she would have sex with an unconscious man, totally dominate the most powerful man in the world, which is kind of a high unto itself. But also do it while a dead woman is lying on the floor nearby to show her complete and utter disregard for that woman's value. I know it could seem like I threw it in for gratuitous sex, but the way I did it was so controversial, if I'd done it just for that I probably would have done it another way.

MURPHY: *After the opening scene, the plot really goes in a couple of directions. One, where the president and others are chasing Luther Whitney, and the other is the investigation of the murder by the detective from the local police department. How did these distinct plot lines come about?*

BALDACCI: I read a lot of different genres. I like the thrillers, the police procedurals. I'm a big fan of Patricia Cornwell, for instance. What I wanted to do here was combine elements from all of those different genres. The chase books are, in effect, a device. What you really want to write is an action-packed sort of thriller. It's a good device to get the adrenaline going. So I wanted to have that segment as well. But I also wanted to have the police procedural with the investigative techniques. I'm fascinated with stuff like forensics and ballistics and fingerprinting. I really had read a lot about it and had a good grasp of the material. I think people are fascinated by how detectives use cutting-edge technology to track down people. As long as you don't turn it into a textbook, and you don't hit them over the head with it. You let it subtly flow into the material and the dialogue. So I wanted to have a smart detective employing some interesting devices in order to track down the criminal. Not to mention the fact that multiple subplots are good to keep people's interest because you can address a number of different characters and different actions. I like to think of it as three or four freight trains headed down parallel tracks. You know they're going to collide somewhere down the road, you just don't know where.

MURPHY: *The detective, Seth Frank, seemed to me to be one of the more interesting characters. He's not very flashy, does his job, almost a Colombo-type character.*

BALDACCI: Yeah, he is. He's very much like that. I wanted a guy who was tenacious, who may not be the most brilliant character in the world, but who perseveres. A lot in life depends on perseverance. It carries over to writing too; ninety percent of it is sweat equity. And you get the occasional flashes of inspiration here and there, but a lot of it is sitting down at your desk and writing each day. I think a lot of being a detective and trying to track down people is tedious, monotonous work, but it is the only way to do it effectively. You have to approach it every day. I didn't want this big, handsome, brilliant hero; I just wanted a guy who I thought would be very close to what a detective actually is. Just a guy with some good instincts, who is tenacious, goes to work every day, does his job and works very hard at it. He may be successful or he may not, but he is going to give it a good shot.

MURPHY: *Seth Frank seemed to be a contrast to most of the other characters, like Jack Graham and his fiancée, Jennifer Baldwin, who are high achievers. Jack is an all-American athlete, a top student in law school, works at a top* *law firm; Jennifer is beautiful and the daughter of a successful businessman. I was curious as to why you chose to portray these characters as such high achievers.*

BALDACCI: I wanted to show some extremes, I guess. And having Jack be a high achiever—which a lot of people in Washington, D.C., and major metropolitan areas, including San Francisco, are. There is exciting and challenging work there, so the best and brightest tend to go to those areas. I wanted to show a high achiever who is presented with a couple of different choices in life. He started out as a public defender. Even though it was very hard work, he enjoyed it. But at the other end of the spectrum is the life Jennifer Baldwin offered to him. It was an interesting choice. A lot of people would say, "That's a hell of a life, I could do what I want to do." A lot of people's dream in life is to end up wealthy, and that's the only thing they really work for. They figure the rest of the happiness will fall into place. So that was Jack's choice. The ultimate destiny of many high achievers in the United States, which is a capitalist economy, is to be wealthy, affluent, and influential in a lot of different areas. Jack was presented with all of that. So I took a high achiever and I gave him the typical goal of a high achiever. Jack had to make that difficult choice.

MURPHY: *You mention in an afterword of the book the portrayal of the Secret Service and how you obviously didn't intend that to be realistic. Have you had any feedback from Secret Service people about the book?*

BALDACCI: I haven't. I've heard thirdhand that at least some of them didn't have any problem with the book. I put that author's note in the end well after I'd written the book, a few months before publication. I did it because I felt kind of weird writing about the service that way. I don't know if you've read James Patterson's book, *Along Came a Spider,* which came out a few years ago. In that book, there are Secret Service agents who are murderers, blackmailers, kidnappers, and they do it solely for money. I read the book and really liked the story, but I felt kind of unusual reading about the Secret Service in that light, because they are supposed to be the good guys, the white knights, who can do no wrong. But I put that author's note in because I felt just a little unusual about portraying them that way. But then I thought, this is fiction and these people are human beings.

The way I set the plot up, they did their job and now they could be in terrible trouble if the truth is found out. And I presented a choice to let the reader decide: What would you do if you were a Secret Service agent, you did your job, you killed somebody, and if you told the truth, regardless of whether what you did was right or wrong, your career would be over? What would you do? Would you cover it up or not? But then if you cover it up with a killing, you have to find this person who is going to blackmail the president. Now it's too late to come forward. If this guy comes out with the truth, you're going to be in even worse trouble because you obstructed justice. In law school they teach you that the slippery slopes can be very slippery. You take that first step, you take that second step, and the additional steps after that become very much easier to take. In the end all you're trying to do is survive and that's a very strong instinct with people. With Bill Burton I set him up as the moral thermometer for the whole book. He didn't like what he was doing but he kept doing it because he wanted to survive. He didn't want to disappoint his family. And for me those are very strong influences.

MURPHY: *Looking back, now that you've finished the book and read the reviews, is there anything in hindsight you would change?*
BALDACCI: It's difficult in four or five hundred pages to write a story that is a "page-turner," has a lot of action, a lot of plot, and at the same time develop all of your characters. For the most part the reviews have been very strong. I haven't received that many bad reviews. There have been a couple reviews, including yours—and that's why I wrote to you—that I thought were fair, pointing out that some of the characters were not as well developed as they could have been. In *Total Control* I spent more time developing the two major characters, making them more well rounded. So in *Absolute Power* I felt like I'd developed the characters as well as I could, under

the circumstances, without giving up some of the other strengths of the book.

———————

MURPHY: Total Control *in many ways is similar to* Absolute Power, *but also in many ways different. One obvious difference is that the protagonist, Sydney Archer, is a female. Did you consciously decide to switch gears in terms of the protagonist?*

BALDACCI: I did. I wanted to write from the other gender's point of view. When you spend a year and a half writing a book, you try to make it as challenging as you can to keep your interest. And one way I made it challenging was trying to write from a woman's perspective. It was difficult at times but I got a lot of input from my wife on different things—the more subtle things that men wouldn't necessarily pick up on with the character, but it really kept my interest.

MURPHY: *Sydney Archer is also an attorney and mother. Toward the end of the book, she becomes very physical. Have you received any reaction from anybody about how she acted in terms of overcoming the bad guys?*

BALDACCI: Yeah. I did. I mean, some reactions I got were funny. And most of these were from men. They were incredulous that a woman could actually wield a gun to defend herself, or think quickly on her feet in pressure situations. But the bottom line was I didn't want to write a "damsel in distress" story, because she wasn't a damsel in distress and I don't happen to know any women who are damsels in distress. I know a lot of guys who could use some help every now and then. But she was a character who was intelligent and quick-witted. She built a career for herself. She was independent and didn't need anyone else, or didn't think she needed anyone else to help her. That's what I wanted to come through in the book. I didn't want her to be smart and quick on her feet throughout three-quarters of the book and then at the end have to hand off to somebody else to finish it up. That's why I expanded her role to make her more physical and take matters into her own hands. And she had a lot at stake; it was her husband, her daughter, and her own life as well.

MURPHY: Total Control *deals with the Federal Reserve Bank and high tech, especially the computer industry. Were those your primary interests in writing the book?*

BALDACCI: Those were the two technical issues that I wanted to talk about. The Fed I really didn't think had been explored well in fiction before, and I had always been interested in high technology, the privacy issues but also the control of information and how powerful those forces can be. The one theme I did want to explore was the faith of one spouse for the other, and how strong that faith can be. How far it would go when tested against really traumatic situations. What I set up for Sydney Archer was every person's worst nightmare of having someone that you love and care about disappear, and then be accused of all these things that you can't believe they could have done, but all the evidence shows that they did do it.

MURPHY: *In Robert Reich's book, he said the Federal Reserve Board chairman was the most powerful man in the country. It seemed like your book was set out to prove that.*

BALDACCI: I spent a lot of time reading and studying the financial world just because it seemed very intriguing to me. But the Fed is a unique institution. Other countries have central banks, but the Fed's purpose is to monitor and keep running smoothly the American economy, which is the largest in the world. A dozen or so people meet in secrecy, supervised by no one. Yet a Fed chairman can act alone at times and control the interest rates. If you can control the flow of information and make an unanticipated change, then that's real power. And when you're talking about the dollars that the Fed controls because they have the pulse of the American economy, it's staggering how much is at stake there. It just seemed to me that this was something to provide rich fodder for a story.

MURPHY: *You did show how information being controlled affects reality, both with the Fed and with Triton Global, the high-tech company. In many ways it seems similar to the way an author can create his own reality by deciding what information to give the reader.*

BALDACCI: It does. So much of writing fiction, and particularly a mystery, is knowing when to give something and when to withhold something. You're limited, too. You try to be fair with the reader and give them as much information as you can without giving away the whole ball of wax from the very beginning. But you create the world and you create the reality. You're judged on how you do. Some people may think you didn't give enough information along the way, some will think that you gave too much, but it's a tricky fence to straddle, but that's part of the challenge.

MURPHY: *There are some interesting characters in* Total Control, *particularly Quentin Rowe and Nathan Gamble, the Triton executives. But it seemed to me that, as in* Absolute Power, *you did your best characterization with the law enforcement character, FBI agent Lee Sawyer. Has anybody else said that to you?*

BALDACCI: You're not the first one to observe that. They're good characters because they've seen a lot and they've done a lot of things that ordinary people wouldn't do. They have this cynical humor side to help them get through their job and let them show other people they are not going to be easily intimidated. Those are just fun characters. I think characters who are a little bit out of the mainstream, who don't walk to the same beat that everybody else does, are fun characters to write about. In thrillers, humor has to be carefully injected. You can't have a joke on every page and you can't have a wisecrack in every paragraph. But law enforcement people are an ideal way, at least for me, to get a bit of dark humor in, lighten the mood a little.

MURPHY: *I wouldn't call* Total Control *a traditional mystery, but you use many of the elements of traditional mysteries. Particularly the ending, when Lee Sawyer solves the puzzle by explaining what happened to the characters. But it's obvious he's talking to the readers. How hard did you have to work on resolving the mystery in* Total Control?

BALDACCI: There were a lot of threads in the story that needed to be tied up at the end. Not that every thread needs to be tied up, but I don't like it when a lot of them are dangling loose. So I tend to try to tie up just about everything that I can. I love foreshadowing in books. A lot of the stuff that Lee Sawyer figured out along the way, a very astute reader could have picked up and followed. I'm not saying solve, but they could at least have gotten close to what was going on. But the bottom line for *Total Control* was: the first thing you read in the book—the Federal Reserve chairman getting on a plane and being killed—that was the heart of the mystery. But my assumption was that people never believe the first thing you throw out at them is what the book is really about.

I threw that out first to everybody to get them to nibble on it and they would think, "Oh, I'm waiting for the real thing." Here comes Jason Archer and everybody thinks, Oh, it's just a coincidence the Fed chairman was on that plane, not remembering that in the first couple of pages something was up with this Fed chairman. He was going to do something big and they would forget that and focus on Archer because they figured this has to be the real thing, the first thing is always the red herring. So I was trying to make the reader make assumptions about the plot, but at the end of the book they would realize they had no basis to make those assumptions.

A lot of tying up loose ends is just going back through the book and making sure you, as a writer, haven't forgotten something, too. And I also went back through the book and made sure that the deductions Lee Sawyer had made at the end were things that he, with his special knowledge and the observations he had made, legitimately could have done. He was trained to pick up the small things that, quite frankly, a lot of other people would have passed over.

MURPHY: *How about your next book? Is that based at all on your success with* Absolute Power *and* Total Control?
BALDACCI: No. My third book is completely different from the first two. There are no lawyers, no politicians. It's about a girl who was born dirt poor in Georgia. She will live and die in poverty, just like her parents did. One day a mysterious stranger comes by and makes

her an offer. And she need do only one thing, it's not legal, but nobody will know except him and her. And if she does it, the payoff is she will be instantly wealthy, incredibly wealthy, all of her dreams realized. And a tragedy forces her to accept that offer and then the story picks up from there ten years later when she has transformed herself. But as you can realize, nothing is really free in life. The title of the book is *The Winner* because in certain respects she is the winner.

It allowed me to write more about the South, which I am familiar with. I didn't grow up in poverty, but wasn't far from it. I was able to put some of my experiences, and also my mother's, into the things that this character does. When you read the book you'll understand the premise behind it. How she is able to get this wealth. But it's a universal theme and it's something that everybody would instantly recognize and be intrigued by.

I wanted to write a story very different from the first two. One reason why is that the publisher would like me to turn out a book a year and thus far I've been able to do that. But one thing I don't want to be is formulaic. In *Absolute Power* I wrote a story that was not your traditional mystery because you knew everything that happened in the beginning and you looked over the shoulder of the detectives who solved it. With *Total Control* I wrote from a woman's point of view and perspective and wrote a more traditional mystery where you have all these clues and all these things happen. You have no idea why but then everything's resolved in the end. And in this third book I wanted to write about people other than lawyers and again from a woman's point of view. But this time not from an educated, fairly affluent woman, but from a dirt-poor, ill-educated woman with no prospects in life. I did that because I don't want to get into a formula. That's the last thing I want to do. I don't want people to start saying, "He's just writing for the bucks now; the quality has gone down."

A lot of times when I'm setting up my plots I think to myself, What plot is going to make me do something different this time? That's very important to me because I want to be challenged. I want to be forced to write different things each time. I think that will keep the quality in the books and stop me from dropping into being just another formula writer.

MURPHY: *It seems that even though* Total Control *is much different from* Absolute Power, *they do share common themes of greed and power. Does* The Winner *also share those themes?*

BALDACCI: It does. With *The Winner* what I'm trying to do is get into the reader's psyche a little bit. I figure if I can make people ask themselves this question, What would I do if I were this character? then I've got them through the entire book. They're going to want to know what happened to that character. Like, in *The Winner,* instant wealth. Who hasn't thought about waking up in the morning and being wealthy with no money problems? You don't have to worry about mortgages anymore. You put that dream smack in the middle of a unique and original thriller and I think readers will enjoy it. But greed, power, and money are things that motivate a lot of people. You're going to find those themes in a lot of fiction.

MURPHY: *You've finished* The Winner *so I assume you're working on yet a fourth book. What's that about?*

BALDACCI: This one actually takes you back to my hometown of Richmond, Virginia. It's about a terrible injustice that was done a long time ago to somebody. And how you can commit a crime, but not really be guilty of it. This one deals more with lawyers than the third book. I'm actually writing about a character from my hometown and about a lot of things that I know well, having been brought up there. If you read *The Winner,* you'll see a lot of differences in the writing and differences in how I approach the characters in the book and the things that I make them do. I try to get better as I go along. It's about as much as any writer can do, so it's something new for me each day.

LOUIS BEGLEY

In 1954 two English majors graduated from Harvard University summa cum laude. One was John Updike. The other was Louis Begley. Updike went on to international fame as a writer. Begley went to Harvard Law School and became an attorney practicing international law with New York's Debevoise and Plimpton. But in 1991 Begley took his place beside his college classmate with the publication of his first novel, *Wartime Lies,* a compelling account of the Nazi takeover of Poland from the point of view of a young Jewish boy. *Wartime Lies* won the 1991 PEN Hemingway Award and the Aer Lingus/Trial Times International Prize, and was a finalist for the National Book Award and the National Critics' Circle Award.

Begley's novel *About Schmidt,* which was a finalist for the National Critics' Circle Award, concerns a lawyer, Albert Schmidt, who finds himself at the end of his career, without his recently deceased wife, but with a daughter who annoys him. He disagrees with his daughter Charlotte's decision to marry a Jewish associate in his firm. Charlotte thinks she knows why Schmidt does not like her fiancé:

Mom brought me up to admire the Jewish tradition and to think your Jew baiting is disgusting. Just listen to yourself: one mention of the word rabbi and the real Albert Schmidt Esquire comes out of the closet! Then it's goodbye caterers and nice short white dress: not for the daughter who's marrying a Jew and wants to bring a rabbi onto her father's lawn!

Mr. Begley continues to practice law with Debevoise and Plimpton in New York. This interview took place in 1998.

FICTION: *Wartime Lies* (1991) ▪ *The Man Who Was Late* (1992) ▪ *As Max Saw It* (1994) ▪ *About Schmidt* (1996) ▪ *Mistler's Exit* (1998) ▪ *Schmidt Delivered* (2000)

MURPHY: *You have been compared to another New York lawyer-author, Louis Auchincloss, because your novels involve in part the upper class and social manners. Do you think that's a fair comparison?*

BEGLEY: It's a flattering one. I admire Louis Auchincloss deeply. Also, I'm not sure that my point of view on the world is as good-natured or benevolent as Louis's. It is also true that one of my books certainly does not deal with New York's upper class or the Eastern Seaboard upper class, and that is my first book.

MURPHY: *You have quite a bit more sex and lust in your books than Mr. Auchincloss.*

BEGLEY: That's true. But there is also a simply darker vision of the world than Louis's.

MURPHY: *Are you a reader of Mr. Auchincloss's books?*

BEGLEY: Yes. I've not read all of them. As you know, he's written over fifty books. But I've read a good many of them.

MURPHY: *He told me in an interview that you're the only lawyer-author he reads but he doesn't consider you a lawyer-dash-author, but simply an author.*

BEGLEY: Perfect mutuality! He is the only lawyer-author I read. And I consider him an author rather than a lawyer-author too. He is immensely gifted.

MURPHY: *Your latest novel is entitled* About Schmidt, *which is an interesting title because it indicates the book is more a character study, rather than plot-driven. Albert Schmidt is a recently retired senior partner from the Wood and King law firm in New York. What was it about Albert Schmidt that interested you?*

BEGLEY: You might say that I met him while I was walking on the beach. I have a house on the south shore of the eastern end of Long Island and have a passion for walking up and down the beach. While I was walking, Schmidt—complete with his name—introduced himself into my head. There he was, very difficult, in fact impossible, to evict. I was interested principally in certain questions that Schmidt faces. One question is how does one cope with the decade that opens when one is sixty and one's physical life is not on a slope that mounts toward greater vigor. That was one question. Another question was what does one do at that age if one's life is shattered as Schmidt's is by the loss of his wife, by the drying up of his professional activity, by disagreement with his daughter. These were questions that obsessed me. How does one exit from the stage? What can happen to such a man other than simply depression, if not despair?

MURPHY: *One thing that happens to him is that he has an affair with a young Puerto Rican waitress named Carrie. Why would a girl like this be attracted to an older man like Schmidt?*

BEGLEY: It's an interesting phenomenon that there are quite a lot of young women who are attracted to older men. Fortunately for older men. The reason may be a combination of factors. Some are attracted by a certain kind of glamour, some by a certain kind of power, some by a more skillful or more understanding way that older men may have of dealing with women. They may be less selfish, they may be less impatient, they may be more considerate.

MURPHY: *Schmidt also is wooed by his daughter Charlotte's future mother-in-law, Renata. So it's not just the younger woman who is attracted to him but the older woman as well.*

BEGLEY: It may be that he is a rather attractive fellow.

MURPHY: *And despite these advances by older and younger women, he's still fighting the misery of not just his wife's death, but his life and how he has spent his life.*

BEGLEY: Yes. I think that is precisely the case. I think that people are rarely monoliths and they rarely experience only one feeling. Very often they experience simultaneous contradictory feelings.

MURPHY: *Were you concerned, in writing the book, that this sense of gloom and darkness about Schmidt would make it difficult to carry the story?*
BEGLEY: No, I don't think so. The story was one that I had in my mind as a whole. I think it's a rather humorous book about a rather difficult subject. I find it funny, don't you?

MURPHY: *Certain parts of it definitely are funny: Schmidt's attempts to deal with Carrie's old boyfriend Bryan, a drug dealer, I think are terrific. But there's also an element in* About Schmidt, *as there is in your first book, of anti-Semitism. He's upset that his daughter, Charlotte, is engaged to a Jewish attorney in Schmidt's firm. But Schmidt doesn't think he's anti-Semitic. Was this a major reason for your writing the book?*
BEGLEY: No, I think that I was interested in showing how the power of eros—love—can unlock someone's heart. I consider that Schmidt's anti-Semitism, which is of the numb, some would say benevolent social kind, is actually rather odious and a symptom of emotional immaturity, of a heart that hasn't ripened. I thought that it would be interesting to show—I don't want to sound pompous about it at all—how the things that happened to Schmidt, his difficulties with his daughter, his love affair with this young girl, his feeling of rejection, could make him see that his anti-Semitism was not exactly a private and indifferent matter. This happens toward the end of the book, but I don't make it very loud or explicit. It wouldn't be; Schmidt is not that kind of fellow.

MURPHY: *You seem to have come full circle from* Wartime Lies, *where the anti-Semitism involved the Nazis, to the more subtle anti-Semitism of somebody like Schmidt.*
BEGLEY: That's right. The two things are not comparable. Nevertheless, anti-Semitism and any other kind of racial prejudice or, if you like, stereotyping and therefore dehumanizing people, disliking national

groups en bloc—all these things are hateful. They have in common the rejection of life, refusal to acknowledge the diversity of humanity, the refusal to treat your neighbor as a neighbor or your fellow human being as a brother. I'm not a holocaust writer. I wrote *Wartime Lies* and I've had my say on the subject of the massacre of European Jews by Germans during World War II. But the evil of prejudice and the damage done by it are omnipresent.

MURPHY: *In your future books, do you plan on pursuing this theme of prejudice?*
BEGLEY: I'm not a programmatic writer. I have a book that I finished during the last summer that will come out this summer or fall. Unless I'm very much mistaken, that theme does not at all appear. And I've just begun to write another book in which I doubt that this theme will be of any great consequence.

But if you consider *The Man Who Came Late,* you will find that I'm very much interested in the ability to accept life as it is, to accept human beings as they are, and of possessing a sufficient degree of humility to love and to accept being loved. And these qualities are stark and complete opposition to bigotry and anti–Semitism.

MURPHY: *You started writing late in life and I know that you were an English major at Harvard with John Updike. Did you have thoughts at that time of being a writer?*
BEGLEY: No. In fact, I came to the conclusion that I wouldn't be a writer. I didn't have a very clear idea at all of what I should do when I graduated from college. I vaguely thought of being a college teacher. And then when I was serving in the army, that idea evaporated from my head and I was, as it often happens to people of that age, quite uncertain about how I would earn my living. Something inspired me with the thought of going to law school. Luckily, it turned out that I loved law school. I have also loved the practice of law.

MURPHY: *Before writing* Wartime Lies, *did you have in mind that someday you would sit down and write a novel?*
BEGLEY: No, I didn't think so.

MURPHY: *And yet since* Wartime Lies *came out in 1991, you have been prolific.*

BEGLEY: I thought I had nothing to say, but found that I was wrong. I've also found that I am happy writing novels. In fact I would be hard put to say which I enjoy more, writing novels or practicing law.

MURPHY: *Do you think becoming a novelist has made you a better lawyer?*

BEGLEY: At the risk of seeming immodest, I would say that I have always been a very good lawyer.

MURPHY: *Your first novel,* Wartime Lies, *won many awards and your style seemed so well developed and sophisticated right from the start. Were you surprised that* Wartime Lies *came out as well as it did?*

BEGLEY: Of course I was. One always has the jitters when a book appears. Publication is a little bit like going out into the street and taking off your clothes, exposing yourself naked to public view. But it went well and my jitters have diminished over the years.

MURPHY: *Do you think that your style is evolving at all as a writer?*

BEGLEY: I'm told it is. The style of *Wartime Lies* is rather special because I was writing in the first-person voice of a young child, so I had to be careful not to make the child express himself in a way that was not appropriate to the child's age. I wasn't able to achieve this always but I tried very hard. I also was writing in English about things that were taking place in Polish, and that's one reason I avoided dialogue. With a couple of exceptions the only dialogue in *Wartime Lies* is interior. The reason is that I did not know how to make Polish speech sound good in English. So you see those were things that marked very much the style of *Wartime Lies.* The style of my subsequent books is much more natural to me.

MURPHY: *In* About Schmidt, *one stylistic device you use is you omit quotation marks.*

BEGLEY: I've never used quotation marks in my novels to set off dialogue. The reason is aesthetic. I don't like their looks.

MURPHY: *Another thing you do—in chapter six of* About Schmidt—*is change from the third person to the first person where Schmidt's diary comes into play. Why did you decide to change point of view there?*

BEGLEY: I felt there was a need for a certain kind of relief or a change of pace. It wasn't that I could not have said those things without the use of the diaries. I also have some letters in that book. I could have done without the letters, but when one writes one acts to a great extent on impulse.

MURPHY: *When you write a book do you have in mind a particular reader?*

BEGLEY: No, not really.

MURPHY: *For example, do you write for literary readers . . . ?*

BEGLEY: I just write the way I write. I am extremely interested in my readers. I love hearing from them. I answer all their letters. But I think that one has to write for oneself. I can't imagine how I would write a novel for a particular audience.

MURPHY: Wartime Lies *has been called a semiautobiographical novel. Would you consider your other books also semiautobiographical?*

BEGLEY: I don't know what semiautobiographical means. Perhaps something like light classical music. *Wartime Lies* is a book in which I drew on my experiences during the war in Poland, but it is not a memoir or an autobiography.

MURPHY: *Who influenced your writing career in terms of writers you admired?*

BEGLEY: I can tell you the names of writers I admire and it would be a long list, but I'm not certain that any writer especially influenced me. I could begin with Dante and work my way through Shakespeare to Yeats, Tolstoy, and Dostoevski, Flaubert, Dickens, George Eliot, Henry James, Conrad, on and on. These writers and many others shaped my taste, the way I judge my own writing and that of others. I do not try to write in their manner.

WILLIAM BERNHARDT

William Bernhardt has enjoyed considerable success in his two chosen professions. As a lawyer, he won an award from the Oklahoma Bar Association for Outstanding Service to the Public and was named Outstanding Young Lawyer by the Tulsa County Bar Association. As an author, he has won critical acclaim for his "Justice" novels, all featuring lawyer Ben Kincaid. His novel *Double Jeopardy* introduced a new protagonist, Travis Byrne, a novice but savvy criminal defense attorney.

While defending mobster Alberto Moroconi on a brutal gang rape charge, Byrne becomes immersed in a battle between feuding Mafia leaders and crooked FBI agents. The gangsters suspect Byrne has a list containing the locations of participants in the government's witness relocation program, and the FBI thinks Byrne killed one of their agents. Before long, everyone is trying to kill Byrne. Byrne obtains the assistance of Laverne Cavanaugh, the assistant United States attorney prosecuting Moroconi, by tying her up in her own apartment. As this unlikely pair runs from their many pursuers, they narrowly escape exploding cars, bumbling mobsters, vengeful hitmen, and crooked FBI agents.

William Bernhardt is a graduate of the University of Oklahoma College of Law. Since 1986, he has been a trial attorney at a large Tulsa law firm.

This interview took place in 1995.

FICTION: *Primary Justice* (1992) ▪ *Blind Justice* (1992) ▪ *Deadly Justice* (1993) ▪ *The Code of Buddyhood* (1993) ▪ *Perfect Justice* (1994) ▪ *Double Jeopardy* (1995) ▪ *Cruel Justice* (1996) ▪ *Naked Justice* (1997) ▪ *Extreme Justice* (1998) ▪ *The Midnight Before Christmas* (1998) ▪ *Legal Briefs: Stories by Today's Best*

Thriller Writers (ed., 1999) ▪ *Dark Justice* (1999) ▪ *Silent Justice* (2000) ▪ *Murder One* (2001)

―――――――――

MURPHY: *You've written a number of the "Justice" novels about attorney Ben Kincaid and with* Double Jeopardy *you've introduced a new character, Travis Byrne. Why did you decide to switch characters in this book?*

BERNHARDT: I really just wanted to do something different—stretch my writing muscles a little bit. It wasn't out of any dislike for the Ben Kincaid books. In fact, I've written another one that will be published next February. But I did want to try something different after having done several of those and *Double Jeopardy* was what I came up with. I've always been a fan of thrillers, and of course they seem to be popular right now. The genesis of it really began during a conversation with my editor at Ballantine, Joe Blades. He was a film major and I'm kind of a film buff and we started talking about movies that we liked, old movies, and particularly the Hitchcock movies, and I thought, Wouldn't it be fun to write a book like that? That's what got me thinking about *Double Jeopardy*.

MURPHY: *Travis Byrne's an ex-cop, he's somewhat out of shape, a first-year trial attorney, but a very successful one. How does he differ from Ben Kincaid?*

BERNHARDT: I think they're like night and day. Travis is very proficient in the courtroom, even though he's only been out of school a short time. Ben, on the other hand, is on the normal learning curve. When you see him in the first book—*Primary Justice*—he's not very good in the courtroom at all. He's a total novice, tends to be nervous and not very confident, and makes mistakes. Through the course of the series he's become more proficient, but he didn't start out that way. I intentionally wanted a character who wasn't Perry Mason, who wasn't flawless, but could grow and find himself over time.

Travis is in his second career. He's been a police officer but quit after a tragic accident. He's already been through years of disillusionment and naïveté, the stage that Ben Kincaid's still experiencing in the "Justice" books. What we see in *Double Jeopardy* is Travis's response.

MURPHY: *Did you anticipate that Travis Byrne would appeal to different readers than Ben Kincaid?*

BERNHARDT: I don't know. That's an interesting question. It's possible. I don't know that I planned it that way, but it could be. I think the important thing is just that the reader be able to empathize with your main character in one way or another. I hope that both Travis and Ben are likable although their personality types are quite different. I think *Double Jeopardy* has a bit more of a hard edge than the "Justice" books. It's a little meaner and tougher. There's certainly more action, more emphasis on the thriller aspects—the chase rather than the justice system. I haven't heard this, but I guess I can conceive that someone who might think Ben is just too lightfooted or too naive or too whatever, might find Travis, who's more grizzled, experienced, and hard-edged, more appealing. As far as I can tell, though, the people who've read the "Justice" books have also followed up with *Double Jeopardy*. If anything, I've probably picked up a few more readers along the way.

MURPHY: *It seemed that in* Double Jeopardy *you borrowed a number of plot ideas from John Grisham, in that there's a horrible gang rape, a trial, and then the chase by both the Mafia and the FBI. It reminded me of parts of* The Firm *and* The Pelican Brief, *and perhaps* A Time to Kill, *with a gang rape. Are you a Grisham fan?*

BERNHARDT: I've read *A Time to Kill* and I thought it was very good. And I've seen the film of *The Firm,* of course. I wasn't aware of being influenced by *A Time to Kill,* but perhaps so—I thought it was a very good book. I doubt if there were that many similarities.

I thought you were going to ask me about the movies because, as I said before, Hitchcock was really the instigator of this thing. In fact, if you're keyed to that you can see in *Double Jeopardy* there are something like fifteen to twenty homages to Hitchcock films that I dropped in to see if my editor would notice. Of course he did. Just little things, like a flurry of umbrellas on the staircase—a reference to a famous scene in *Foreign Correspondents*—or the aunt's name being Marnie. I won't list them here but they're all through the book. That was intentional. That was just having a bit of fun.

MURPHY: *Did you devise any plot turns or twists with Hitchcock in mind?*
BERNHARDT: I don't know if I plotted with him in mind, but I think the whole concept—the innocent man on the run from bad guys who think he's got something which in fact he doesn't have—that's pretty much a thriller standard. Gosh, that would fit *North by Northwest, The Man Who Knew Too Much,* and probably others I'm not thinking of.

MURPHY: *There are some humorous aspects of* **Double Jeopardy,** *too, despite the heinousness of the crime. Travis ties up the prosecuting attorney, Cavanaugh, and tapes her mouth shut when he's in her apartment. Then there's the Mafia boss who's got a dolt for a nephew and involved in a lot of humorous scenes. Were you making a satire of these people?*
BERNHARDT: I've always put humor in my books and in fact there's probably much less humor in *Double Jeopardy* than in the "Justice" books, but because *Double Jeopardy* was more hard-edged, I restrained myself. Still, there were a few times when I couldn't help but write something that struck me as funny. This is dangerous because I know some people don't like humor in books. Particularly in a suspense/thriller book. And it seems to be men who complain. I've never heard it from a woman, but occasionally you'll find a man whose reaction is basically, "What's this funny stuff doing in my thriller? It's supposed to be serious." My own standpoint as an author is that novels should reflect life and life is sometimes funny and sometimes tragic, and so I try to put some of both in my books.

MURPHY: *There are a lot of lawyers writing novels these days and many of them tend to portray lawyers in a negative light for various reasons. You have a couple of lawyers who are positively portrayed—Travis and Cavanaugh.*
BERNHARDT: That's consistent throughout the "Justice" books as well. I can understand lawyer bashing in the world at large, but I don't

understand why other lawyers do it. In fact—I won't name any other writers—but I think some have jumped on the bandwagon of criticizing lawyers because it seems that's what you hear on television and that's what you hear from news media and they just want to try to cash in on that and give their books an easy appeal to a certain element. Criticism is so easy and so cheap. I'm more interested in trying to show people what it is lawyers really do. Although the "Justice" books are entertainment, they're also an exploration of the justice system. What works and what doesn't. Instead of just blanket cynicism, I'd rather say, Let's figure out what could be changed, what could be improved. Instead of just labeling all lawyers as bad people, why don't we see what specifically should not be permitted, and try to address it in an intelligent fashion? I think there are aspects of the legal system that could be reformed and improved and I have occasionally seen lawyers do things I didn't approve of. But I don't see why I should focus only on the negative.

MURPHY: *It sounds like you, as a lawyer and author, believe you have some responsibility to educate the public in your books.*
BERNHARDT: Absolutely. I don't want to sound preachy but I think that's absolutely right. I've heard time and time again when I'm speaking, or at signings, that people are really interested in what goes on in courtrooms, what goes on behind closed doors, in chambers. They'd like to get beyond the superficial "lawyers are all crooks" media level, and find out what really happens. I think that's one reason people read my books, because they know that although I write books I also still practice law. I'm still a trial lawyer. I didn't quit the instant the first book hit the bestseller list and I still don't plan to.

MURPHY: *There's a chapter in* **Double Jeopardy** *on telephone tracing equipment that goes into quite a detailed description. In some sense I got the idea that you put this in there for reasons that may be in addition to the plot.*
BERNHARDT: I was fascinated by that. I mentioned in the acknowledgments that I got to tour WilTel, now a major long distance carrier;

they're located right in Tulsa where I live. So I was able to tour their facility and learn a lot of the stuff about how it's all done, and I thought that was interesting and that's why I put it in the book.

MURPHY: *You're fairly young by successful author standards. How did you get into writing legal thrillers?*

BERNHARDT: I was fortunate in that I always knew that I wanted to write. When I was growing up, and I was in college and went to law school and did other things, I knew writing was really what I wanted to do so I set a goal and went after it. I started trying to write what would be my first book, *Primary Justice,* almost immediately after I got out of law school. Really, the only thing that kept me from trying a novel before then was that I didn't have a clue what I would write about. But after I'd gotten out of law school, in eighty-six, and practiced for a while with a big firm and been associated with cases and clients and found out a little bit about what goes on out there, I thought this was something I could write about. I could write about law firms and courtrooms and I could write about the experience of the young lawyer working in a big firm and all of those elements mixed together to give me *Primary Justice.* I should point out I'd started writing the book in 1987, which was well before I knew about John Grisham and before even Scott Turow. I picked my subject because it was my subject, it was something I knew about, and it was strictly fortuitous that it turned out to be such a popular subject.

MURPHY: *In law school you won awards for your legal writing. Has your ability as a legal writer helped you in writing fiction?*

BERNHARDT: I think if you can write one you can write the other. They're different, but still, a lot of it is just fundamental good writing skills. I wouldn't make anything more of it. I was on the Moot Court National Championship Team when I was in law school. I'm not sure that means I'm a brilliant talker. We were just fortunate to win the competition.

MURPHY: *You mentioned earlier that you're working on another Ben Kincaid novel.*

BERNHARDT: It will be titled *Cruel Justice,* and it will be out next February. It will be the fifth outing for Ben, and writers should never say anything like this, but I think it's the best book I've written. It's the longest and probably the most complex. My editor thinks it's the best one I've ever done. I hope he's right.

MURPHY: *What will the theme of* **Cruel Justice** *be?*

BERNHARDT: I hate to put that in boldface law kind of terms. When people go looking for big themes, they sometimes seem a bit artificial. But I could say that my wife and I have two small children at home and I'm a relatively new father. So issues having to do with children and child welfare, and what it is to be a father, are important to me right now, and I think that will be reflected in the book.

JAY BRANDON

Jay Brandon's fourth novel, *Fade the Heat,* involves Mark Blackwell, Bexar County district attorney, whose son is charged with raping a black maid at his downtown San Antonio office. The defendant claims the victim appeared at his office door, ripped off her own clothes, and screamed, "Rape!" As Blackwell helps his son prepare for trial, he experiences regret at the kind of father he's been.

> *I realized I didn't really know how smart David was. He was always so unobtrusive. Standing there, I wished I could live twenty years over again in an instant, live them differently so David would be a different person and so would I, so we'd be standing somewhere other than where we were, having a witty conversation and laughing and clapping each other on the shoulder.*

Brandon received his law degree from the University of Houston in 1985, bachelor's degree from the University of Texas, Austin, in 1975, and master's degree in writing from Johns Hopkins University in 1979.

His legal experience includes working as a briefing attorney at the Texas Court of Criminal Appeals and as an assistant district attorney in Bexar County, Texas. In 1989–90 he worked as a staff attorney at the court of appeals in San Antonio. He now limits his practice to handling family law matters and occasional criminal appeals.

This interview took place in 1990.

FICTION: *Deadbolt* (1985) ▪ *Tripwire* (1987) ▪ *Predator's Waltz* (1989) ▪ *Fade the Heat* (1990) ▪ *Rules of Evidence* (1992) ▪ *Loose Among the Lambs* (1993) ▪

Local Rules (1995) ▪ *Defiance County* (1996) ▪ *Angel of Death* (1998) ▪ *After Image* (2000) ▪ *Executive Privilege* (2001)

MURPHY: *Several critics, as well as your own publisher, have compared you to Scott Turow. Do you believe that comparison is a fair one? Are you as good a writer as Turow?*

BRANDON: I've only read *Presumed Innocent,* not his other two books, so I'm not very authoritative, and certainly not objective, but I'll give you an answer. Yes, I'm as good a writer as he is.

I'm not a lawyer who decided to write a novel. I'm a writer who became a lawyer. I've been writing since I was ten years old, so I've been at this a long time. I had two novels published before *Presumed Innocent* appeared. When it did, I already had the idea for *Fade the Heat* and was making notes for it. I read *Presumed Innocent* and liked it, I thought it very well written. But its enormous success disheartened me a little. I would have liked to be the first to publish a novel about a prosecutor becoming personally enmeshed in the criminal justice system, but Mr. Turow was a few years ahead of me in his own legal experience and he beat me to it. Consequently, nearly every review of *Fade the Heat* I've had has compared me to him. I'd much rather stand on my own, but I'm not afraid of the comparisons.

MURPHY: *The term* fade the heat *is used many times in the book. What does the term mean?*

BRANDON: It means to handle pressure, particularly the pressure of adverse publicity or bad public reaction. I've only heard it used by lawyers or criminals, for that matter, or police. I've read that it's a prison slang term. The way I've heard it used is, for example, if a lawyer has a motion to suppress evidence and he thinks it's a good motion, he may wonder if, in spite of the validity of his claim, the judge will have the courage to grant it and "fade the heat" from the public.

MURPHY: *I've not heard the term used around here. Do you know if it's just a Texas term?*

BRANDON: I don't know. I've heard it in Houston and I've heard it here in San Antonio and my father said he heard it in Dallas in the fifties. My publisher in New York hadn't heard of it. There was some talk about changing the title, but I thought it was the kind of phrase that was intriguing, even if you didn't know what it meant.

MURPHY: *The book involves the son of a district attorney who is accused of rape and the efforts of the DA to, essentially, "fade the heat" from him. What theme did you have in mind in writing the book?*

BRANDON: I had the idea before I went to work in the DA's office in San Antonio but I didn't start writing it until I was already working there. What I wanted was a main character, in this case, the district attorney himself, who is also the narrator, who is a real veteran of the system, so much so that he is rather cynical about it. But I wanted him to have a case where he would care about the outcome again. Something that hadn't happened to him in quite a while.

MURPHY: *The district attorney, Mark Blackwell, says straight out that he will do anything, even if it is illegal, to get his son off. What moral message did you want to send with this kind of attitude?*

BRANDON: Here is a man who understands how the system works and how the system could possibly convict his son, even if his son was innocent. But more importantly, he cares more about his son than he does justice in this particular case. That is the only moral message, that the family is more important than the integrity of the system. Even, as in this case, when Mark has serious doubts about his son's innocence.

MURPHY: *All of your books, in one way or another, involve threats against a family member. Is the subject of family something that particularly interests you in your writing?*

BRANDON: I hadn't realized that. You're right. That's true. And I'm running out of family members, too. Children, wives, son. Yes, family is something I'm really interested in, more so as I get older. For example, I think the best novel I've read in the past ten years is John Irving's *The Hotel New Hampshire.* It was all about family. Frankly, I'd like to write more just about family than about crime and suspense. I'd like to do that someday. Just a mainstream, family novel and I'd like to cover a longer time period. As I get older, I find out that I think family is more important, particularly now that I am a parent as well as a child. I want to write something about how parents' lives affect what their children become. I guess that I have used that a lot in suspense novels just because that seems to me the greatest threat there is, particularly a threat against your child.

MURPHY: *In* Fade the Heat, *you have a number of courtroom scenes which the critics have hailed as being authentic and vividly real. Yet, in the actual trial of Mark Blackwell's son, you don't include anything about voir dire or opening statement. Why did you omit those aspects of the trial?*
BRANDON: Because they're so boring. Most of my work in the law has been in appeals, and so I've read a lot of transcripts of trials and that stuff is just so boring. One of things that I wanted to do in *Fade the Heat* was to see if I could write trial scenes that were correct by the rules of evidence, because I see so much on television that I just can't even watch because it is so violative of the rules of evidence. So I wanted to be faithful to the rules and yet try to be entertaining at the same time, of course. And I've found that one of the best ways of doing that was to omit a lot of the boring stuff. Although in my next book, of which I just finished writing the first draft, I did spend some time on the jury selection process. I realize that it's important but it's not a real crowd pleaser.

MURPHY: *Were there any aspects of the courtroom scenes that you thought came out particularly well?*
BRANDON: One thing that has always bothered me about watching courtroom scenes, particularly television lawyer shows, is how much surprise there always is. If you have been a trial lawyer, you know that by the time it comes to trial, there should be very little in the way of surprise. I have always seen these shows where the defense lawyer still

had investigators out investigating the case while the trial is going on, and that seems ludicrous to me. But you have to have some kind of surprise, it seems. The part that I thought came out well, particularly in *Fade the Heat,* was the victim's testimony, Mandy Jackson, the woman who is accusing the district attorney's son of raping her. That was another thing I did sort of inadvertently, which I thought in retrospect was good. Most mysteries are murder mysteries. In this one, the central crime is rape, so the victim is still around to tell her story. I liked that. It set up much more of a dramatic confrontation.

MURPHY: *In that particular scene, you conveyed a lot of skill on the part of the defense lawyer in shedding doubt on the victim's testimony. Was that difficult to do? The reader already knew pretty much what the victim would say.*

BRANDON: It was a little bit hard to do. But I had seen a lot of cases where even when I was certain someone was telling the truth, I saw how easy it would be for a lawyer to pick at discrepancies in the testimony, because a lot of things usually don't happen entirely logically. Events are always idiosyncratic and I saw how even if someone was telling the truth, and of course in this case there is a question as to whether she is telling the truth, it could be made to look suspicious.

MURPHY: *After the trial, a mysterious short man appears basically out of nowhere, like the* **deus ex machina** *from Greek tragedy, to tell Mark Blackwell about some evidence that may assist his son. Why did you choose to use this kind of technique to basically turn the plot around?*

BRANDON: I've been complimented on the plot of *Fade the Heat,* but to tell you the truth, I don't think plotting is really my strong point. I just brought in another character at that point because Mark Blackwell had come to a dead end. There is some behind-the-scenes maneuvering going on and I thought that the person behind that would also have come to the point where he or she was very nervous and would send an emissary to jog the proceedings along.

MURPHY: *It seems that that really is the turning point in the book. The first half is the trial of David Blackwell; the second half involves to a great extent*

Clyde Malish, a criminal who was being prosecuted by Mark Blackwell's office. When you started writing the book, did you anticipate that you would have essentially two story lines, or did that come about in the middle of your writing?

BRANDON: No. I had a fairly thorough outline of *Fade the Heat* before I started writing it. Some things changed in the course of writing it, as they always do, but I knew pretty much that that was going on all along. That is one of the only rules I've discovered in writing suspense, that once you have one good idea you should wait until you have a second one because it's much better if there are two plots going on. It seems to take up the slack. When your first plot goes on hold, your second one starts up again. I think I've tried to do that in all my books.

MURPHY: *You went to law school at the University of Houston, graduating in 1985, but you'd already gotten a master's degree in writing from Johns Hopkins. What led to your decision to attend law school?*

BRANDON: When I got the master's degree in writing, the work itself that I did at Johns Hopkins was a great experience, spending that year with other people who were interested in writing. I've missed that because it was the only time I got to spend around other writers. But the degree itself didn't get me anywhere. I know a couple of people from my class who got jobs from having that degree but I wasn't looking for something academic. I just wanted to be a writer.

What happened was that I wrote a couple of books after that and nothing happened to them. I moved to Houston and a lawyer there hired me to write what turned out to be two books about former clients of his. Nothing happened with those either, but I started spending a lot of time hanging around law offices and I discovered that I was the smartest person there but they were all making a lot more money than I was. I decided to go to law school.

Then toward the end of my second year of law school, I changed agents and my new agent sold both of those books I had written after Johns Hopkins. The first one was *Deadbolt,* which came out in 1985 right after I graduated from law school. So I began my law career and my publishing career right about the same time, just coincidentally.

But I knew even when I started law school that I was going to keep writing.

MURPHY: Deadbolt *involves a criminal defense attorney who is harassed and threatened by a former client who had been convicted of a crime and sent to prison. Was this story based on an actual case?*
BRANDON: No, it wasn't. I wrote that before I went to law school and before I spent much time with lawyers. Once I was working in the law office I realized that it was a possibility and I was surprised it didn't happen more often—clients coming back to haunt criminal lawyers—but no, I didn't know of anything specific like that. It was kind of an odd coincidence that I wrote that book before I had any idea of going to law school and before I was married and lived in Austin. By the time it came out, I was married and a lawyer and living in Austin just like the main character in my book. It was kind of eerie.

MURPHY: *In fact, in* Fade the Heat, *there is a threat to the family of Mark Blackwell, apparently by one of Clyde Malish's associates. Is this a continuation of the types of threats that you first started writing about in* Deadbolt?
BRANDON: Maybe it is a continuation but I have been writing suspense novels right along and you've got to have a villain. It does seem like the most likely type.

MURPHY: *Was it your intention to write suspense novels once you completed the master's program at Johns Hopkins?*
BRANDON: No, it wasn't. I had written a couple of other novels, mainstream sort of novels, and nothing happened to them. I read, or someone told me, that it is easier to get a first novel published in a particular genre like science fiction or mystery or romance. And I had an idea for a suspense novel. The first idea I had was *Tripwire,* which came out second. So, I wrote that and got stuck in the genre.

MURPHY: *All of your books involve, it seems to me, a sense of paranoia. Either private attorneys or district attorneys or family members being threatened by someone from their past or because of something they witnessed, as in* Tripwire, *where a woman witnessed a murder. Do you purposely instill this sense of paranoia in your novels for suspense reasons?*

BRANDON: Sure. But frankly, I've had that same sense of paranoia instilled in me, too. It doesn't take too many years of working in criminal law, or much imagination, to imagine yourself a victim. I've seen so many cases of absolutely senseless, random horror. And often the victim hadn't done anything wrong, or even anything stupid.

I think this sense of insecurity is most effective in *Fade the Heat,* because what is threatening Mark Blackwell isn't any particular person, it's his knowledge of how the criminal justice system works. This threat is so amorphous that it's hard even for someone with his supposed power to fight it. Mark knows the system very well, he's spent twenty years in it, to the point that he's very cynical about it. But when the defendant is his own son, his attitude changes. People keep telling him to let the system take its course, but he says, "I can't afford to let the system take its course. I know what its course is."

He knows the odds that are stacked against the defendant. Defendants get ground up like sausage. And rightfully so, because ninety-something percent of them are guilty. But the odds remain the same even when the defendant may be innocent, or when someone with authority is willing to do something to save him.

MURPHY: *You worked for a short period of time as an assistant district attorney. Did you get to try cases in that short period?*

BRANDON: When I started I was in county court. I was county court prosecutor on misdemeanors and I tried a lot of cases. At that time about twenty jury trials and at least twenty nonjury trials. Motions to suppress hearings and things like that. One reason I went to the district attorney's is because I wanted to get a lot of trial experience and I did—enough to get real tired of it after a few months. So from there, I went into the appellate section and spent the rest of my time in the DA's office there, another two and a half years.

MURPHY: *And you most recently were working as the staff attorney for a Texas court of appeals?*

BRANDON: Yes. After the DA's office I went to an intermediate court of appeals here in San Antonio, where I was a staff attorney. It was when I was at the court of appeals that I worked on both criminal and civil cases. The Court of Criminal Appeals, where I worked when I first graduated from law school, is something that is almost unique to Texas. I think there is one other state that has one. It is the equivalent of our supreme court for criminal cases. Our supreme court only handles civil appeals. So the Court of Criminal Appeals here in Texas is the court of last resort for state appeals in criminal cases.

MURPHY: *In that position, as well as your position as staff attorney at the court of appeals, I assume you did a lot of legal research and writing. How did you find the shift from legal writing to fiction writing?*

BRANDON: It was never a problem for me, but I didn't think it was a help, either. They are very dissimilar. For example, in writing drafts of opinions for judges, you try always to call whatever you are talking about by the same name. You deliberately depersonalize them by calling them the Appellant, or Plaintiff, and try to have no variety about it so that it will be absolutely clear what you are talking about. From that kind of writing it was a relief on weekends to write fiction and try to introduce some variety into what I was writing. But the two are very dissimilar.

MURPHY: *Getting back to the plots of your novels, the one we haven't mentioned,* Predator's Waltz, *concerned a couple in Houston who got involved in Vietnamese gang wars, and the wife's life was threatened. That theme or plot seems very similar to the others, and I can't help but compare them to Elmore Leonard. I don't know if you have read any Elmore Leonard, but he is a crime writer from Detroit whose characters are always average people confronted by threatening circumstances. Was he an influence in your writing at all?*

BRANDON: No. I've read a couple of Elmore Leonard's novels, but not very many. In fact, I don't read that much suspense. I have read a fair amount of mystery and suspense, but it's not the major portion of what I read now. I probably shy away from suspense novels since I started writing them.

Having ordinary people confronting extraordinary danger just goes with the territory when you write the kind of suspense I do. I never was interested in spies or Tom Clancy–style hardware thrillers. You could easily say I've been influenced by Hitchcock as by Elmore Leonard.

MURPHY: *Three of your four books have a Texas setting. How important is that setting to the plots of your novels?*

BRANDON: I think in *Fade the Heat* the setting is very important because it's set in San Antonio, which is my hometown. It wasn't until my fourth novel that I wrote a book that was set here. I was deliberately saving San Antonio as a setting. San Antonio is an interesting place and it certainly has not been done to death in fiction. I wanted to save it until I had a plot that was intrinsically San Antonio. I think that a lot of things in *Fade the Heat* about how law is practiced apply particularly to San Antonio, particularly to the business of trading favors, for example, which is almost a way of life in San Antonio.

MURPHY: *I imagine with* **Predator's Waltz** *that Houston was important for the presence of the Vietnamese population there.*

BRANDON: Yes, I got the idea for that when I was living in Houston, which I did from 1980 to 1985, and the influx of Vietnamese into the area was very noticeable. When I used to drive to law school every day I saw this giant sign going up at one end of downtown that at first said VIET and later VIETNAM and then VIETNAM PLAZA and finally VIETNAM PLAZA INCORPORATED. It was fascinating to watch and wonder what was going on. The sign was rising from one little section of downtown that went Vietnamese. In the course of a few weeks or months for some reason a lot of Vietnamese merchants moved in there and the whole character of the neighborhood changed. It was really strange. If you got into those streets you wouldn't have had any idea where you were.

That was what started the idea for *Predator's Waltz*. I thought, How strange to have this culture here so isolated from the city around it. I wondered what would happen if there was one last American who was caught in a neighborhood like that, which is what happens to Daniel, the main character in *Predator's Waltz*. He owns a pawnshop in a neighborhood like that and suddenly the whole neighborhood around him has gone Vietnamese except for him and accidentally he becomes involved in a Vietnamese gang war.

MURPHY: *What are your future plans? Do you have another novel in the works?*

BRANDON: I just finished the first draft of another novel that is also set in the courthouse here in San Antonio but with different characters. Two or three of the main characters in *Fade the Heat* are minor characters in this one. They pass in the hallways the way they do in real life. Then I'm going to write a sequel to *Fade the Heat*. After that I don't know. I'd like to write about someone other than lawyers. I think my publisher would like me to keep writing courtroom dramas, though.

RICHARD DOOLING

Nebraska attorney Richard Dooling's second novel, *White Man's Grave* (1994), was nominated for the prestigious National Book Award. The book chronicles the search for Peace Corps volunteer Michael Killigan, who disappeared from his village in the West African country of Sierra Leone. Killigan's best friend, Boone Westfall, travels to Sierra Leone, becoming immersed in native culture and superstitions. Meanwhile, Killigan's father, Indianapolis bankruptcy attorney Randall Killigan, conducts his own search from home, throwing around money and influence wherever he thinks it will do some good.

Dooling vividly describes Randall Killigan's love of bankruptcy practice:

> *Randall lived and breathed the Bankruptcy Code, and intimidated anybody who crossed him by quoting it chapter, section, and verse. . . . When Randall Killigan slept, he dreamed sections of the U.S. Bankruptcy Code, and woke up to discover money—lots of it—eagerly paid by clients who had insatiable appetites for his special insights into the Code. . . . In Randall's hands, the U.S. Bankruptcy Code was a weapon, anything from a blazing scimitar to a neutron bomb, depending upon how much destruction he was being paid to inflict on his client's adversaries.*

Richard Dooling graduated from St. Louis University Law School and practiced civil litigation for several years in St. Louis. Before entering law school, he worked as a respiratory therapist, an experience that led to the publication of his first novel, *Critical Care*.

This interview took place in 1995.

FICTION: *Critical Care* (1992) ▪ *White Man's Grave* (1994) ▪ *Brain Storm* (1998) ▪ *Bet Your Life* (2002)

NONFICTION: *Blue Streak: Swearing, Free Speech, and Sexual Harassment* (1996)

MURPHY: *White Man's Grave is set primarily in the West African country of Sierra Leone, a relatively unknown country. What made you think Americans would be interested in reading about Sierra Leone?*

DOOLING: I didn't really approach it from what I thought they would be interested in; it was just a place that I was familiar with. I wanted to write about Africa and that was the country I was most familiar with. I spent about seven months in Sierra Leone in 1981 and 1982. I traveled through a lot of other countries as well, but I spent most of my time there. I also became most familiar with certain tribes that live there, especially the Mende tribe. So that was the main reason that I selected it; it was the one I knew the most about.

MURPHY: *I understand you were there visiting a friend in the Peace Corps. Did you actually start writing the book back then?*

DOOLING: No, not really, but I always write, so I had sort of a journal that I kept and I eventually used some of that material in the novel.

MURPHY: *The book begins, actually, with Indianapolis bankruptcy lawyer Randall Killigan, who receives a strange package from West Africa which is described as being a black bundle of tightly wrapped rags with a hollow red tube in it. I thought it was interesting that the dust jacket for your book has a black wrapping around it. Was this intended to symbolize the bundle that Randall Killigan received?*

DOOLING: I've never heard that before. I kind of like the idea. That's interesting! I know for sure that they wanted something that was, if you will, "interactive" in a way. In other words, you've got to pick it up and play with it before you see what it is. And you're tempted to look behind the creature and unwrap it to see what it's made out of, but I get a lot of comments on the jacket. I like it, too. I've heard all different kinds of theories. There is another one—somebody told me that this is called "an exquisite corpse" when you have a figure that's made out of three different parts like that. I meant to look it up, and I still have never done it. But it's an art term, "exquisite corpse," so I'll track that down for you.

MURPHY: *The book features a lot of interesting characters in Sierra Leone— witch finders, juju men, baboon men, bush devils, looking-around men—and focuses a great deal on witchcraft. You use two characters—Randall Killigan, the lawyer, and Boone Westfall, the failed insurance agent—to interact with Sierra Leone. Were you trying to draw any kind of parallels between witchcraft and the practice of law or insurance?*

DOOLING: Actually, law, insurance, and medicine I thought would be interesting parallels because there are similarities between those three fields of knowledge and what goes on in witchcraft and magic, in my opinion. So I was drawing parallels between all of them. Actually, I was just comparing the way Africans organize reality, which for them is often chaos and poverty and violence, and the way we organize reality, using different sciences and world views. But there are similarities in the way that they operate. You assign evil to certain things and certain people and label them and try to get some control over them by doing certain rituals or using certain words. You've heard the expression "You've got to know the magic words" for a certain area of the law in order to practice it properly. It's the same sort of thing. There are a lot of similarities that occurred to me while I was there.

MURPHY: *For the readers who haven't had a chance to read your book yet, can you talk a little bit about the similarities that you explore between witchcraft and law?*

DOOLING: If a villager is bent on harming someone, there are a number of ways to do it. First of all, if they want to harm somebody, it's probably going to be bad medicine or illegal medicine, so they would go and consult a witch doctor—what we'd call a witch doctor—called really a "bad medicine" man. And the bad medicine man would make some concoction, like the bundle that Randall received, or some other kind of poultice. It doesn't really matter what it is. You find different things used in different parts of the country, in different tribes, and in different parts of Africa, but ultimately it's something that really operates outside of the person. So it doesn't matter if it's a charm, an amulet, a bundle of rags, a snake's skin, or some creature's head or something. But you are going to use this thing to get power over someone else and to harm them.

Now, what happens, though, is, inevitably in the close-knit community of a village, the person that is the target of this bad medicine hears about it. Or the other person looks at him funny—the evil eye, that type of thing. One way or another they are given to understand that this mischief is afoot. So they go hire their own "bad medicine" man who concocts a defensive medicine that is designed to either protect the person from the initial curse or swear or bad medicine, or is designed to counterattack.

When I came back home, I went to law school, and it just dawned on me every time I got involved in a lawsuit, the emotions were so similar. The American litigant says, "This person has destroyed my life and now I want to destroy their life and just tell me what I have to do. I don't care how much it costs." It's the same thing, then it's a suit, countersuit, swear, counterswear, the same dynamic. It's asking the wrong question to ask who won the lawsuit. I think it was Voltaire who said, "I was only ruined twice: once when I won a lawsuit and once when I lost one." So it's really a purgation of some kind—you have to exorcize this feeling of hatred that you have. It doesn't matter if you win or not, you have to go through it and a lawyer helps you do that, just as a bad medicine man or a medicine man would help you do it over there. The same thing is true with insurance. In fact, that's probably the closest similarity—between insurance here and beneficial magic over there. The kind of magic where you're going on a journey or you're uncertain about something—things just aren't going right. And you're afraid that something bad is going to happen to you so you pay money to this looking-around man who comes in and looks into the future for you and says, "Well, if you go to the market, buy a white chicken, kill it, cook it, and serve it to the first three strangers you see walking down the road, your journey will be a safe one and you will accomplish the purpose of your journey." So then you go and do all that stuff and you feel so much better. Journeys are inherently hazardous, especially over there.

Then if something goes wrong later on, well, there will always be an explanation, either you had committed adultery and you didn't tell the looking-around man about it before you consulted him, or some witch or an ancestor interfered with the whole divination process for its own evil purposes. There's always an explanation, but that's not the point. The point is that you have this peace of mind, which is just what you get when you buy insurance. Disasters still can strike. It's just that you can comfort yourself with the illusion that you've taken steps to protect yourself and your family from whatever, all these unknown terrors and catastrophes lurking out there.

MURPHY: *You've got a great scene in the book where Boone Westfall's brother explains to him that the purpose of insurance is not to pay claims, but to give people peace of mind.*
DOOLING: Isn't that the truth! And that's the purpose over there, too.

MURPHY: *Why did you choose a bankruptcy lawyer to explore the parallel between law and witchcraft?*
DOOLING: I had done some bankruptcy law. I was in a bigger firm, and we rotated through departments, and that was one of the departments that I rotated through. At least in our firm, bankruptcy lawyers had the reputation for being almost rock 'em sock 'em litigators. I didn't know if it was because the Code was so new that it still needs to be fleshed out so you can do creative things with it that you can't do with older statutes or the common law. Mainly I wanted a particular

body of law that I could refer to throughout, and this bankruptcy lawyer would draw all his power from it. It's so nice to call it "the Code." That's his little fetish, the Bankruptcy Code. There are guys who memorize it. They not only know the Code, they know all the annotations to it, they carry it around with them. So, I think I just picked it because I knew something about it and because it was relatively compact and manageable.

MURPHY: *On the surface the book is about the search for Michael Killigan, but it seems that Randall, his father, and Boone Westfall really are searching for something much deeper. Is that accurate?*

DOOLING: They are searching for Michael, but once all this other stuff starts happening, certain issues supersede. Randall thinks he's going to die, partly because he's a hypochondriac, but partly because he has a real fear that there's something wrong with him, and there could be. Through most of the book you're uncertain about whether he's imagining things or is there really something wrong with him, because of this CT scan that's done to him with equivocal results. So he's in peril of his life. He's not only trying to find his son, but he's also facing death. Again, that's the parallel: when a villager is confronted with the prospect of dying from a disease, what do they do to protect themselves as opposed to what we do over here? Is it any better or is it just different? Because when Randall goes to see his looking-around man or medicine man, he gets equally conflicting advice. It doesn't put his mind at ease, it's just more complex, it's just more technological and scientific. The same sort of equivocal result would probably occur in a village setting where a guy would say, "I had this terrible dream last night—I dreamed a snake bit me. What does that mean?" It's the same sort of thing: it could be this, it could be that, could be this, could be that, and so forth.

MURPHY: *Also, in the process of dealing with his own problems, Randall seems to confront the choices he's made in life in terms of his role as an attorney and the fact that he caused an opposing attorney to have a heart attack and die. He* *even goes to church; receives Communion, and gives confession. You were drawing a parallel there, too, between the Catholic Church rituals and beliefs and the witchcraft in Africa.*

DOOLING: Right.

MURPHY: *As far as Boone Westfall goes, in his search through Africa for Michael Killigan he began to confront what it meant to be an American. Was that part of your purpose in putting him there?*

DOOLING: Yes. I wanted someone from the Midwest who was just completely naive about the rest of the world, and then drop him into this setting where he is forced to ask himself all the time: "Do I adopt the African method to find my best friend?" I mean, he starts out trying to find his best friend but pretty soon he's just trying to survive. "Do I adopt all this superstitious mumbo-jumbo? Is that the thing that works over here, or is it better just to remain skeptical about that and stay with scientific rationalism?"

So he's feeling torn between those two ways of looking at the world. And he thinks that he's always able to keep his distance, but by the time he gets to the end he's completely swept up into it. There's no question—at least in my mind—that the African dynamic of the village has subdued him completely.

MURPHY: *You have two American expatriates in Sierra Leone: Sam Lewis, who essentially scoffs at the Mende superstitions, and Aruna Sisay, who has learned to adapt to them. Did you intend these characters to be symbolic of the two kinds of American reaction to the superstitions?*

DOOLING: Yes. I traveled all through Africa and it seemed that so many Peace Corps volunteers would fall into those two types. It's very common for Americans to go over there and either totally embrace the whole going-native scene, or else they don't—they're more like the British, where they have as little to do with it as possible, associate with their own kind, and set up a separate little area of town to live in. Or if they're forced to live in a village, they still get out of there as often as possible. But Americans are different. I'd even meet Americans who would no longer speak English because they had forsworn any contact with America, and they only spoke Arabic if it was Morocco or Mende if it was Africa or something. It's an interesting thing to watch happen to people.

MURPHY: *You mentioned at the beginning that you wanted to write about Sierra Leone. It occurred to me that you give a lot of detail about the Sierra Leone people, its customs, history, and the language. Did you start out writing an ethnography of the Sierra Leone people, or did you start out with the idea of writing the novel that it turned out to be?*

DOOLING: No, I started out with a novel. It's just that before I began the book I did a lot of anthropological research. Most of it I've listed in the back there, the good books I found. I was surprised to find any. But when I was in Sierra Leone I would hear about baboon men and bush devils and all this kind of thing, and I thought, well, I'm going to go look these up in the library and I won't find anything. But I was really surprised to find a lot about it actually.

MURPHY: *In the acknowledgments at the end of the book you mention that the manuscript was a lot shallower until it reached your editor, John Glusman. What contribution did Glusman make?*

DOOLING: He mainly encouraged me to develop the character of Randall Killigan, who was really sort of a framing presence in the initial draft. He offset all the things that happened in Africa and there wasn't this whole feeling of a parallel plot. I think he was in the first chapter or the last chapter and maybe two very short ones in the middle. I know it was a good idea in retrospect to have it be more a Ping-Pong effect—go over there and see how they do it; then come back over here and see how we do it. I had to write another four or five chapters to do that and I was unsure whether it would work. But, in retrospect, it was a great idea because Randall was the most fun character.

MURPHY: *I have to ask you about chapter nine, which I call "the latrine scene." Did any of your editors raise any objection to your vivid descriptions of Boone Westfall visiting the latrine?*

DOOLING: No, no, there was very little editing there. Some of the chapters were heavily edited, and by editing I don't mean pen and pencil. It's more: "I think you'd better take another run at this." So you do six, seven drafts of one chapter. But the latrine chapter I don't think was edited hardly at all. The only comment he made was that Henry Miller would really love this!

MURPHY: *You were fortunate to receive a nomination for the National Book Award. Has that nomination helped your sales at all?*
DOOLING: Yes, it has, on the hardcover. But I think you see the most dramatic results when the paperback comes out. It's due out in June. We were very lucky. I was amazed.

MURPHY: *Have you sold any books in Sierra Leone?*
DOOLING: It's coming out in England, and Sierra Leone was a British colony, so I think some might make their way to Sierra Leone one way or another, but they don't really have printing presses. I think there's one at the university in Freetown. But I don't think they'd do a project like this. They do more collections of folk proverbs and all that kind of thing.

Michael C. Eberhardt

Criminal defense attorney Michael Eberhardt based his first novel, *Body of a Crime,* on his experience trying *State v. Jackson,* a "no body" murder case. After twenty-three months, the trial resulted in the acquittal of Eberhardt's client in 1985.

His second novel, *Against the Law,* involving the assassination of the governor of Hawaii, is completely fictional. The suspect is Peter Maikai, a leader of the movement to preserve native Hawaiian rights. Maikai is the godfather of prosecuting attorney Dan Carrier, who is forced to balance family loyalties with his professional duties. As his colleagues push for the prosecution of Maikai, Carrier conducts his own investigation, uncovering evidence that shatters the power structure in Hawaiian politics and changes his own life forever.

In addition to writing mystery novels, Eberhardt practices criminal defense law in Lancaster, California, where he has practiced since graduating from the University of LaVerne Law School in 1975.

This interview took place in 1995.

FICTION: *Body of a Crime* (1994) ▪ *Against the Law* (1995) ▪ *Witness for the Defense* (1997)

MURPHY: Against the Law *features a Hawaiian prosecutor investigating the murder of the governor of Hawaii. The theme is predominantly related to Hawaiian nationalism and issues of Hawaiian identity. What interested you in this theme?*

EBERHARDT: Quite frankly, you try to find a theme that fits your story or plot. I'm not from Hawaii, I just feel their plight isn't any different than the American Indian out here, or anybody else whose land has been somewhat usurped and used for purposes other than what they feel is good for them. In Hawaii, the land is being turned into an economic situation for lining people's pockets, for development. I'd like to say there's really something more noble than that, but it was really just something that worked in with the theme of my story, not that I have any great interest in that.

MURPHY: *You do pepper the book with a lot of references to Hawaiian culture, Hawaiian language, the taro crop, canoe racing, things like that. You must have done some research or had some personal experience to enable you to do that.*

EBERHARDT: I try to go to Hawaii quite a bit, number one; number two, I have a high school friend, John Tullius, who actually lives in Hawaii. He helped me with a lot of it, not only with the story but with the Hawaiian background. I did have a lot of help.

MURPHY: *I notice that he shares the copyright with you. Is there any reason he wasn't listed as a coauthor on the cover?*

EBERHARDT: When an attorney gets involved in writing, everything they do, quite frankly, appears like a legal brief. And they need some assistance. I think anybody in New York who does any publishing will tell you everything they get from attorneys normally needs somebody to help with the prose and the creative writing aspect of it. And that's what I used John for on the first three books, but the fourth book, I'm on my own. John's been a writer since high school; he graduated in creative writing from UCLA. He's written nothing but nonfiction so fiction was a new venture for him. It really worked out as somewhat of a partnership for those first three ventures, but the more I write, the less I use him.

MURPHY: *Other than the Hawaiian atmosphere, did you have to get assistance or do any research in terms of the criminal law aspect of* **Against the Law?**

EBERHARDT: No, the one great thing about writing on something you do for a living is it doesn't require research. The only research was finding out if they have prosecuting attorneys instead of district attorneys, things of that nature. Otherwise, everything was the same. I had to do a little research in that regard. I think I ended up calling the local attorney there and just trying to find out if they have superior courts. I basically wrote the book based upon California law. I didn't have to get into any real details in that regard.

MURPHY: *The murder victim, as I mentioned, is the governor of Hawaii, and the accused is a Hawaiian nationalist named Peter Maikai. Why did you decide to have such a high-profile murder victim in this novel?*
EBERHARDT: I'm not trying to write *War and Peace,* I'm doing it commercially. It's just what's referred to as "a hook," what would draw the attention of some would-be reader when they read the flap cover of the book. Something like a governor being murdered draws attention. The first novel I wrote was drawn mostly from personal experience and had the premise of a "no body murder," which was, again, a novel idea. My third book had to do with the president of the United States suspected of murder. So . . .

MURPHY: *You keep moving up.*
EBERHARDT: As you can see, I went even higher the third time. Now, the fourth won't have political figures of any nature. But it was just something that I felt would draw the attention of readers. When you're a first- or second-time author, readers don't recognize names so they only see if the story would in fact interest them.

But the governor of Hawaii is not a real participant in the book, except for the fact that he was the one who was murdered. It just created a bigger hook than having a district attorney killed or something of that nature.

MURPHY: *One thing I noticed in* Against the Law *is the murder weapon is a hog boning knife and blood is found on the knife which is identified as that of* *the governor. It was curious, especially after the O. J. Simpson trial, there was no mention of any DNA testing being done.*

EBERHARDT: DNA testing and all modern sciences have wreaked havoc on writing novels. They really have. I think you're going to find a lot of novelists will be writing in the 1950s and '60s and '70s, before DNA, because it takes away a lot of the suspense. All you can do a lot of the time is what I did and ignore it. You've got to remember, I wrote that thing two years ago and DNA really wasn't the thing two years ago. It's only recently come into play. I mean, I've been a criminal lawyer for twenty years almost, and I've never had occasion to deal with DNA. So it's really very seldom used, although you do hear a lot about it now because of the O. J. case.

MURPHY: *In* Against the Law, *one of the interesting plot twists is Dan Carrier, the prosecuting attorney, meets up with Lily Maikai, his teenage sweetheart. But they haven't seen each other for some eighteen years. In a small state like Hawaii, what difficulties did you have with the plot in making that credible?*

EBERHARDT: That's always something you have to be very careful of. And I'm not saying I even pulled it off. I mean, some readers would say it is contrived. The first draft of the book quite frankly had them brother and sister. And at the end of the book you'd only found out that they were brother and sister, that Peter Maikai had an affair with Dan's mother. You just have to be very careful. I'm not saying it's credible, all I'm saying is sometimes you have to stretch it and hopefully it doesn't bother the reader. That is the toughest, most difficult part about writing what I call a plot-driven book. My books are not character-driven, they're plot-driven. Sometimes you stretch it and you might stretch it too far and a reader is going to close the book because they just don't buy it. Now, I'm not saying it worked in this case or it didn't; only the reader can decide that. But in every story such as this, there's got to be some coincidence. The rule of thumb is as long as there's only one, you're all right. A reader can buy one coincidence, but when you start throwing in coincidence after coincidence, then it becomes very difficult. I don't know if I pulled it off or not!

MURPHY: *I think you're right, it does depend on the reader. I know reading the book, I thought sometimes it was realistic and other times I wondered.*

EBERHARDT: That's the problem you run in to. But the more you try and put in twists and turns, that's going to happen with plot-driven books. More so than with character-driven books, where the story surrounds the character and the character's motivations. Whereas in my books, the characters are not as important, and that could work to my detriment. I know when I get bad reviews, that's the first thing they jump on is that I don't get deep enough into my characters. Now, the fourth book I'm doing as a character-driven book, so I'm going to try something different.

Not that the others haven't worked. My first book, *Body of a Crime,* hit some bestseller lists, which is very unusual for a first-time author. It's a bestseller even overseas in some countries. So sometimes it works, sometimes it doesn't. Some readers just like to turn the pages; other readers like to get behind the characters. If you like to get behind a character, my stuff is not what you want to read. My feeling is that readers nowadays are becoming directed more toward turning the pages of a plot-driven book. You can just look at the successes of some authors; somebody like Grisham is not a character author. He has stick characters. *The Firm* was a plot-driven book. That's what started Grisham off. His first book wasn't plot-driven and it wasn't a success at all until *The Firm* made it! Guys like Michael Crichton, they have mostly plot-driven books.

I just feel people nowadays are in such a rush that they're not as concerned with how somebody got to be that way, why they act that way; they would rather see them act it out rather than know why they're acting that way. And I don't think that New York feels that way; I think New York is still trying to hold on to the idea that the public wants character-driven books. I don't agree with that. The one thing you look at in a book in New York is what's called the "sales-through figure," meaning what percentage of your books sold versus the number printed. They try and maintain fifty percent; they figure a fifty-percent sales-through is a good figure. *Body of a Crime* was over seventy percent and I don't know what's going to happen with *Against the Law* yet, it's just too new. I'm not saying that means anything; I'm just saying that I think that—when compared to the number of copies that were printed—some word of mouth is being generated, and it helps with the overall success of the book.

MURPHY: *After practicing criminal law for about twenty years, what led you into writing novels?*

EBERHARDT: It goes back to the first book, *Body of a Crime.* I represented an individual named Steve Jackson, back in 1982, who was accused of killing a girlfriend acquaintance of his. But they could not find her body. It's called a "no body murder." The trial itself went on for a national record of twenty-three months. From the day we started picking a jury to the day the jury came back with a not guilty verdict, the trial lasted twenty-three months. The longest in U.S. history for a trial in which somebody was acquitted. The jury selection alone took nine months. It got a lot of publicity.

All the participants in the trial—like investigators, the DA, everybody—said, "Ah! Somebody's got to write about this." Well, nobody did and then four or five years later I was talking to the homicide investigator and he said, "Didn't anybody ever write a story about it?" I said no. They still hadn't found the body six years later, and I was constantly being asked questions every time a corpse would be unearthed in the desert. They would wonder if it was her and so the press would get ahold of me again. And it got to the point where I was forgetting a lot of the facts of the case. So one day I sat down just to sort of draw myself an outline or make some notes so I wouldn't forget some of these things. To make a long story short, that outline turned into a true-life account of the trial. But I found it to be a little bit boring, and wanted to spruce it up. All of a sudden I'm writing a fictionalized account of this trial and the rest is history. I finished it and got a six-figure advance in New

York. Now, *Against the Law* is different. I never personally experienced any of that.

MURPHY: *I understand where the title* Body of a Crime *came from. Where does* Against the Law *come from?*

EBERHARDT: It was just something that I decided on. I couldn't come up with a title, quite frankly! You have to understand they have me pigeonholed into doing courtroom legal thrillers and they like to have something that has to do with the law, some type of title. And almost everything is used and quite frankly I picked *Against the Law* because there is a passage in the book in which Peter Maikai is talking about what they've done to him. He's saying, "It's against God's law." He really wasn't even referring to the cops and robbers–type thing—it's against God's law what they're doing to Hawaii. So it was just sort of hit and miss. The toughest part of writing a book is coming up with a name.

MURPHY: *You mentioned Grisham and Crichton. Have you tried to emulate any authors in your writing style?*

EBERHARDT: As a matter of fact, when I wrote my first book, *Body of a Crime,* I'd never heard of Grisham, and I wasn't familiar with Crichton. I didn't do much reading as an attorney; leisure reading is not what I look forward to. You do so much reading on the job that you don't want to go home and curl up with a book. So, I did hardly any reading and I haven't tried to follow anybody. As a matter of fact, I was very naive; I thought if somebody took the time to write a story, that somebody would publish it. I'm since finding out (because I have been asked to give a couple talks at some writers' conferences) that maybe one out of a hundred books are ever even published. The rest sit in somebody's closet.

MURPHY: *Do you plan on continuing to write in the criminal law vein?*

EBERHARDT: Yes. Either the criminal law or legal thriller type. It's very difficult to write plot-driven stories that are based in a courtroom, because there is only so much you can do. You run out of things. It's hard to keep a reader's interest for four hundred pages when you're stuck in a courtroom the whole time. So I think you have to deviate from that somewhat. But the problem is, normally, your publishers, who hire you to be a courtroom drama writer. They pigeonhole you into that and it's difficult to break away. That's what they want you to write, even though you might not feel that that would be the most interesting story you could write. In other words, maybe I think I could write a better story about a serial killer and it's not based in a courtroom, but you're taking a chance if you do that. You might lose your publisher.

MURPHY: *Isn't one of the problems that when you do courtroom scenes you're often giving the reader information they already have, or should have?*
EBERHARDT: Yes. And, like I said, it becomes boring after a while. You can only read so much. I have a difficult time, especially when I tried to write the third and fourth book, doing courtroom scenes because I feel like I've done it already. There's only so many ways you can make questioning interesting. So it is a problem for me anyway. I don't know if it is for some of the others.

LINDA FAIRSTEIN

New York City prosecutor Linda Fairstein has turned her extensive experience prosecuting sex crimes into compelling fiction featuring Alexandra Cooper, not coincidently also a New York prosecutor. The third book in the series, *Cold Hit,* begins with the murder of wealthy socialite Denise Caxton, whose husband, Lowell, is a famous art collector. Though still occupying the same apartment, the couple lived in separate rooms and were planning to divorce. Cooper's investigation takes her and her two police officer sidekicks into the seamy side of the art world where lives are lost for the price of an obscure Rembrandt and where money doesn't talk, it swears. Her investigation takes a surprising turn when the crime lab reports a "cold hit" and a new suspect enters the picture. Whether questioning the victim's boyfriends or dodging an assassin's bullets, Cooper always keeps her cool, though rarely cool enough to beat her sidekicks in a game of Final Jeopardy!

A graduate of Vassar College and the University of Virginia School of Law, Fairstein joined the New York District Attorney's Office in 1972. Since 1976 she has been bureau chief of Manhattan's Sex Crimes Prosecution unit, prosecuting rape, sexual assault, and domestic violence.

This interview took place in 2000.

FICTION: *Final Jeopardy* (1996) ▪ *Likely to Die* (1998) ▪ *Cold Hit* (2000) ▪ *The Dead House* (2001)

NONFICTION: *Sexual Violence: Our War Against Rape* (1993)

MURPHY: *Let's start with your protagonist, Alexandra Cooper, a thirty-five-year-old sex crimes prosecutor. All three of your novels focus on her. What interests you in her as a character?*

FAIRSTEIN: When I started to write the first book, *Final Jeopardy,* I intended to write a series. I love the crime novel genre and I especially like procedurals because—being in law enforcement for so long—I enjoy things that have the technical accuracy of real police and prosecutorial work. The natural thing was to make my protagonist a prosecutor—it's the old write-what-you-know axiom. I write them from a first-person point of view, from Alex Cooper's perspective. I felt very comfortable creating a protagonist who was the woman in charge of a sex crimes unit in the Manhattan DA's office.

MURPHY: *The prosecutor, generally, is not going to be at the scene during a murder or a rape, but will come in later and have to reconstruct it. Do you find that limiting in any way as a writer?*

FAIRSTEIN: Not for the reason you suggest, but certainly it is much more limiting to write in the first person than in the third person. Obviously, in many murder/crime novels, you are not at the crime scene. Depending on how the writer constructs and solves it, whether it's an amateur sleuth or a prosecutor, the protagonist is not there. It is certainly very limiting. As one of my favorite lawyer-authors, Lisa Scottoline, said when she switched to the third person in her last book, it's more liberating; it gives you more points of view, more omnipotence as the writer. She said—I'm smiling through the tape recorder that you can't see—it's much easier to write in the first person because you don't have to deal with layering and when different people find out about things and what their feelings are and what their thoughts are. So maybe I've taken the easier route by doing the first person, but that's very much the way, of course, how my colleagues and I learn about and investigate cases. And that's, again, the perspective that I wanted to present. It was a very conscious decision when I sat down to write and I went back and forth about whether this would be a third-person perspective or the first.

MURPHY: *The term* cold hit *refers to a match between a computer profile data-base DNA and the crime scene DNA. It's a term that, as a civil lawyer, I've never heard before. Why did you, first of all, entitle the book* Cold Hit, *and secondly, focus the plot around the cold hit?*

FAIRSTEIN: You are not alone in not having heard of it before. It's a very new forensic term. In fact, when I started writing the book, which was in 1997, the term was not even in use in the forensic and law enforcement community. It's a forensic science, FBI term that means a computer databank actually makes the DNA match rather than human beings analyzing and comparing the evidence. It's so-called cutting-edge technology. This morning, January twelfth, I got two phone calls: one was a case that happened last night, but the second was the M.E.'s office calling me—life imitating art—to say that they had a cold hit on an unsolved case from June of 1998 in which a fifteen-year-old girl had been attacked. A new DNA sample on a defendant, who was just arrested in a neighboring town on a murder case, went into the computer databank and matched this unsolved rape case from the summer of ninety-eight. So, that's a cold hit. It is cutting-edge technology. It is a new forensic term. And that was a prime reason I wanted to use it.

The second reason is that my other two titles had double entendres in them. In this book, the question about the victim's murder is whether or not the killer is someone she knew or whether it was a hired killer, whether it was a hit, in fact. And so, it was a very cold hit for someone to do and that's sort of the double entendre aspect that I liked. And some of it is just that I think it's a strong title; as a reader I would pick the book up and explore it.

MURPHY: *The cold hit in the book leads Alex Cooper to the art world in New York City, both the high aspects and the low aspects. Is art a particular interest of yours?*

FAIRSTEIN: Art is an interest of mine in a much more amateur sense than I use in the book. There were two things that drew me to it. One is that having had this prosecutorial job for twenty-eight years, living in New York as well as working here, I always found the artwork in the city—both our wonderful array of museums, large and small, and the galleries (there are so many galleries in this town)—an escape from my world. It's very elegant, very calm, and a wonderful refuge for me on weekends with either my husband or my friends. The second aspect began to surprise me almost fifteen years ago when one of the most sensational murder cases that happened in New York State, in a neighboring county, involved a crime that was committed by the same man in Manhattan that I investigated. It was alleged to have been committed by one of the most prominent art dealers in the country. What I found fascinating was that this world, which was so elegant on the surface, had beneath this veneer a really dark underbelly. It had much crime and intrigue—stolen paintings, false provenances, great auction houses such as Christie's and Sotheby's being used by dealers for scams to drive up the price of art. All of these things were happening in this world that I thought was a complete escape from my criminal surroundings. Those were the two reasons, the surface and below the surface, that drew me in.

MURPHY: *It's certainly an interesting contrast where you have people of wealth and fame, living in high society, who are in many ways as unseemly as the people that you deal with on a day-to-day basis.*

FAIRSTEIN: Yes. It was a shock to me as a young prosecutor. When I began to do the research for this book, I can't tell you how many times I was amazed. The research that I did, both in museums and in libraries, then was supplemented by actual cases that I would take out of the *New York Times,* the *New York Law Journal,* the *American Bar Association Journal,* and art magazines about thefts and frauds and crimes in the art world. What real life provided me to layer in my fictional background was just extraordinary.

MURPHY: *You also get the opportunity to bring in some historical details like the Nazi plundering of Russian artwork and the Isabella Stewart Gardner theft, which I understand is still unsolved.*

FAIRSTEIN: Correct. I love research. It was one of the things that I liked as a student many, many years ago. The Gardner, as you may know, is a jewel of a little museum in Boston and was very undersecured in the estate of Mrs. Gardner. There was a heist a little over ten years ago during which one of the centerpieces of the museum, and of the book—Rembrandt's only seascape, worth millions of dollars—disappeared during an armed theft. It has never resurfaced, which is quite unusual because most of the art thefts are about acquiring the painting for someone else, or it sleeps for a while but there're rumors on the hot market off in a bar in Europe or Asia that the piece is available for a private collector. And there has not been a whisper [of the stolen Rembrandt] in more than ten years. The FBI reward is up to five million dollars. I love taking real facts like that and an actual painting, using the history of the actual theft, and then doing a what-if or where I think it might be now. I want this painting to be restored to the world someday; that would be wonderful. But I had this fear that it would be a week before pub date for *Cold Hit*. It might ruin the plot . . . but still no suggestion of solution on the missing Rembrandt or that beautiful little Vermeer that was stolen during the same heist.

MURPHY: *I want to ask you about the victim, Denise Caxton. She's the third wife of wealthy art dealer Lowell Caxton. Apparently, all three of his wives were beautiful young women. When I was reading the book, I had in mind some famous Hollywood people that may fit that category. I wonder if you were modeling those characters after any real people.*

FAIRSTEIN: Caxton's not any particular individual, and it was less Hollywood actually than New York business world in which the same kind of thing has happened. In fact, there were, within the last five years, some very well publicized divorces in the art world that were similar in terms of background. The husband and wife had separate apartments and had amazing private art collections. The man whom I stole some life facts from literally had, for example, a Renoir bedroom and a Boudin dining room. In his private home each room was lined with some great and some minor paintings of great artists. These characters are wholly fictional. But I do like to draw—when I read a profile in a magazine or in a newspaper frequently or in an obituary—an interesting detail about somebody's life that I find fascinating. I like to weave it into my fiction.

MURPHY: *Toward the end of* Cold Hit, *Alex Cooper finds herself in the middle of gunfire, shot at, and her life threatened. I assume that you're taking a literary license here and that Manhattan prosecutors typically don't find themselves in that situation?*

FAIRSTEIN: Yes, I would have lost my job a long time ago. The only time I was ever accidentally involved in a shoot-out was because I was riding in the back of a police car about eighteen months after I had started in the office. The police actually apprehended someone and the officer's gun went off accidentally in the police car. I think it was because he was so nervous. He drew the car into park and the gun was in his hands—the hand he was driving with—and the bullet blew out the windshield of the car. I was cowering on the floor of the backseat. The then–district attorney, the great Frank Hogan, called me in and said, "If you want to go to the police academy, go to the police academy. If you want to be a prosecutor, stay at your desk." And yes, I've taken fictional liberties in the crime novel genre. Part of what readers like is for the main character to be in jeopardy at some point throughout the book. Part of the challenge of writing these books, now that I'm in the middle of working on a fourth one, is to find other realistic ways that Alex Cooper would find herself in a dangerous situation and be able to extricate herself from it as well.

MURPHY: *It seems to me that it's particularly challenging with a female protagonist whom you don't normally associate with getting into life-threatening gunfights or even fistfights. It reminded me a little bit of Lisa Scottoline's last book, where she had her protagonist take boxing lessons.*

FAIRSTEIN: Yes, I think it is more challenging with a woman protagonist. One of the series that I most admired, which most drew me to the crime novel series genre, was Patricia Cornwell's procedurals with a forensic pathologist named Kay Scarpetta. Scarpetta, who is a lawyer-physician, is an expert gunwoman who has licensed guns and is well trained and knows how to use them. My character isn't a gun carrier and will never be a gun carrier. It's a little easier to get oneself out of danger when a situation confronts you and you've got guns in your home and a gun in your car. I find it even more challenging. Though Alex is athletic and swims and takes dance lessons and is a lot more fit than her creator, she has to get herself out of these situations generally with her wiles and good judgment.

MURPHY: *She does spend a lot of time with her police officer buddies, not only on investigations, but hanging around bars watching* Jeopardy!

FAIRSTEIN: We have a very interesting system here in Manhattan. Having traveled around the country and done a lot of work with other prosecutors throughout the U.S., including San Francisco, we have a very interactive relationship with the NYPD, especially on our homicides and major felony cases like the sexual assault cases. And pretty much, most of the time, from the time that the murder occurred, we are involved with the investigation. We are on twenty-four-hour call, we respond to crime scenes, we respond to the precinct, we question defendants on videotape. While some prosecutors across the country do this, most don't and most police departments don't bring in prosecutors until the arrest has been made. Historically, for more than thirty years, we have found it much more useful to have this cooperative collegial arrangement from the get-go because it makes sure that things are done with the view to getting the evidence admitted at trial. We do search warrants, subpoenas; we work with the police from the beginning to make sure that there's a legal propriety to the steps.

As a result of what I try to reflect through Alex Cooper and especially the two detectives, Mike Chapman and Mercer Wallace, who have tracked the crook in these books, there is an enormously profound respect between the two and among the three and a friendship that has developed as well as the professional relationship. They're part of a team and perform different tasks within that team. But these are really the people who watch Alex's back; they are her social friends as well, they are her drinking buddies.

The *Jeopardy!* theme is something that I started in the first book and it's a motif that a lot of fans who like the show have associated with the characters. It's just that Alex and Mike are addicted to the Final Jeopardy! question. They can both skip the whole show, but they bet money on the Final Jeopardy! question. Alex is a little more tasteful about it and can skip the show, but Mike—from the first book on—will frequently step over a dead body at a crime scene if he can turn that television on and watch the question. It's one of the leitmotifs that's supposed to provide a little humor and just a personal trait of Mike's that has now become closely identified with his character.

MURPHY: *A lot of lawyers have confessed to wanting to write novels after the success of* Presumed Innocent. *You're the first lawyer I know of who decided to write a novel during the filming of* Presumed Innocent.
FAIRSTEIN: [Laughter] A good point! Nobody's ever made that point, very good.

MURPHY: *Tell me about that.*
FAIRSTEIN: I do think *Presumed Innocent* is truly the best lawyer-novelist book that I've ever read. I think it was just a brilliant and a beautifully written book. I was a great fan of the book quite by coincidence. Alan Pakula, the late director who directed the movie, called me out of the blue because of the work I've done. That book, as many of your readers will recall, was about the murder of a sex crimes prosecutor. Pakula knew my work in New York and called and asked if I would have time to spend with the young actress who was playing the murdered prosecutor. That actress is Greta Scacci, who was fairly unknown in the States at the time and a wonderful actress and just a lovely human being. She came down here to shadow me around, as we call it, and to see how a prosecutor behaves in court. Just the basic things of what the office is like, a little of the language, how we relate to things. It's because she was going to be shown in flashback in a courtroom trial scene.

And while this was going on, we actually had an unstable fan who was stalking her. I suggested that she use the house that my husband and I have on Martha's Vineyard near another San Francisco author-lawyer whom I admire greatly, Richard North Patterson. This was back in eighty-nine, ninety and I offered Greta the use of the house, which is, for those readers who have and will read *Final Jeopardy,* pretty much how the house is described in my book. It is on a very remote part of the island, really tranquil, peaceful, quite apart from neighbors. I said to Greta, "You can get away from everything in New York and from this crazy guy and you can just go up there and relax." I was telling my husband I had made this offer and I was up the whole night worried about it because it is so remote. All I could think of was if the bad guy ever found her and followed her to this little country road on Martha's Vineyard, there would really be no one there to help her. Something terrible could happen to her without anybody knowing. I told her that the next day and retracted the offer. The situation was resolved.

But that what-if stayed in my mind and became, without giving anything away, the opening scene of *Final Jeopardy,* which is exactly that of the prosecutor's offer to a young actress of her home on the Vineyard. *Final Jeopardy* begins with Alex reading her own obituary. The actress was shot in the head on the way into the house and the local police assumed it was Alex Cooper, the prosecutor who had many enemies in prosecuting these cases for years, who had been killed in the drive. The police get the call and Alex gets the *New York Post* headline that says she's been shot to death. I used the filming of *Presumed Innocent* to begin my fictional career. You are right.

MURPHY: *You must have a wealth of material on a day-to-day basis for novels. How do you decide which of these experiences to fictionalize?*
FAIRSTEIN: That's a very good question. The murders in each of the three books I've written are completely fictitious. Those are created and made up. They're not cases that ever happened. But then I like to draw from examples in my work of things that could happen, or motives for crimes that have been committed and that I have investi-

gated to layer in. Most of the work is somewhat creative. What I've always found so fascinating for years is that my colleagues and I have had a fairly interesting backlog of cases. Screenwriters, TV writers, novelists will come and pick our brains and pick our files or just use our headlines and create their own stories. I'm sitting here, as we speak, looking at part of my archives of twenty-eight years: twelve file cabinets just in my view that have everything that I've ever worked on going back to the seventies. There's just a wealth of information.

Sometimes I'll tell a story at a dinner table about something that happened during my day that I wouldn't even think to include as a detail. Somebody else writes a screenplay about it just based on the anecdote. That's happened to me. It's just a matter of what people find interesting or different. I've written the series to be entertainment, for people to buy and read and enjoy the way I buy them and read them and chew them up like candy. But I also like to inform. I like books like the Cornwell series that have a reality-based texture so that at the end of the three or four hours that I've been reading the book or the end of the airplane trip or a day at the beach, I've not only been entertained but learned a little something as well. That's where taking a lot of the real detail and using real motives or interesting aspects of cases I've worked on and putting it in these books comes together for me.

MURPHY: *That motivation sounds similar to an author I interviewed last year who also was a Manhattan DA, Robert Tannenbaum. I wonder if you've worked with him.*

FAIRSTEIN: Bob Tannenbaum—and I'm saying this with a big smile, in case he reads this—is much older than I am. But Bob was one of my, I like to say, mentors, when I first arrived here. He was one of the most well respected members of our homicide bureau in the Manhattan DA's office. When I first got here, Bob was trying some of the most high profile murder cases in New York. I used to sit and watch him in the courtroom to learn from him. He was a wonderfully helpful teacher to me. Neither one of us at the time, I think, ever dreamed that either of us would be writing about these experiences one day. But long before I started writing, I started reading his series and I've enjoyed them enormously.

MURPHY: *Tell me about your fourth book, which I understand you're working on.*
FAIRSTEIN: Yes. It's untitled at the moment, which is one of the most difficult aspects of the book. It involves the murder of a professor at something called Kings College in Manhattan, which looks a lot like Columbia University. My second book, *Likely to Die,* was an exploration of the medical community with a murder that happened in the hospital. It let me examine the hospital as a crime scene because we've had many cases that've happened there. The third one was the art world. This one is sort of the academic community. We've had so many cases in our large urban campuses of crimes that happened in dormitories, because of the neighborhoods (people who have nothing to do with the college coming onto the campus), because of the administration in running the colleges, domestic cases, homicides. So I just found academia another world for me to explore in the same way that I did the art world in this case. And I've killed a professor. I'm trying to figure out who did it, but at this point I've killed her.

MURPHY: *I'm curious, as I am with most of the lawyer-authors, and you particularly because you seem to have such a hectic schedule, how you fit in time to write. What's your writing routine?*
FAIRSTEIN: My writing routine is very irregular. I realize that many, many writers, especially lawyer-writers, do two things. I think for me, as I said off the tape in the beginning of this, it's really not that my job is harder than other lawyers', but it's terrifically unpredictable. In the middle of the night last night we had a call and one of my lawyers had to go out and take a statement for two hours from a defendant who was arrested, having attacked a woman in her home. Her employer came to her aid and he turned out to be a network producer. He broke up the assault and he was slashed across his face by the rapist and needed fifty stitches. We're dealing with that one this morning as well as a cold hit on an unsolved homicide. The body

was found at six, and all of these things continue to go on. For me, the writing is certainly never at the workplace, where I have to be completely religious about separating the city job, the government job, from fiction. Nights I reserve for family and friends. It's become my husband's joke. My husband is a litigator, but a civil litigator, mostly securities regulations. Most of my work is done, as he likes to say, on *his* time. I write on vacations, I write on weekends, and, occasionally, I write early in the mornings. It's going to be a long time between books. It's more like two years between books whereas most series authors try to do one book every year. But it's weekends, vacations, and very early in the morning.

PHILIP FRIEDMAN

Philip Friedman's novel *Reasonable Doubt* was on the *New York Times* paper-back bestseller list for fifteen weeks. The book opens with the brutal murder of the son of former U.S. Attorney Michael Ryan in a Soho art gallery. Ryan's daughter-in-law is charged with the murder. When she asks Ryan to defend her, Ryan is forced to confront his own failures as a father and husband. During his investigation into his son's murder, Ryan for the first time begins to understand his son. Friedman skillfully intertwines Ryan's defense of his daughter-in-law with his own search into the life of his son.

Friedman's novels include *Termination Order,* which the *New York Times Book Review* called "one of the best spy stories of the year"; *Act of Love, Act of War,* about a National Security Council member involved in the aftermath of the JFK assassination; and *Rage,* which was made into a movie starring George C. Scott.

Philip Friedman is a sole practitioner in New York City. After graduating from Princeton, he studied mathematics at Stanford and Berkeley before obtaining his law degree at New York University.

This interview took place in 1991.

FICTION: *Rage* (1972) ▪ *Termination Order* (1979) ▪ *Act of Love, Act of War* (1979) [reissued as *Wall of Silence* (1994)] ▪ *Reasonable Doubt* (1990) ▪ *Inadmissible Evidence* (1992) ▪ *Grand Jury* (1996) ▪ *No Higher Law* (1999)

MURPHY: *You'd written three novels before* Reasonable Doubt, *but* Reasonable Doubt *was the first one that involved the court system and lawyers. Why did you wait so long to write about the law?*

FRIEDMAN: It took me that long to write about the law because I was busy writing about other things. But some of the other things that I was writing about were things in which I had been educated in one fashion or another. I actually got the idea for *Reasonable Doubt* a good many years ago, and I wrote an outline and even talked to a publisher about it. He was interested in publishing it, but it was his style not to pay very large advances. I knew that it was going to be a very tough book to write so I turned down the offer he made. At the same time I became involved in other work which was actually related more to my college education than to my law school education. So I embarked upon a period of going in that other direction. It was only when that was over and when I had done some other things—in television writing and some other work—that I found myself in a place where I was looking for something to write. So at that time I turned back to this old idea and began to look at it again. That was the genesis of it and in any case it was a good many years after law school that I began to do it.

The man who published the hardcover edition of *Rage* was talking to me about other books he might like to see me write. He suggested I write a novel about a corrupt Supreme Court justice, and that would have been within a very few years after my graduation from law school. It struck me at the time that I wouldn't do such a thing without getting it right and that it would involve research of a kind I was unwilling to undertake, and so I turned it down. I think it was a matter of my not being ready to address making fiction out of something which had seemed to me vastly complicated and full of nuances. It would have been very important to get it right. Not a scruple that everyone who writes fiction based in the legal system bothers about. That's one thing that kept me away from doing it. It struck me as a rather large undertaking.

MURPHY: Reasonable Doubt *involves a rather unique conflict situation where the defense attorney, Michael Ryan, is representing his daughter-in-law, who is accused of killing his son. Did you base the factual situation on any real case?*
FRIEDMAN: No.

MURPHY: *How did you come up with this scenario?*

FRIEDMAN: I don't remember. I'm never quite sure. You sit around and you think about something that will be an interesting dilemma for your characters, and that will go to the heart of whatever it is you want to explore, and be dramatic. It's more than ten years ago that that part of the idea first occurred to me, and I really don't have a clue where it came from. It proved to be even a more interesting situation than I had anticipated at the time I first thought of it. The fun part of writing the book was exploring the nuances of the legal status of an attorney who was attempting to defend someone accused of killing his son. Not an easy question. A very close question. And of course close questions make good drama.

MURPHY: *You have basically been in part-time legal practice since getting out of law school. Did you have to get any expert consultations in order to write this novel, or did you rely on your own background and knowledge?*

FRIEDMAN: No, I depended almost exclusively on expert consultations and extensive legal research. While I have been practicing law, it hasn't been criminal law. So what I had was the ability as a practitioner, and also as a client, to understand some things about attorney/client relationships. And also as a person educated in the law, the ability to know what kinds of questions to ask when I was talking to people who did the kinds of things that I was going to write about. I don't think I could have done the research I did—both in the standard sort of legal library research way, and also in the way of interviewing people and getting help—if I hadn't been a lawyer. Because I (*a*) wouldn't have known what questions to ask and (*b*) wouldn't have understood the answers. As it happens, though, I benefited from the remarkable generosity of the people I talked to. I also benefited a good deal from continuing legal education programs put on by organizations like the New York State Association of Criminal Defense Lawyers, which are superb and very helpful.

MURPHY: *You spend a lot of time in the beginning of* Reasonable Doubt *going over Ryan's decision to accept the case and defend his daughter-in-law.*

And, of course, there's a hearing before the trial judge to decide whether he can even do that. Did you recognize that the premise may be a difficult one for the reader to swallow?

FRIEDMAN: It's a funny thing. When I started out, it struck me that it was a fun notion and it would lead to very interesting places. As I began to write it, and as I began to investigate it, both as a personal, moral question and as a legal question, I began to see it was a higher, steeper hill than I had perhaps realized at the outset. And, in fact, some people did comment on what they felt was the improbability of such representation occurring. Perhaps different people reacted differently to how I presented it. But it seemed to me that the reasons I gave Michael Ryan were sufficient. I thought a real person could do that. I don't think it's something that happens every day, but given the multiplicity of reasons that Michael Ryan had, I thought he might do it.

And as to the difficulty from a legal point of view, I didn't fully anticipate that until I was in the midst of it and the deeper I got into that the more fascinated I was by it. It is, in New York, ultimately a question for the judge. Criminal defense lawyer friends of mine, who were my consultants, did me the favor of asking several judges what they would do if the question arose in their courtroom. To my enormous relief, they all said they'd allow the case to go forward.

MURPHY: *There's another conflict built into the beginning of the story when Ryan meets with the assistant district attorney, basically as the victim's father, and talks about the case. Then later he turns around and decides to be the defense attorney. Did you find that this would be an ethical problem or a conflict that the courts would allow?*

FRIEDMAN: What I learned is that it would probably be determined by the facts of the case. It would depend on how much Ryan had learned, what had been disclosed to him that wouldn't have been available to him if he hadn't been a parent. In the case and the facts as I have them, his one interview had given him no information that wasn't pretty much available to him as a member of the public. I don't address the question of whether if he had been given some kind of inside information that would disqualify him. I rather think it might.

MURPHY: *There is a tension throughout the book about whether Jennifer Knee-land Ryan is guilty. And it's much like, I'm sure you've been told this, the tension in* Presumed Innocent *about whether Rusty Sabich was guilty. Did you decide early on the guilt or innocence of Jennifer Kneeland or did that come about toward the end of your writing?*

FRIEDMAN: No, I decided right away. I knew from the beginning who did it.

MURPHY: *There's also a hint of a romantic relationship between Michael Ryan and Jennifer. Why did you feel a need to put that in?*

FRIEDMAN: [Laughter] Feel the need. I don't know about feel the need. I would say, however, that it's very sharp reading on your part to get that because I think it's there and it's meant to be there. I was very straightforward about knowing who did it from the beginning. But which of the two women—Jennifer or his cocounsel, Kassia Miller—Michael Ryan was going to get romantically involved with was not a decision I made right away. It wasn't clear to me and I didn't want it to be clear to the reader, so when I decided it would be Kassia Miller and not Jennifer Ryan I did not want to extinguish all of the hints that there might be something more between them. Ultimately it seemed to me that it was just going too far to do that and the relationship with Ryan and his cocounsel seemed to me much more plausible and much more interesting. But I did flirt with that other alternative, and having decided it was the wrong thing to do, I left the vestiges (*a*) because I thought they were humanly possible and they made sense given the people, given the characters; and (*b*) because I wanted there to be some ambiguity. I didn't want it to be a foregone conclusion that he would end up with Kassia Miller if he ended up with anybody.

MURPHY: *Was the need for this romantic relationship with Kassia Miller the reason you chose a female as Ryan's assistant?*

FRIEDMAN: No. You know it's hard to ascribe reasons in some unitary way. These things are determined over a period of time. It isn't all quite so calculated. It's a little different from playing chess. He was a person who had some difficulty in his relationships with women, so it seemed important for me to give him a chance to grow in that direction.

Also, I wanted to have someone who was a nice interface between him and Jennifer because it struck me that there were going to be difficulties with them talking to each other for a whole lot of reasons. He needed someone who could be an intermediary there, and it seemed to me a woman would be better. If I were Michael Ryan I would probably want a female cocounsel.

MURPHY: *In many ways Ryan represents some of the problems that lawyers many times undergo. Formerly he was a federal prosecutor who worked so hard he alienated his wife. His marriage breaks down and eventually results in tragedy. Were you trying to make any particular point here about lawyers' lifestyles?*

FRIEDMAN: The law, they say, is a jealous mistress. I guess I was, sure. I was trying to make a point about it. I was also trying to use the reality, again, for what it was worth, from a dramatic point of view. It would have been impossible to give Michael Ryan a successful marriage which didn't end in tragedy. It would have been a very different book. It might be interesting to know how the book would have gone. One of the things about writing novels is that it's all about making choices. It's like life a little bit—you make one choice, you're stuck with it, you follow that path and you never find out what the other road would have been like.

MURPHY: *As Ryan gets more involved in the defense of Jennifer, of course he learns a lot more about his own son, Ned, and part of this involves a hint of Mafia activity. The Mafia, of course, is prominently mentioned in John Grisham's novel,* **The Firm,** *which is currently on the bestseller list. Did you inject the Mafia into this book for purposes of increasing sales or because you thought that would be of interest to the reader?*

FRIEDMAN: The primary criminal involvement that Ned has is with Latin American drug dealers, although the Mafia, the Mob, comes into it a little bit. I did not want to write a book about the Mafia and so it's a little piece of reality that comes in. The drug deal's the same.

There had to be criminal activity involved; there was criminal activity of several kinds. But these things are intertwined and interlocked inevitably, and you can't engage in large-scale criminal activity in some of the arenas in which my characters find themselves without running into the Mob and/or drug money. I think clearly Mr. Grisham's very successful novel is—what the blurb line is—a combination of *L.A. Law* and *The Godfather,* or something. I had no such thing in mind. The important things for me were the personal relationships, as you say, with Michael Ryan learning about his son in the course of defending his son's accused murderer. An interesting irony, it seems to me. And all the legal stuff. And the rest is necessary, perhaps inevitable, but not part of what interested me about the book.

MURPHY: *In a way the trial of Jennifer Ryan is secondary to Michael Ryan's own search for the identity of his son. As he goes through the trial, he learns more and more about his son and it's not until after the trial that he really discovers who his son was. Did you consciously juxtapose these two plot lines?*

FRIEDMAN: Yes, absolutely. Yes. That's so as to make one search for the truth serve the other. Yes, definitely.

MURPHY: *Do you think that's the primary reason* Reasonable Doubt *has been so successful?*

FRIEDMAN: I wish I could answer that. I really wish I could answer that. I don't know what the primary reason is *Reasonable Doubt* has been so successful. It's very gratifying to me that people respond to the book and it's been a delight to work with the people at Donald I. Fine and especially the people at Ballantine and Ivy Books, who have been most wonderful in their support for the book and have demonstrated all that is good in publishing. But as to what the reasons are, I wish I could answer that because it would make the next book a lot easier.

MURPHY: *In terms of the style of* Reasonable Doubt, *it seemed to me there was a lot of dialogue, much like books by George Higgins, the Boston attorney and writer. Is that your general style or did you use more dialogue in this book?*

FRIEDMAN: I think I used more dialogue in this book. I generally tend to a rather spare sort of style. I'm not a writer of elaborate descriptions, although there's some of that in the book. But again it's the nature of the kind of book that much of the action is forwarded, and would be in the life of real characters doing the thing that the book is about, by conversation. It certainly is in the courtroom. Really it's all about dialogue. I mean that's what it is, it's words in the courtroom. It's demeanor as well, to be sure, and nuances of that sort, which here and there I try to bring out. But it seems to me that that's true to the lives of the characters and true to the story. Not a lot of car chases in the courtroom.

MURPHY: *You mentioned that you don't practice criminal law. What areas of law have you practiced?*

FRIEDMAN: At the beginning I did general, mostly commercial types of things, also a little bit of real estate and one interesting trust document. But, basically, I've practiced commercial law for show business–related, entertainment business–related clients. In the past few years, I've represented writers exclusively. A lot of negotiation. Also, I spent some years turning my legal talents, such as they are, toward the drafting of offering memorandums for motion picture development companies of which I was a principal. So that kind of law.

MURPHY: *It's interesting that you haven't practiced criminal law, because Ballantine sent me a list of suggested interview questions. The first time I've ever gotten that from a publisher. And they all involve the criminal justice system— prosecutors and police. Did you participate in preparing those kinds of questions? Because they don't seem to be relevant to your practice.*

FRIEDMAN: Well, they're not. What they're relevant to is the practice of all the people that I spent so much time on brain-picking expeditions with while I was doing research for *Reasonable Doubt,* and concerns that have developed in me as a result of that work and the work I'm doing on this next book, which will be called *Inadmissible Evidence* and which is about prosecutors. These questions were originally developed when I went out on media tour for *Reasonable Doubt,* and that seemed to be the area that was of interest to people, since it was related to the book. And I did a good deal of research in the direction indicated by those questions.

MURPHY: *Is* Inadmissible Evidence *going to be another criminal trial kind of book?*

FRIEDMAN: Yes, it's going to be a book about a murder trial, and it's going to be this time from the prosecutor's point of view and not the defense lawyer's point of view. It will be about a New York City assistant district attorney who is assigned a case for retrial—it was reversed on appeal—which seems to him to be the case of a lifetime until he gets into it and discovers there's a lot more going on and a lot more to trying it than he had presumed at the outset.

MURPHY: *Your other novels,* Termination Order, *which has been called one of the best spy stories of the year, and* Rage, *involve completely different subject matters.* Termination Order *dealt with espionage and* Rage *involved military systems to a certain extent. Why did you write novels on these subjects?*

FRIEDMAN: Taking the more recent one first, *Termination Order,* that novel was about espionage. Espionage had been part of my life in a way since college, at which time I was involved in the recruiting process for the CIA for a little while. I found myself in the years after that with a larger than you would expect, or that I would have expected in any case, number of friends who were or had been in that business. And it fascinated me. So, ultimately I could not resist writing about it. As to why I wrote about the military and nerve gas and those kinds of things for my first work, I'm not as clear about all the reasons. I was fascinated by the question of people who were basically, I guess for want of a better word, patriotic people who believed in the system in which they lived and in which they had been raised who were in some manner betrayed by that system. That was one of the things that drove me to investigate that question. And the whole question of governmental response to its own sometimes unintentional role fascinated me, too, and the two came together.

That was interestingly a story about a governmental coverup that was written before the Watergate burglary happened—or at least the idea was concocted and the outline was written and the screenplay, in fact. The novel was written between the burglary and the time when the cover-up started to come unraveled. The book was published and the movie was released before the cover-up was made public. So it was remarkably timely, or perhaps it was just a little bit ahead of its time. But those were all issues that were very much on my mind. The whole question of people being betrayed by large institutions and wanting to fight back. So, that gave birth to *Rage.*

Act of Love, Act of War, which was about the John Kennedy assassination, grew out of my fascination with that and also with the way in which those same themes took a part in the investigation, the way the government works with what information it wants or doesn't want to be public. But those are things which I'm not so concerned about anymore. Doing *Reasonable Doubt* really was like coming home. That goes back to your much earlier question about why it took me so long. I had to grow up a little to be ready to deal with these questions. I've been interested in the legal system since high school, which is how after trying to become a mathematician I ended up in law school. I find it endlessly fascinating to investigate the nuances of the legal system and to become involved in questions that are both legally and ethically and also morally interesting.

STEPHEN GREENLEAF

Former California attorney Stephen Greenleaf has received critical acclaim for his hard-boiled series featuring San Francisco private investigator John Marshall Tanner. *Bookcase* involves Tanner's search for the writer of a manuscript mysteriously left at a small publishing house.

Like his creator, Tanner is a former lawyer. The practice of law is a favorite target for Tanner's cynicism: "The law was a decidedly mixed blessing, stimulating intellectually but not psychologically, exciting philosophically yet intimidating pedagogically, august in the abstract and slimy in too many of its earthly manifestations." When referring to the senior partner in a large law firm, Tanner observes, "The senior partner resides in the bowels of a law firm the way a pearl nestles within the clammy flesh of an oyster."

Greenleaf is a graduate of Boalt Hall School of Law. From 1970 to 1976 he practiced antitrust, securities, and business litigation in San Francisco and Monterey before turning his attention full-time to writing.

This interview took place in 1991.

FICTION: Tanner novels: *Grave Error* (1979) ▪ *Death Bed* (1980) ▪ *State's Evidence* (1982) ▪ *Fatal Obsession* (1983) ▪ *Beyond Blame* (1985) ▪ *Toll Call* (1987) ▪ *Bookcase* (1991) ▪ *Blood Type* (1992) ▪ *Southern Cross* (1993) ▪ *False Conception* (1994) ▪ *Flesh Wounds* (1996) ▪ *Past Tense* (1997) ▪ *Strawberry Sunday* (1999) ▪ *Ellipsis* (2000)

Non-Tanner novels: *The Ditto List* (1985) ▪ *Impact* (1989)

MURPHY: *Your Tanner novels have been compared to the writings of Hammett and Chandler. Did you expect to get these kinds of accolades when you began writing?*

GREENLEAF: I'm not sure that that comparison is an accolade anymore. I think every private eye novelist's work is compared to Hammett and Chandler these days by critics who are too lazy to do much more analysis than that.

But when I began writing, the avalanche of mystery novels that is currently in vogue was not at all present. I was advised by almost everybody I talked to that the private eye genre was dead. It was a 1950s form of literature and it was a big mistake to even try it. Because I was a fan of that type of book, I thought I'd try to write a novel very much in that tradition, just so it wouldn't die out.

That's what people were talking about—that once Ross MacDonald passed on, nobody would write these books anymore and I thought that would be a shame. Of course, as it turns out, everybody's writing these books these days. But, in terms of quality, no, I didn't have the hubris to imagine that anybody would seriously compare my work with theirs and I'm not sure it's an apt comparison anyway.

MURPHY: *When you stopped practicing law and began writing the Tanner novels, did you expect you'd ever be able to make your living writing?*

GREENLEAF: No, I didn't. What's true is that, in terms of book sales, I barely do make a living at writing. If it hadn't been for the movie deals with the two non-Tanner books I've written, I would have to be doing something else probably in addition to writing. Book sales alone would not have been enough to sustain a family, even in a place like Oregon, where the cost of living is significantly less than it is in San Francisco.

MURPHY: *John Marshall Tanner bears a lot of similarities to the old private eyes Marlowe and Spade—he's hard-boiled but he's sensitive. In your mind, what makes him distinctive?*

GREENLEAF: In terms of the attributes that he has, I purposely made him a generic figure. I didn't really want him to differ in any material respects from the traditional figure, again, for the reasons I mentioned earlier. I think what makes him different, primarily, is that the world around him is different. As I see his function and the function of any detective, he is really an interpreter of the world in which he lives, and that world has changed.

So, what Tanner has to say about the world differs from what those other two detectives or any other detectives have to say about the world. He was a former lawyer so I suppose that legal matters are more prominent in his world or in these books than in some of the others. But, basically, I feel that these books are at their best when they're not so much about the detective but about the world around them. Spending too much time talking about the detective and what he eats and what he drinks and who he sleeps with and all that, is really a distraction from the main purpose of these books, which is to give a certain kind of perspective on the world.

MURPHY: *Your latest Tanner novel,* Bookcase, *involves a manuscript left at a publisher's office and Tanner is hired to find the author. What kind of messages about the world around Tanner did you want to convey in this novel?*

GREENLEAF: There are several subthemes in that book—homelessness, the publishing world, the world of adolescence, the world of the rich and poor. Generally, the way I start to write is to pick a couple of themes that I want to introduce and then try to figure out a factual framework on which to hang those themes. And nine or ten books down the road, when I start casting about for background material that I know something about, I'm down to the publishing business. So in terms of what background to frame all these concepts in, the publishing industry came to mind. That's the way the book begins, with the problem in a small publishing house.

MURPHY: *It seemed, in my reading of the book, that there was a thread that ran through all the themes—of Tanner looking at the art world, the publishing world, the legal profession, and decrying the phoniness he found there. Am I accurately reading that?*

GREENLEAF: I think that's true. There's a general sense when you write about something and—it may not be a good impulse, but the impulse is to criticize rather than to praise. I guess it's easier to be a critic than an applauder. Of course, all these aspects do have elements that are easily criticized. But Tanner's a cynic and iconoclast and that's generally his take on things. I think that's right. I think phoniness and materialism push his buttons pretty rapidly.

MURPHY: *In* Bookcase, *Tanner reveals—I think for the first time—that he has always had a hidden ambition to write a novel. It seemed to me, after having read most of the other Tanner books, that this was perhaps the most autobiographical. Would you agree with that?*

GREENLEAF: In part. There's some autobiography in all of them, of course. I think the other one that is, perhaps as much or more so than *Bookcase,* is *Fatal Obsession,* where Tanner goes back to the Midwest to a small town that's quite similar in some respects to the town I was raised in. So that book aside, *Bookcase*—in terms of maybe his adult concerns—is probably more autobiographical.

But not entirely so. Tanner is not me and while some of the things he says and does are things that I say or do or would do in those circumstances, others are entirely otherwise. I'm primarily conscious of him being a fictional character. But, of course, I did at some point in time want to write a novel because, after all, that's what I've done. So that impulse is certainly autobiographical in this case.

MURPHY: *The manuscript that is the subject of* Bookcase, *entitled* Homage to Hammurabi, *provides a counterplot to the plot that Tanner is investigating. Was this actually a manuscript that you prepared for publication?*

GREENLEAF: No. The only part of that manuscript that exists are the little parts that are sprinkled throughout the book. I felt that you couldn't really talk about a manuscript as being a potential big deal without showing parts of it to the reader. You couldn't expect the reader to take your word for it, that this manuscript that sent Tanner off on his odyssey was something important without at least making some effort to show the reader what was important about it.

Now, whether or not I've succeeded in that is another story. But I felt an obligation to dangle a portion of this manuscript in front of the reader so they would know specifically what was going on and why people were excited about this book. But, no, it's not a real book. I've had people say that my next book should be that book, however.

MURPHY: *In* Homage to Hammurabi, *a teacher is accused of sexual misconduct with his student. Then Tanner tries to find out if this is a real person and a real case. In the course of doing that, he comes across Marvin Gillis, a senior partner in a big law firm and an administrator of a private school, and, basically, makes a lot of cynical comments against lawyers and the practice of law. Is Tanner's attitude with regard to the legal practice a reflection of your own?*

GREENLEAF: It is and it isn't. Law practice is easy to take shots at and a lot of the shots are accurate. But overall my attitude about lawyers and the practice of law is not as negative as Tanner's appears to be. In the early books, he cites a specific incident that drove him out of the practice and I never had anything like that happen to me. The fact that I'm not a lawyer anymore really has more to do with my inability to be as good a lawyer as I wanted to be. The fact is that I'm a much better writer than I am a lawyer. There's a lot of ways to practice law and a lot of the ways are perfectly honorable things to do with your life. But on the other hand, where Tanner does take a shot, I think most of the time, he does reflect my views.

MURPHY: *What ultimately made you decide to leave the practice and start writing?*

GREENLEAF: It was a complex decision but part of it was the reason that I mentioned before—I just didn't feel I was achieving that much personally in terms of my ability as a lawyer. A rather big part of it was an urge to get more in control of my life and not be at the beck and call of clients and other lawyers in the firm and judges and all kinds of people. I just didn't deal very well with that kind of atmosphere— coming and going at the behest of all kinds of other people.

So writing, of course, is the extreme opposite of that—you're at nobody's beck and call, except your own. I get up and go to the next room, write, and I submit a book once a year and that's about it. I find this a lot more conducive to my personality than the practice of law.

MURPHY: *Tanner's story, of course, is set in San Francisco and you haven't lived here for a number of years. Does the fact that you've been away from the city yourself create any problems in writing the Tanner stories?*

GREENLEAF: It does a little bit. But I visit periodically and I lived in San Francisco for six months, just in this last year, between roughly December and June of this year, 1991. So, I kind of keep up to date. I probably make some mistakes—I've mentioned restaurants that have gone out of business or some building that had the name changed or something like that from time to time.

But I've tried to keep up to date and I've visited periodically over the years. But I'll have to keep doing that, obviously. I have subscribed to the *Chronicle* most of the time while I've been writing to keep up with political matters and the general sense of what's going on in the city. But it would be a mistake if I keep setting the books there and lose touch entirely. I don't plan to do that.

MURPHY: *In* Bookcase, *there is a passage involving an art gallery where Tanner walks in the front door and sees a wall painted to look like a bookcase, which opened up and a young woman walked out. This seemed to me to be an excellent symbol of the book itself, in that* Homage to Hammurabi *really wasn't the primary subject of Tanner's investigation—it was the schools. Do you often use symbolism as a device in your novels?*

GREENLEAF: I think most of it is unconscious rather than conscious. There are symbols but I don't try to overdo it certainly. But there's no question that a main issue in this book was the difference between art and reality, both in the manuscript and what lay behind the manuscript that the book was about. And some of the questions you asked about the difference between the Tanner character and me as his author—and what's really me and what's not really me. That whole issue, of course, can be approached in various ways and I tried to illustrate some of them in this book.

MURPHY: *You've written two books that did not involve John Marshall Tanner,* The Ditto List *and* Impact—Ditto List *being a book about a divorce lawyer and* Impact *about an airplane crash and personal injury trial. Why did you decide to diverge from the Tanner novels in these two books?*

GREENLEAF: There were several reasons—one, my mystery books were not reaching a particularly wide audience so I hoped that maybe a general fiction, mainstream novel would broaden my audience, even though I didn't intend to abandon mysteries entirely. I also wanted to write something that was not in the first person—to use a third-person narrative that was a little more expansive in scope than the detective form.

With *The Ditto List*—a divorce novel—I wanted to write about relationships between men and women and I didn't feel a lot of those subjects fit very well in the detective format. So there were a variety of reasons. *The Ditto List,* while not a comic novel, was a lot lighter in tone for the most part than the Tanner books. I felt an urge to write a book with a different voice, with a different feel to it. So there were both practical and creative reasons for doing it.

MURPHY: *In* Impact, *you go through the course of litigation for the airplane crash up through the trial. You quote interrogatories, answers, and complaints and actually put them in there in complete form. Why did you use this technique?*

GREENLEAF: One of the impulses behind *Impact* was this sense that you read in the paper about the "million-dollar verdict" and, if you read it from the insurance point of view, how awful that is; or from the plaintiff's point of view, how essential that is. I felt a lot of people didn't understand that process very well, how you go from an accident that happens to somebody to the end where some jury says, "Yes, you get a million dollars."

So part of *Impact* was an attempt to explain that process. I felt that you really can't explain any kind of major litigation—which, of course, air disaster litigation is—without showing some of the paperwork. As a matter of fact, my editor wanted me to take those pages out. He felt they got in the way of the flow of the narrative, and slowed the reader down, that a lot of people wouldn't read them and would be bored by them and wouldn't understand them. But I felt that to come out of that book with the best understanding possible—given that it was a novel and you can't really fully explain anything like a five- or six-year course of litigation in the course of a novel—it was essential to give somebody a taste of what the documents look like. And that's what I tried to do.

MURPHY: *You've now been writing since 1976 when you left the practice of law. How do you believe your writing style has changed over the years—or has it?*
GREENLEAF: I had occasion to go back and read the early Tanners, which are being reissued just about now by Bantam, along with the paperback of *Bookcase.* So there'll be a new set of the first four Tanners, plus the *Bookcase* paperback, out there shortly. But in the process of that—I proofread the new galleys—I noticed that the Tanner book styles have changed. I think my style has gotten a little more sophisticated, a little bit away from the traditions of the genre, the similes, and the hard-boiled talk and the smart-aleck responses.

I think, basically, without really setting out to do it, the Tanner books have become written in a style that is more like the other books. In a more literary style—for lack of a better term—even though they are really not literary. But I'm not conscious now as much, when I set out to write a mystery, that I'm doing something different than I was in writing the other books. I'm just setting out to try to write a good book. Even though with the Tanners, you have to have a mystery—a crime of some sort is involved—the style relies less on the conventions of the genre than it did in the early days.

MURPHY: *From the very beginning you've received quite complimentary reviews. Yet your sales haven't been that big. Do you have an explanation* *why other lawyer-authors, such as Grisham and Turow, have had big sales while you have not?*

GREENLEAF: No, I don't have an easy explanation for that. I think part of it has to do with me writing both in and out of a genre—some people assume I'm a mystery writer and yet, the other books come along and other people read them but not the mystery ones. I get whipsawed. I'm half in one school and half in another school. That's part of it. I'm not sure I've written anything as good as the Turow books—I haven't read the Grisham book—but his were perfectly good books and deserve the attention they got.

But I don't think anybody really knows why one book takes off and another book that seems similar just lies there. If they did, there'd be a lot more bestsellers around. It's a real mystery; it's been frustrating for me. But I've tried to do things—I've changed publishers, I've gotten an agent, I've done whatever I thought I could do as a practical matter to make things change. But, basically, they haven't changed that much. For the most part, publishers have wanted me to succeed—I mean, that's why they publish books—but whatever they've done hasn't been effective.

I'm hoping this reissue of the Tanners by Bantam, with a set of attractive covers that are coordinated, will help boost me, at least to the next higher level. But I have no idea whether that will actually prove to be the case.

JOHN GRISHAM

INTERVIEW BY OWEN PRELL

Imagine you're a newly minted Ivy League lawyer, top of your class, heading for the big bucks of Wall Street, when an obscure, medium-sized Memphis tax firm comes courting. Not worth a second glance, right? But what if they pitch a starting salary of $80,000, a low-interest mortgage, and a leased BMW, when you've got a mountain of student loans and a decrepit Mazda that has to be jump-started? You're interested enough to fly down south for a visit, where the firm wines and dines you and your spouse and all but guarantees you'll be a millionaire by forty-five. So what if the billable hours are long? They're no better on Wall Street. And in Memphis you can buy a nice three-bedroom house in a good neighborhood right away. Sounds too good to pass up, right?

Mitchell McDeere, the protagonist in John Grisham's novel *The Firm,* certainly thinks so. But then the missing pieces begin to fall into place. No one ever resigns from Bendini, Lambert, and Locke; mysterious death or retirement are the only ways out. Then the FBI contacts Mitch and tells him the firm's been under investigation. Soon the dreadful truth seems inescapable to Mitch and his wife, Abby — the firm is just a front for a Chicago Mafia family. The young associates handle mostly legitimate client matters, but before too long they've been sucked into the firm's money-laundering activities for the Mob and there's no way out. Considering the less than attractive early retirement plan, most opt to swallow their scruples and stick it out, consoling themselves with massive billable hours and equally hefty partner draws. But Mitchell has other plans, prompted by the FBI probe. His dilemma: if he stays, the FBI will nail him; if he squeals, then the Mob will. But surely a bright lawyer like Mitch can find a solution.

I spoke with John Grisham by telephone from his home in Oxford, Mississippi, where he lives with his wife and two children. A criminal defense lawyer

out of Ole Miss, who served two terms in the Mississippi House of Representa-
tives, Grisham speaks with a mellow southern drawl, his words flowing with
equal clarity and languor.

This interview took place in 1991.

FICTION: *A Time to Kill* (1988) ▪ *The Firm* (1991) ▪ *The Pelican Brief* (1992) ▪ *The
Client* (1993) ▪ *The Chamber* (1994) ▪ *The Rainmaker* (1995) ▪ *Runaway Jury*
(1996) ▪ *The Partner* (1997) ▪ *The Street Lawyer* (1998) ▪ *The Testament* (1999)
▪ *The Brethren* (2000) ▪ *A Painted House* (2001) ▪ *Skipping Christmas* (2001) ▪
The Summons (2002)

––––––––––

PRELL: *You have a runaway bestseller on your hands. You've already given up
your political career. Will you give up lawyering as well and concentrate on
writing?*
GRISHAM: I closed my office at the end of December and I've been out
of the practice for three months. I tell folks I'm a recovering lawyer.

PRELL: *Did you have your own practice?*
GRISHAM: I practiced for ten years. The first four years I had a partner.
I really enjoyed the practice. I'm going to keep my license current. If
the books stop selling I'll have to go back and make a living.

PRELL: *How did you gain insight into the operation of a big firm for your book?*
GRISHAM: I was never in a firm like "the Firm." I never interviewed
with a big firm, never had any interest. I had a lot of buddies from
law school in big firms and came up against lawyers in those firms. I
spent a lot of time in their offices over the years. You pick up a lot of
stuff.

PRELL: *The firm in your book is not the typical firm. I'm sure its behavior
exceeds what most firms consider proper legal conduct but how much of it is
fiction?*
GRISHAM: I'm sure there's a firm like that somewhere but I don't want
to know where it is. I'm certain there are a lot of attorneys and

accountants doing dirty work, but the book is purely fiction. I've had a lot of attorneys in Memphis ask me if there's any truth to it and I just protest as loud as I can. I think a lot of the legal stuff is fairly realistic—the workload, files, and things like that.

PRELL: *At one point a partner is tutoring Mitch in the fine art of padding hours. I doubt many firms are as explicit, but do you think that sort of thing is common?*

GRISHAM: I think the abuse is terrible. I was always on the receiving end, mainly from personal injury trials where the case could have been settled early on, even before suit sometimes. They were not settled until a sufficient number of hours were billed and padded to the file and the lawyers were happy and at that point the defense attorneys would start talking. I saw a lot of abuses on the plaintiff's side, too.

PRELL: *Say that Mitch had joined a firm just like Bendini, except it was a legitimate firm. Would he have stayed there, even with the workload and his wife chafing at home?*

GRISHAM: Oh, yeah.

PRELL: *Why? The money?*

GRISHAM: The money. I think Mitch would have hung in there a long time. He can take it. I don't know what would have happened at home but I think he would have worked it out. After a couple of babies, probably.

PRELL: *You used to live near Memphis. Is that why you based the novel in Memphis?*

GRISHAM: I'm really lazy when it comes to researching. When I start writing a book I really hate to stop and go look something up. I think it goes back to law school. I used to hate legal research. Memphis is one of my favorite cities—I grew up there. It was very easy to write about. I got so lazy. I wouldn't even go check some facts in Memphis. No one's caught me in a discrepancy yet so I think I'm home free.

PRELL: *Do you enjoy the actual writing?*

GRISHAM: I love the writing when it's easy and good, which is about half the time. The other half it's work, it's slow, nothing sounds good. I can't say I really enjoy sitting down and putting the words on the paper. I do enjoy when the book comes out and sells well and I get to be interviewed on television. That's fun.

PRELL: *You've published one previous novel,* **A Time to Kill.** *What was that about?*

GRISHAM: It was purely a southern book. It's about a capital murder trial set in a small Mississippi town in modern times, told through the eyes of a young attorney who represents the accused. The lawyer really wants to do a good job—it's a notorious case—and he starts drinking too much and cracking up from the pressure. It's a real good dose of the legal system and of the deep South. It sold five thousand copies and took a year and a half to do that so I moved on to something that would sell.

PRELL: *Did that discourage you from writing that type of book?*

GRISHAM: The book will come out in paperback shortly. It never had a decent chance in hardback. It was published by a very small, very new publishing company. I guess it will always be my favorite book because it was my first one. It was entirely different from *The Firm.* I'd like to write more books of the first type.

PRELL: *Do you feel part of the literary tradition of Oxford?*

GRISHAM: Not really. Oxford's got a lot of writers. It's a university town. Of course, you've got Faulkner—he put the place on the map. He was a great literary artist, dedicated to his craft, and he wrote what I consider to be literary works. Most of the writers here do that or attempt to do that. I don't aspire to do that. I think *The Firm* is high-quality commercial fiction. That's all it's intended to be. I just wanted something that was a real good story and, hopefully, well written, that people could enjoy.

PRELL: *Do you consider Faulkner one of the writers you admire most?*

GRISHAM: No. I had a great deal of difficulty reading Faulkner. Steinbeck has always been my favorite. I was exposed to him in high school and I fell in love with him after reading *Tortilla Flat*. I think that's because of his characters and his writing style, which is very clear.

PRELL: *You sold the film rights to* **The Firm** *before the book was published. Did you have an inkling that might happen?*

GRISHAM: Not at all. I didn't know it was being negotiated because my agent handled it. I thought the book would be sold to a publishing company and I wanted a better contract than my first book. I thought the movie people might look at it once it came out. You always like to think about those things. After I wrote *The Firm* I was—I wasn't going to give up, but I was about to take a serious look at the writing. I was practicing law full-time and serving in the legislature part-time and spending a lot of time writing. I wanted to write something that would sell a few copies. When a writer says he doesn't write for money, I think basically he's lying. It's no fun if no one's reading your work. But I never thought it would happen this fast.

PRELL: *How much time did you devote to the writing?*

GRISHAM: It took two years to write *The Firm* and I devoted on average an hour a day. I was very disciplined about it. I learned early on that a page a day will get you a book a year. Of course, nobody can publish a book a year, except maybe Stephen King or Danielle Steel. I got into a real routine. I wrote my first draft for *The Firm* in longhand with a fountain pen and a legal pad.

PRELL: *Has that become your lucky fountain pen?*

GRISHAM: I would have a hard time getting rid of it.

PRELL: *Would you consider writing exclusively for Hollywood?*

GRISHAM: When we sold the film rights to *The Firm,* no one ever asked me about the screenplay. I brought it up once or twice and was told that, since I've never written a screenplay, I couldn't do it. I said, Well, that's true, and I'd never written a novel before either, but I didn't get anywhere with that. So then I sat down and started reading screenplays and books about screenplays. Then I wrote one and there's an agent in Hollywood who's got it and is getting ready to sell it. I really enjoyed it. If I have any talent, it's in writing dialogue and a screenplay's about ninety percent dialogue.

PRELL: *Is the screenplay about lawyers?*

GRISHAM: Yeah, and it's also set in Memphis, about a lawyer my age who gets into a case he shouldn't get into, with a lot of suspense. I like stories with people on the run, like Mitch and Abby, who'd never imagine that they would literally be on the run.

PRELL: *I can't imagine being more on the run than having both the FBI and the Mob after you.*

GRISHAM: He really was in a heck of a bind. I worried about him appearing to be too smart and too cool. A couple of book reviews mention that. But the reviews have been kind. I haven't had a bad one yet except for the *New York Times*. The *San Francisco Chronicle* was the first one I saw and it had a pretty good review.

PRELL: *Do you think the lawyers portrayed in movies and on television are fairly accurately portrayed?*

GRISHAM: I think most of the depictions are deplorable. Most of the lawyer movies I've seen are really bad. I guess as lawyers we tend to be too critical of movies about trials but I think sometimes Hollywood must not even consult with attorneys. My first book is a courtroom novel and my editor loved the legal stuff. It's deadly accurate because I know what I'm writing about—I've handled murder trials. I liked *L.A. Law* for the first year and then it got outrageous.

PRELL: *Any favorite lawyer movies?*

GRISHAM: *Anatomy of a Murder,* the old James Stewart movie. I liked most of Al Pacino's movie, *And Justice for All.* I liked *The Verdict.* I thought *Jagged Edge* was really stupid.

PRELL: *Your first book sounds not too dissimilar from* To Kill a Mockingbird.

GRISHAM: It has similarities and I was flattered by those comparisons. *To Kill a Mockingbird* is one of my favorite books—it's a classic. I thought there were really no comparisons because that book was set in the deep South forty years ago when race relations were a lot different, but the comparison was nice. Today people ask me about Scott Turow. It's nice to be mentioned along with Scott Turow, but I don't think there's anything similar about us.

PRELL: *How do you think you and he are alike?*

GRISHAM: I haven't read his second book but I read *Presumed Innocent* and I thought the legal stuff was really great. I read it in two days and I'm a slow reader so that says a lot. I thought it was a heck of a mystery. I read his book about law school when I was in law school. I think the only similarity is that we're both attorneys and we've both written two books. His first one sold five million copies and my first one sold five thousand copies.

PRELL: *Why did you make Mitch a Harvard lawyer?*

GRISHAM: I guess because it's perceived to be the elite, top law school. Believe it or not, there's a fair number of Harvard lawyers around here, in Jackson and in Memphis.

PRELL: *Does the community actually tolerate them?*

GRISHAM: They're in the big firms, so they're sort of insulated. They wouldn't survive long out here with the rest of us street lawyers.

PRELL: *Is there anything you would identify in yourself in Mitch? Were you a college athlete? Do you have a dog named Hearsay?*

GRISHAM: No. We both have beautiful wives—I guess that's the only thing. Maybe that we're both from humble backgrounds, but mine is not nearly as humble. The first book had a lot of autobiographical material.

PRELL: *What about the next book?*

GRISHAM: It's set in New Orleans and Washington, D.C. I'm not famil-iar with those cities at all but I just couldn't set the book anywhere around here. So I've got to spend some time there learning the alleys and the beer joints to make the book work. Believe it or not, I don't really enjoy that research, but I've got to do it. At least I've got more time to do it now.

JEREMIAH HEALY

Jeremiah E. Healy III, a graduate of Rutgers College and Harvard Law School, is a former professor of civil procedure, evidence, and modern remedies at New England School of Law in Boston. Professor Healy is the creator of an award-winning series of mystery novels featuring John Francis Cuddy, a Boston private investigator.

In *Right to Die,* Cuddy is hired by law professor and right-to-die advocate Maisy Andrus to find the person who has been sending her threatening letters. In the process of investigating various suspects, Cuddy struggles with his own feelings on the right to die, especially relating to the suffering endured by his late wife. In an informative and suspenseful style, Healy uses his many unusual characters to debate various issues concerning the right to die.

Healy has been nominated several times for the Shamus Award for the Best Private Eye Novel of the Year, winning in 1986 for *The Staked Goat.* His short stories have also been nominated for the Edgar Award by the Mystery Writers of America.

This interview took place in 1991.

FICTION: Cuddy novels: *Blunt Darts* (1984) • *The Staked Goat* (1986) • *So Like Sleep* (1987) • *Swan Dive* (1988) • *Yesterday's News* (1989) • *Right to Die* (1991) • *Shallow Graves* (1992) • *Foursome* (1993) • *Act of God* (1994) • *Rescue* (1995) • *Invasion of Privacy* (1996) • *The Only Good Lawyer* (1998) • *The Concise Cuddy: A Collection of John Francis Cuddy Stories* (1998) • *Spiral* (1999)

Non-Cuddy novels: *The Stalking of Sheilah Quinn* (1998) • *Turnabout* (2001) • *Uncommon Justice* (under the pseudonym Terry Devane, 2001)

———————

MURPHY: *Most lawyers who write novels use another lawyer as their protagonist but you've chosen to use a private investigator. Why have you done that?*
HEALY: A couple of reasons. First of all, as a trial lawyer, I tended to find that the system dealt pretty well with ninety-eight percent of the cases but not well at all with two percent of the cases. And what I thought would be interesting, as a law professor who writes mystery novels, is to explore the two percent of the cases that the system doesn't deal with well. I use a private investigator on the theory that, at least in the literature, a private investigator is kind of the righter of wrongs when the system itself has failed the people caught up in it.

MURPHY: *So is your main interest people who do not even enter the criminal justice system?*
HEALY: My main interest is people for whom either the criminal justice system, or some other aspect of the legal system, whether it be judicial, bureaucratic, or legislative, doesn't work well or effectively.

MURPHY: *Even though your main protagonist, John Francis Cuddy, is a private investigator, he also had a year of law school. What added dimension did his year of legal training give him?*
HEALY: Two things: first, it allows me to have other characters in the book—perhaps lawyers, perhaps not—speak with him in more legally oriented terms. Secondly, it allows him, since it's a first-person narrative, to explain to the reader what some of the legal terms mean, without it seeming incredible that a private investigator would understand subtle legal concepts.

MURPHY: Right to Die *involves a law professor, Maisy Andrus, who is a proponent of euthanasia and is being threatened by anonymous letters. What sparked your interest in the right to die?*
HEALY: First of all, the simple media coverage of the different cases involving the right to die over the last few years. Secondly, I had a

pretty good friend, who was a Boston area mystery writer, who developed AIDS and passed away. Before he developed AIDS, he and I talked about the AIDS crisis and talked about concepts like right to die, assisted suicide, and that sort of thing.

MURPHY: *Did you do any legal research in connection with the right to die?*

HEALY: Yes, I did. What I found was, to me, kind of surprising. Over forty states, even before the *Cruzan* decision last summer, had some form of either living wills, durable power of attorney, or health care proxy, depending on the state. But even in the states that had those—usually legislative—options, only about ten to fifteen percent of the population in those states ever took advantage. I guess that shouldn't be too surprising to us, as lawyers, in that nationwide something like only thirty percent of the people have any kind of will at all.

MURPHY: *The news stories have had a number of cases recently of assisted suicide, which is different than the right to die or mercy killing. Did that subject interest you as well?*

HEALY: Yes, it did. With respect to the right to die, there are a number of different aspects. First of all, it was pretty well established over the years that a competent adult could decline medical treatment, so long as that adult was competent at the time the treatment was appropriate. The classic example would probably be the Jehovah's Witness, who could decline a blood transfusion. Now some states made exceptions to the right to die of a competent adult if the death of the adult would lead to children, say, being a burden on society. The second aspect of the right to die is children. Generally, the parents of a child can't decline clearly appropriate medical treatment for a child. A classic example here would be parents who are Christian Scientists, not being allowed to ignore the medical needs of their children. These cases often result in criminal prosecutions if the parents don't take the sick child for some sort of medical treatment. An example from the Boston area would be the Twitchell couple, who were convicted of manslaughter. An exam-

ple from your area would be the Rippberger Middleton case, in
which the parents were acquitted of manslaughter but convicted of
felony child endangerment.

Those two areas of the right to die are fairly clear—the competent
adult and the child who is in need of medical care. What's less clear is
when the adult is currently incompetent and some treatment would
be medically appropriate. Here is where the living will and durable
power of attorney kick in. However, some states have case law or
statutory law, allowing for the parents, spouse, etc. of the incompetent
patient to provide information that the incompetent patient—at
some time prior to his or her incompetence—in fact provided infor-
mal information that he or she really would prefer to die. The *Cruzan*
case is the now classic example of that. The Supreme Court of the
United States, back in 1990, said that there was a liberty interest
under the Fourteenth Amendment to decline medical treatment,
although the states, obviously, can require a fairly high standard of
proof on that incompetent person's wishes. Now, it's a lot harder to
discontinue current treatment than to decline treatment initially,
partly because doctors and hospitals are so concerned about civil suits
for malpractice, criminal prosecutions, and, indeed, even professional
society censure.

The real question, it seems to me, and the tough question in the
1990s and beyond, is going to be whether or not there's a right to
assisted suicide—the so-called Dr. Kevorkian situation. If the
patient is competent and can pull the lever himself or herself—or
real assisted suicide where the patient, himself or herself, is physically incapable of pulling a lever or injecting himself or herself or
swallowing an overdose. That incompetent patient, therefore, needs
active help to inject or terminate in some way. Now, as I understand
it, in California, assisting a suicide is a felony. In Michigan, there
happens not to be a statutory provision on it, a loophole. They had
situations like the Harper case from California, interestingly
enough, of a seventy-two year-old husband and a sixty-eight-year-
old wife and their forty-year-old daughter, traveling from Califor-

nia to Michigan so that the husband could assist in the wife's suicide. Apparently it was done by suffocation in a motel room. Now, that spouse was indicted for second-degree murder but the jury found the spouse innocent in Michigan.

MURPHY: *In* Right to Die, *you cover a lot of different social issues, usually in the form of either friends of the professor or suspects in the threats on her life. For example, there's a gay man dying of AIDS; there's a law professor who was sexually harassing students; there's a Nazi bigot; an overprotective father whose daughter commits suicide; an antiabortionist; a handicapped bodyguard. Why so many of these unusual characters?*

HEALY: First of all, I think whenever one writes a series character, meaning a continuing character who appears in a number of books, you need to vary the supporting cast in some way. A lot of us who are mystery novelists probably could be more fairly characterized as playwrights for a repertory company. It's very easy to accidentally repeat your characters, book after book, and just have, if you will, your stock character playing a slightly different role. Accordingly, I think you try to vary, no matter what the book is, the characters who appear in it.

What I found when I was doing the research for *Right to Die* is that there are a number of different viewpoints that are appropriate to represent, whether you're an advocate for the right to die or a complete opponent of the right to die. I think you have to recognize that there are a number of different viewpoints in society, which, in a literal sense, the novelist can represent through characters who have other roles to play as well in the book.

MURPHY: *And so you use these characters to debate the issues surrounding the right to die?*

HEALY: At least I tried to. My feeling was that each major character in the book should be both a suspect in the threats against the law professor's life as well as a representative spokesman or -woman for some aspect of the right to die that I had come across in my research on it.

MURPHY: *There's a side plot in* Right to Die *of Cuddy training for the Boston Marathon. It's interesting that one of the characters is a homeless man, a former teacher and track coach, who gives Cuddy some advice on running marathons. Why did you include this side plot and this homeless person?*

HEALY: First of all, you try to have, I think, in every mystery book that you hope is a novel on its own, some aspect of subplot. Secondly, the Cuddy character in the books was someone who had been getting into better physical condition, once his nine-to-five job ended and he had the flexibility to run and do Nautilus and so forth. Third, my wife and I have lived around the corner from the finish line of the Boston Marathon for twelve years. The year I was turning forty, I finally decided that if I didn't run the marathon that year, I never would. So I trained for it. Given the amount of time I spent on it and running the marathon itself, frankly I had to use that experience in some way in the book. Otherwise, it would have been in a sense a little bit wasted. So to some extent the subplot is in the book because I had that more or less happen to me as I was training for the marathon.

MURPHY: *But I imagine you didn't run the marathon with a bullet wound.*
HEALY: [Laughter] No.

MURPHY: *And the homeless person who gives advice to Cuddy on marathons— was this just a statement on homeless people?*
HEALY: I tried to think of a way to weave in people who were alive and perfectly healthy but whose enjoyment of life was somewhat curtailed. It seems to me a homeless person is a pretty good example of the healthy but not happy person, as opposed to, perhaps, the unhealthy but happy person who doesn't want to prolong his or her life, due to the medical difficulties he or she suffers from. Also, to some extent running the marathon is the closest thing one gets to death and still be alive. It's a long, slow, agonizing process of actually running twenty-six miles. I've found, at least personally, that it was worse training for the run than doing the run itself. To train for the marathon, you have to do fourteen- and sixteen- and eighteen-mile

runs, interspersed with shorter but almost daily runs, just to build up your legs' endurance to finish a twenty-six-mile course.

MURPHY: *So, not only does a sick person have a right to die but an older man has a right to die by running a marathon.*
HEALY: In a sense, yeah—at least a middle-aged man. [Laughter]

MURPHY: *Not only is Cuddy a jogger, he's also sensitive, romantic, and has a girlfriend. How does Cuddy differ from Robert Parker's Spenser?*
HEALY: There's no question that Bob Parker opened the door to having credible private investigator characters outside of both California and New York, geographically, and outside of the purely tough, hard-boiled character, in particular. When I first got the idea to write, I was in high school and I was reading science fiction but I didn't have the time to write. The same for college, law school, and law practice. By the time I got the opportunity to teach, to have a considerable block of time off in the summer to do other things, I was reading private investigator fiction, Robert B. Parker principal among them. I thought, If this is what I'm enjoying reading, then this is what I'd enjoy writing.

I also found as a law practitioner and, eventually, law professor, that there was an awful lot of sexism in the profession and in the peripheral professions that law tends to become involved with. As a result, I wanted to be sure that I had my character be a little bit different. Not so much politically correct, but attitudinally different, because I thought it would be more interesting. It's one of the reasons why I had Cuddy be a widower, for example. The classic stereotypical private eye is the male who is promiscuous and in pursuit of women at all times. I thought what might be interesting for readers about the Cuddy character would be to have him be a World War II attitude in a Vietnam veteran's body—the concept that you married once, and perhaps you didn't marry again, but if you did marry again, you certainly wouldn't jump to it. You'd wait for someone who really could replace the loved one that you'd lost.

MURPHY: *Cuddy is a widower and spends a great deal of time at his wife's graveside, speaking to her spirit. Why did you insert this dialogue into the book? I know you've done it in other books as well.*

HEALY: That's right. It's a continuing aspect of the series. I did it originally because I thought it would make Cuddy a little different. The actual dialogues at the graveside were sparked as an idea by a funeral that I attended when I was, basically, the shoulder to cry on for someone who had lost someone close to her. But I really didn't know the person who had died and so, like all of us, my attention started to wander at the graveside ceremony. I noticed, a few rows down and over, an older man who was talking to the grave in front of him. It struck me that it wasn't such an odd thing; that in fact a person would talk at the graveside to a loved one who had died. What I discovered over time, in writing the books, was that the graveside dialogue between Cuddy and his wife oftentimes provided me with the opportunity to explore an aspect of the book's plot, which, frankly, I wouldn't have been able to explore in a convenient way through the first-person narrative, the character talking to the reader.

MURPHY: *You change the technique of the dialogue in* Right to Die *so that Cuddy and his deceased wife have, essentially, a conversation, back and forth. In other books, I know, it's Cuddy talking to his wife's spirit and then talking for her as well. Why was that change made?*

HEALY: It felt more comfortable as time went on. The concept of talking at the graveside became established in the books so that an evolution of him hearing her voice wouldn't be so surprising. Frankly, that was what I did without thinking about it. As I went back and checked to make sure I had my chronology facts in the fictional person's life straight, I noticed that. I think it was from book two to three when the change occurred. I decided it is a little odd but, at the same time, it's not unnatural once you buy the premise that someone would speak to his dead spouse's grave.

MURPHY: *One of your earlier novels,* The Staked Goat, *won the Shamus Award and I know you've been nominated for that award several times. What* *made* The Staked Goat *different, in your mind, that allowed it to win this award?*

HEALY: I'm not sure I had a great deal of perspective on why it was better or worse than other books. But my guess is because it dealt with an issue which was just emerging at the time, which was Vietnam veterans who had become not so successful, as opposed to the unfortunate stereotype of "unsuccessful" or "drugged out." They would come back to the U.S. and have the same problems everybody else would. In the case of Al Sachs, the Vietnam veteran who dies in the book, that he would be an unsuccessful steel salesman. In the case of the Cuddy character, that he would be a somewhat successful private investigator and I think that that was a tone whose time had come. What has pleased me is that I've had later books, like *Swan Dive,* in the same series, also nominated for the Shamus Award, as well as short stories involving the Cuddy character.

MURPHY: *Your books all seem to have a strong moral component. In* The Staked Goat, *Cuddy is both the hunter and the hunted. He is involved in finding his friend's killer while, at the same time, he's being hunted by the brother of somebody he put in jail. Were you consciously putting in a moral theme in this story?*

HEALY: I think I was, although, as I think Hemingway once said, you really can't talk about something very much without losing it. When you talk about a moral tone, I think what you have to recognize is that in many books there's a reason why the book got written that has little to do with commercialism or simply continuing the series. In that particular instance, it was my awareness that there are people, like the killer in *The Staked Goat,* who can drift through society and kill a lot of people without being particularly visible.

MURPHY: *You also had elements in the story that differed from other private eye books. That is, the main character, as well as other characters, questioning the use of violence. Is that a theme that you carry throughout the series?*

HEALY: I think that it's odd that, in our society, we sometimes prefer the honest violent person to the dishonest nonviolent person, that, in fact, there's an aspect of the Cuddy character that is as violent as any of the bad people he pursues. But I think that that's something that most of us haven't really thought about and let me give an example, if I can: I think that if you took a poll of people in this country and said, "Is there too much violence in America?" The answer would be yes and a fairly large percentage of people would say that. But if you really ask some subsidiary questions, I think what you discover is that people think there's too much of the wrong kind of violence and not enough of the right kind. Too much of the wrong kind of violence but not enough of somebody on the subway stopping other people from harassing someone by simply slapping them across the face and saying, "If you do it again, it's going to get worse."

In fact, I think that's the beauty of the private investigator character. From the Wild West, we have this view that the cowboy was the person who brought law to a lawless land when, in fact, there was a reason why they were called cowboys and not cowmen. They were thirteen- and fourteen-year-old orphans, who were looking for a job and probably couldn't have hit the broadside of a barn with their six-guns. They used to fire them in the air to try to turn a stampede. If you look at a real-life private investigator, you find that he or she is basically an ambulatory administrative assistant for a lawyer, not anything like the person who, in the fictional account, brings justice to law-bound society. Yet, I think that the reason why people enjoy private investigator books is precisely because they see this kind of knight errant who tries to do the right thing, who tries to see that justice is done, even if it involves violence, and especially if it involves acting outside the system itself.

GEORGE V. HIGGINS

A former assistant state and federal attorney general in Massachusetts, George V. Higgins enjoyed literary success ever since the publication of *Friends of Eddie Coyle* in 1972. A prolific writer, Higgins routinely produced at least one novel a year, including 1992's *Defending Billy Ryan*. When Ryan, the Massachusetts Commissioner of Public Works, is indicted on a corruption charge, he has trouble finding a lawyer to defend him. Ryan finds his way to Jeremiah F. Kennedy, the "classiest sleazy criminal lawyer in Boston" and also the protagonist of two previous Higgins novels.

Kennedy's initial impression of Ryan is decidedly unfavorable; he describes Ryan as having "a face that looked like a headman's double-bitted ax, freshly sharpened on both edges for a very special guest—Anne Boleyn, maybe." Despite Ryan's troublesome facial features, Kennedy takes the case. As Kennedy tries what seems like a hopeless case, help comes from an unexpected source, causing Kennedy to reexamine his own perspective on life. *Defending Billy Ryan* contains the same sharp, authentic dialogue that won Higgins critical acclaim for nearly three decades.

A graduate of Boston College Law School, Higgins had a varied career. In addition to working as a prosecutor and defense attorney, he was a columnist for the *Boston Globe,* a script consultant in Hollywood, and a college English teacher. He also taught creative writing at Boston University. He died on November 6, 1999, at the age of fifty-nine.

This interview took place in 1992.

FICTION: *Friends of Eddie Coyle* (1972) ▪ *The Digger's Game* (1973) ▪ *Cogan's Trade* (1974) ▪ *A City on a Hill* (1975) ▪ *The Judgment of Deke Hunter* (1976) ▪

Dreamland (1977) ▪ *A Year or So with Edgar* (1979) ▪ *Kennedy for the Defense* (1980) ▪ *The Rat on Fire* (1981) ▪ *The Patriot Game* (1982) ▪ *A Choice of Enemies* (1983) ▪ *Style vs. Substance* (1984) ▪ *Penance for Jerry Kennedy* (1985) ▪ *Impostors* (1985) ▪ *Outlaws* (1987) ▪ *The Sins of Their Fathers* (1988) *Trust* (1989) ▪ *Victories* (1990) ▪ *The Mandeville Talent* (1991) ▪ *Defending Billy Ryan* (1992) ▪ *Bomber's Law* (1993) ▪ *Swan Boats at Four* (1995) ▪ *Sandra Nichols Found Dead* (1996) ▪ *A Change of Gravity* (1997) ▪ *The Agent* (1998) ▪ *At End of Day* (2000)

NONFICTION: *The Friends of Richard Nixon* (1975) ▪ *Wonderful Years, Wonderful Years* (1988) ▪ *The Progress of the Seasons* (1989) ▪ *On Writing: Advice for Those Who Write to Publish (or Would Like To)* (1990)

————————

MURPHY: *You've been publishing fiction now for some twenty years. Did you ever think, when you first got published, that so many lawyers would be following in your footsteps?*

HIGGINS: I don't think it was my footsteps they were following. It's sort of a legendary or traditional progress of lawyers communicating back and forth between the law, and making the right marks on the white paper. It goes back a long way. Molière . . . I think Michel de Montaigne was a lawyer, too. A lot of lawyers have gone straight. Thomas Jefferson probably was a novelist-lawyer; he did a lot of writing. Except he wasn't smart enough to get into law school.

MURPHY: *Were you inspired at all when you began writing by any of the lawyer-authors in the past?*

HIGGINS: No, absolutely not. I was like Little Abner, merely fifteen and a half years old when I started writing, or doing what I thought was writing. I wrote fourteen books before I wrote *Friends of Eddie Coyle,* and I rewrote several of them. They were rejected by the most reputable publishers on both sides of the Atlantic, but there was never any connection in my mind between going to law school and somehow getting a novel published. They were completely disparate ambitions. I wanted to try cases, and that's the only way they would allow me to do it in Massachusetts. I had first to go to law school and then pass the bar exam. So I did that, but I didn't do it with the idea that I was going to emerge from the experience writing better novels than I had started writing when I was fifteen—although of course I did. But I think it was more a function of advancing years and having learned my trade than it was of having practiced law.

MURPHY: *After having fourteen novels fail to get published, why do you think* Friends of Eddie Coyle *finally hit the big time?*

HIGGINS: Oh, two reasons, Steve. The first one would be that, as I said, I was learning my trade. It takes a long time to learn how to write stories. We're born with almost none of the equipment. We have to learn the language. Then we have to learn how to use it, and usually we do that by mimicking somebody else's style—initially our parents and then, when we learn to read, the styles of writers whom we admire. When we've done that, we have to develop our own style, which takes a long time. You have to shed all the other styles that you've mimicked and then intentionally tried to emulate. In the meantime you also have the task of gathering stories, because you don't have stories in queues. They're not like the ability to smell or chew or things like that, that just sort of come with the beast when it's born. You have to go out and get the stories.

People have a lot more stories, I'm convinced, than they have any notion that they have. I've reached the point now where I'm convinced I'll never live long enough to tell all the stories that I must know. But it takes a while nevertheless to get them. It's often said of aspiring young writers in creative writing courses that they write the same six stories. Old man dies; old woman dies; why I hate my mother; why I hate my father; how I lost my virginity; how I tried to, and failed. That's it. And, in fact, many of these young people do have a lot of stories, but either they don't yet realize that they have them, or they might—in a shadowy kind of way—realize they possess the stories, but they're not ready to tell them. And that's not at all unusual.

I had a story that I told in the form of a novel, *A Choice of Enemies,* in 1984, but I got that story as a result of a newspaper assignment in

1962. So there's a lot of germination and fermentation that goes on somewhere in the back of the brain, and you shouldn't try to tell a story until you're ready and it's ready.

MURPHY: *Most of your stories focus on criminals—small-time hoods.*
HIGGINS: Not really. Some of the people who are the subjects of my stories commit crimes, but I never met a criminal in all my years as a prosecutor. And then as a defense lawyer I never once met a person who agreed that he was a criminal. Yes, some of them would admit— usually privately—that they committed acts that the law construed to be crimes, and that the government could prove it and in most instances had, or was so plainly about to do so that it would make no sense even to try the case. But that does not impose upon them the status, in their own eyes, of being criminals. They're still human beings, just like you and me.

MURPHY: *What is it about these types of people that has interested you in your writing?*
HIGGINS: The same thing that interested the people who started the myths of Robin Hood, and I suppose Beowulf and Gilgamesh, and all the other legendary beasts and giants and villains and heroes of sagas past. That the people who are violent and unpredictable and who break codes and laws and all sorts of solemn promises are more interesting than the people who behave themselves. Austen's characters— her books are wonderful, her stories are great—but to me it's remarkable that she made such good stories out of such little material. Scarcely anyone gets garroted or throttled.

MURPHY: *Your latest novel,* Defending Billy Ryan, *features an attorney, Jeremiah Kennedy—the third book you've written featuring him. What is there about this character that you find interesting?*
HIGGINS: I suppose in a way it's the alter ego kind of thing. If I had not been uncommonly fortunate coming out of law school, I probably would have had a career something like Jerry Kennedy's, except of course for the fact, too, that I could type. Jerry Kennedy is a talented

enough fellow—he's at least as talented a trial lawyer as I am, or was when I was still trying cases. It's just that he never really has gotten a clean break or never got one at least until Billy Ryan. And I don't know how long the fallout from that redemptive occasion is going to last him either. It's been seven years since Jerry's previous report—he'll probably report in five to seven years more, and I'll find out then what he's been up to.

MURPHY: *Kennedy is Irish, divorced, drinks a bit too much, and has a fledgling law practice. How does he differ from Frank Galvin of* **The Verdict** *fame?*
HIGGINS: Jerry Kennedy, when he goes into the courtroom, what he does is—in my experience, at least—what trial lawyers do. Not all of it, because much of what we do of course is boring. You don't want to sit through it; you pay twenty dollars or more for a book. But what he does, I think that a trial lawyer actually would do, has done, or ought to have done in cases that I've either tried or observed being tried.

But I can't say the same for Frank Galvin. If you recall that movie—for example, that absolutely hilarious scene in which you've got a major Boston law firm chaired, as I recall, by senior partner James Mason. If you've got about thirty-five partners around that table—can you imagine what that meter is with all those guys clicking away? My God, that's a partner conference on a comparatively minuscule case, even though the client is the Diocese of Boston. But on a comparatively minuscule case that hourly fee alone would run somewhere in the neighborhood of twenty-thousand or thirty thousand dollars. You're not going to keep your clients very long racking up that kind of money!

So it was fantasy; it was preposterous; and it was greatly, highly enjoyable. But I don't think it bore much resemblance to what actually happens in the real world of trials.

MURPHY: *In writing legal fiction, is it really that important to be accurate procedurally?*
HIGGINS: Not only legal fiction, Steve. Any kind of data that you use in your fiction *has* to be legit. If one of your characters uses the word

camshaft in a story, you'd better know what a camshaft is and what it does. Don't use it as a synonym for say, tongue depressor—it's not that. The minute you strike a false note like that, your reader is going to know. Even if your reader doesn't really know what a camshaft is, he's probably going to have some vague connection that it has something to do with an internal combustion engine and not with a streptococcus examination. And that's when you've lost him. One false step in fiction, just the same as in nonfiction, you're gone!

And I have this theory which nobody has ever tried to refute to my satisfaction, or at least to my conversion, that people read fiction for very much the same motive that they read nonfiction, and that's to learn something that they didn't know. Generally it's not just about human nature, or emotions, or the meaning of life, or some other ponderous crap like that. They also want to know things. If they pick up, by way of no harm, additional data about the real world around them, they're going to take that with satisfaction and gratitude. And it increases the credibility of the storyteller. It's very important, of course, because when you sit down to write something that's going to be called flat out a "novel," everybody who is involved in the enterprise from the beginning—the writer, the reader, the publisher, the salesman—knows it's a pack of lies. And the minute you lose that suspension of disbelief, you're finished—you might as well take up another line of work.

MURPHY: *What would you expect a reader to learn from reading* Defending Billy Ryan?

HIGGINS: The learning, the didactic bonus, if there is one, is secondary. First of all, I hope the reader is entertained, because it is entertainment. That's what we're after. The second thing would be, of course, that indeed in a trial at law where supposedly we seek the certitude, the truth above all, and all the rest of it—sometimes, quite often in fact, those of us who are engaged most sedulously in the search are furthest removed from the actuality of what we've unearthed. Jerry Kennedy doesn't really know, as Teddy Franklin tells him in the book—and no, I'm not going to give the ending away—he really doesn't know how he won that case that he worked so hard to win. And I've had that feeling a good many times. That after all the hard work was over and the clothes have been sent to the cleaners to have the sweat stains taken out of them, as a matter of fact probably nothing I did really had very much to do with the outcome, even though it was the outcome that I wanted.

It's very hard to maintain—and this notwithstanding the reputation of the breed—it's very hard for an honest trial lawyer to maintain a flourishing ego when he looks in the mirror. He can do it out in public, or in a meeting of other trial lawyers—and he'd better if he knows what's good for him—but it's pretty hard to do it with yourself. We hope that Charlie McCarthy is going to give us the answer that we want when we put our Edgar Bergen to him, but we don't always get it, and we know it! Sometimes we make the most progress toward the outcome we desire when we get an unexpected answer—if we've got brains enough to perceive that that's what's going on.

MURPHY: *You mention that Jerry Kennedy won his case and in fact the very first sentence of the book tells us that Billy Ryan got off. Why did you reveal the result of the trial so early on?*

HIGGINS: Because the story was otherwise. The story is not about how Billy Ryan got off. The story is about how Jerry Kennedy took on this case that nobody else in town wanted because it was hopeless, and won it, and what effect it had on him. That's what the story's about. See, I believe that dialogue is character and character is plot; and I didn't think that up—it was John O'Hara who said that. But I agree with him. And the second thing is what you are after, or what I'm after, when I read a novel is the progress from point A through point B until we reach point C and that's the end. There has to be change in a character in a novel. It's nice if you can get one in a short story, too, but it's very hard to do with a short story. You just don't have room enough.

So, this story is about what happened to Jerry Kennedy when he got this case. It's really not about Billy Ryan or what Billy Ryan did. Billy Ryan was an old crook, there's no question about it, and they finally got him on a pretty good case but they couldn't win it. And the reason they couldn't win it was—well, because something got funny in the trial. But Billy Ryan didn't know what it was and neither did Jerry Kennedy. And that's what the story is about.

MURPHY: *You spend actually very little time in the book on the trial itself. Why is that?*

HIGGINS: Trials are boring and we both know it. When you watch a television show, if it's artistically and aesthetically and artfully done, you're not going to spend much real time in the courtroom unless it's one of those old Perry Mason epics, which are not trial stories, by any means, they're Perry Mason stories. The courtroom scenes in *Perry Mason* are absolutely preposterous. And *L.A. Law,* I'm sorry to say, has gotten very much into the same mode of operation—they're having trial scenes now where there's scarcely an answer given by the witness at all. It's all leading questions and argument to the jury. There's really nothing necessary that occurs between the witnesses and the lawyers. But of course they do have to compress the courtroom action on *L.A. Law,* because so much of the hour is spent with the partners sweatily groping one another or their clients, and there's hardly time for courtroom work. I would like to know how they could run a law firm of that size, with that overhead, purely on lubricious sexual graspings. I've never seen that done. I know you could run a whorehouse that way, but I'm darned if I can understand how you can run a law practice!

MURPHY: *You mention that dialogue is character—you have been particularly praised for your dialogue. The* **New York Times** *referred to it as "impeccable";* Time *magazine has mentioned your "gift of gab." How did you develop such a great dialogue style?*

HIGGINS: I didn't develop it. That sounds as if there were some intention behind it—I had no such thing. What I did was, I was a newspaperman and I learned very early at the *Providence Journal* and then at the Associated Press that the quotes make the story. If you can get a good biting one-liner from the principal character in a news event, that's what you want to lead with. And the second way I had that drummed into me was when I was trying cases, because we both know that when you are trying a case you'd better listen to what those witnesses are saying. If they're your witnesses, you'd better be getting the answers you expect, and you'd better put another question that will get the one you wanted if you didn't. With the other guy's witness, if you plan to cross-examine that gentleman or lady, you'd better listen very carefully to see if a mistake has been made and your opponent doesn't recognize it because that's how you're going to make your money on cross. So you learn to pay attention, and that's where I picked up—quite, as I say, inadvertently—the reliance upon dialogue. That's the way you try cases and that's the way you get newspaper stories. I didn't set out to tell *Friends of Eddie Coyle* completely in dialogue. It seemed to me just like the most economical way of telling a story I wanted to tell. And staying out of it—that's another thing. I think the writer should stay out of the story. If the reader is bright—and I don't know what other kind of a reader there is (well, yes, I do, because the *New York Times* lists the number of books which come out for people who are not terribly bright)—the reader is certainly bright enough to figure out what the moral and ethical implications of the character's actions are. And those are decisions the reader should make, not the writer.

I resent it, for example, if somebody like a historian—like Nigel Hamilton—tells me what I ought to think about John F. Kennedy. I'll decide what I think. You just tell me what facts you've unearthed. It annoys the hell out of me when that's done. And novelists as well, even more so. When they start cooking the books—slanting the evidence—I'm no longer interested in it.

MURPHY: *You mentioned that* Friends of Eddie Coyle *is primarily dialogue. A lot of your novels are predominantly dialogue. I noticed, though, that* Defending Billy Ryan *has more narrative than the others. Was this a conscious choice on your part?*
HIGGINS: No, it was not. It was a conscious choice to the same extent that it was a conscious choice to tell *Friends of Eddie Coyle* almost completely in dialogue. This happened to be a book in which the

first-person narrator was the logical approach to take to it. All the Jerry Kennedy books, the whole three of them, have been first person. The disadvantage to that from an operational viewpoint—from the writer's operational viewpoint—is that you've got to figure out a way for the character to see, hear, or hear about, all the events that are necessary for him to reach the denouement at the end. And that's where your problem is, because occasionally you can find yourself dragging in some completely extraneous character or event in order to obtain a piece of information that the reader really needs to understand why the story turns out as it's going to. Of course, with the omniscient narrator, you can hop around all over the place if you like, but then you have trouble getting inside the thought processes of the major character. So you have to make that choice, or at least I do. I don't approve of shifting viewpoint. I think it's confusing to the reader and I think it can be pretty damn confusing to the writer, too.

MURPHY: *In using Jerry Kennedy as your narrator, you incorporate a lot of digressions.*

HIGGINS: Yeah, I put a lot of digressions in it. It's a lot of interior monologue. He's having a conversation with you.

MURPHY: *He talks about things like his views of judges,* L.A. Law *even, his past cases. Some critics might say this slows the plot. Do you think your digressions slow the plot?*

HIGGINS: A lot of critics have said that I don't have any plot in my books. And these are the critics who either haven't heard of, or don't understand, the maxim which I believe that God meant us all to live, which is "dialogue is character and character is plot." The character—the head guy, who develops into the character that he is, or has become, by the end of the book—is the story, and that's the plot. But I am *not* going to haul you around and bang you on the head with a pig bladder to say, "Now, Dear Reader, our scene switches to the Canary Islands at the turn of the century." The plot is strictly what the character encounters—first, how the character either gets into or has already gotten into an extremely tension-filled, stress-packed situation at the time that the story begins. And, secondly, what he or she does to get out of it. And who the character encounters on this progress and finally whether the character has succeeded or failed. Then you can decide whether it was a flaw in the character or meanness of the fates that brought the result if it's bad, or smiling gods if it's good.

MURPHY: *You say "dialogue is character." Are you including the digressions of the narrator as a type of dialogue?*

HIGGINS: Oh, I think that you can tell something about the way that Jerry Kennedy approaches the witness in the courtroom by the attitudes that he strikes himself in discussing people whom he has met outside the courtroom, people that he knows, and his attitude toward them. I'm sorry to say that I think Jerry (quite understandably, but I'm still sorry to see it) has gone considerably far down the road toward misanthropy in this book, much further than he was in *Penance of Jerry Kennedy* in 1985. He's become bitter and, in many respects, kind of mean. But I think he's had sufficient reason to become bitter and mean. He may come out of it, he may not, I don't know.

MURPHY: *Your dialogue has been compared with another author, Elmore Leonard. Have you read much Leonard?*

HIGGINS: Oh, yeah. And I finally got to meet Dutch up at the Toronto Harbor Fest in ninety-one. He's a delightful man. Dutch has announced to the world in public (I think in *Esquire*), that I taught him how to write dialogue. I didn't mean to do that, either, but I think he got the benefit out of it. God knows, I've stolen everything I thought I might need.

MURPHY: *Do you think he's learned any lessons from you?*

HIGGINS: He had been writing screenplays, you see, until he stumbled onto me or maybe I mugged him in an alley, I don't really know. The lesson that he said he learned from reading my stuff was to start in the middle and let the reader catch up. If you recall, at the beginning of

Friends of Eddie Coyle, there isn't any scene set to it, you don't even know where you are—there's "Jackie Brown at twenty-six with no expression on his face said that he could get some guns." I didn't know where they were, either. I didn't know who the key man was until I finally wrote his name. I think that's in chapter two or three. I didn't know his name was Coyle.

MURPHY: *What's the advantage of starting a book in the middle?*
HIGGINS: I don't start in the middle. I just start with the first sentence. I don't know whether it's the middle. I just start with people talking or something happening to a person and then follow it until I find out how the story ends. First, what the story is about and then how it ends. I have no idea how the story is going to end.

MURPHY: *So you don't outline your novels before you start writing?*
HIGGINS: I couldn't even do that with term papers. When I went to Boston College it was a rule in freshman year that you had to hand in the outline with the term paper. So the first time I tried to do this, I did the outline and then I did the paper and I handed them in. And the professor flunked me because the outline didn't match the paper. They had absolutely no relationship at all. I'm clearly of the school that doesn't know what he thinks until he sees what he's written. And so thereafter I got very good grades in English because of course I would just write the paper and then I'd do the outline, so they matched. And as long as the congruency was there, I was safe. But that's the only way I could give you an outline of my novel—write the novel and then go back and do the outline.

MURPHY: Defending Billy Ryan *starts and ends with Billy Ryan's funeral. Was this symbolic?*
HIGGINS: God, no. That was the seventh draft. That's one great advantage that I did not anticipate when I—most reluctantly, kicking and screaming—went from the typewriter to the computer. For example, *A Choice of Enemies,* which is a very long manuscript—it was six hundred pages plus, and that was in Elite not Pica type, which was

twelve characters to the inch, not ten pitch as Pica is—I wrote that through four drafts. When I talk about a draft, I start at the beginning, word one, and I go through the whole last period on the last page. For a typewriter man, that was difficult. But I'm also, some would say, nasty-neat—the cruel would say, fixated in the anal phase, or something. I like my copy to be neat. I'm a professional writer and I want it clean. So when I would do a draft, either some pages would have, say; the rigidity of shingles because they have so much CorrecType on them or, in the alternative, I'd have to type it all over again. Strikeovers and things like that: I won't have them, and therefore I was hindered in the number of times that I could rewrite a book.

Now, with a computer, I can rewrite an entire novel in two weeks front to back. I'm not nice to be near—I'm not exactly a social lion during those two weeks and you don't especially want to have a social engagement with me—but that's as close as I've been able to get to what somebody or other said would be the ideal world: to write a novel in a single sitting. The same way you read a novel which is particularly enthralling, when you literally cannot put it down. Well, that's the same way it would be to write novels the way I write them, at least. I would like to be able to start at the beginning and write it through to the end to find out how it comes out.

MURPHY: *You've never done a novel from start to finish in one draft then?*
HIGGINS: Oh, yes. *Friends of Eddie Coyle.* I cut 175 words from the first draft—otherwise, it was identical with the paper that came out of my typewriter.

Eddie Coyle was nowhere near as complicated a novel as *Billy Ryan* is, for example. There were very, very few moral choices in *Friends of Eddie Coyle*. Eddie Coyle came into the world of adults with two choices. One of them was to get Mobbed up and the other one was not to get Mobbed up. He chose the Mob. And, once he did that, he was aware that he had made a choice and if he strayed from what the Mob considers to be the straight and narrow, he was dead. That was it. He had subscribed to the code that you get two mistakes in this life, and the second one is making the first one. And he made the first one. He did fink, or he wanted to, and, as a matter of fact, he was not the fink responsible for what angered the bank robbers. But by then he had been rendered sufficiently suspect, so the villain who really had been the fink was able to lay off the action on poor Eddie. He doesn't get into a heck of a lot of rather moral implications. People who have made choices, moral choices that must be made even though they're in terms of comparative grayness. Not which one is pure white and which one is pure black, but which one is less black and more white. That's much more difficult. Jerry Kennedy is one of these people. He has difficult choices.

You could argue—and it has been argued, of course, not only ad infinitum but ad nauseam—that criminal trial lawyers represent people who are guilty, which of course isn't true. They're not guilty until they've been convicted and you can't be convicted in this country—at least theoretically you don't have to be—without a trial lawyer. But, nevertheless, Jerry knows what Billy Ryan is, and in the course of his investigation, he finds out this unsavory background material and specific data which the prosecutor would like very much to have. I refer specifically to the contents of that safe-deposit box, and where that came from.

MURPHY: *Right. And that never came out in the trial.*

HIGGINS: No, it didn't come out in the trial because Jerry Kennedy kept it a secret. That was his obligation as defense counsel. He couldn't reveal that. And as a matter of fact when he got that little benison, let's say, when Jack Bonnie was on the witness stand, he knew that was perjury, or at least he had a strong suspicion that Bonnie was perjuring himself. Except he wasn't perjuring himself the way that Jerry had expected him to, which was perjury in an effort to make the case against Ryan stronger. He was perjuring himself to make the case against Ryan a little weaker. You didn't see Jerry flinging himself upon the floor or weeping salt tears of remorse, any more than you would have seen me. You take what you get in this world.

MURPHY: *In* Defending Billy Ryan, *it seems the judges, the politicians, the prosecutor, the Monsignor appear to be unsympathetic, whereas small-time criminals like Cadillac Teddy and Carlo Donato and a few of Jerry's other clients are far more sympathetic.*

HIGGINS: Now, I don't know about that. The incumbent pastor of St. Matthew's is a very nice fellow and certainly has what I consider to be a balanced and healthy, wholesome view of the universe and how it works. I think the undertaker, who is a man of some stature in the community, certainly has a good attitude and approach toward other human beings.

And I might add here, or interject, because it probably isn't too responsive, I have frequently been truly surprised at the reactions and the judgments that my readers have made about characters whom I had judged to be quite the opposite. And that of course is why we have juries in this world. For example, I might find a character to be completely sympathetic. Cadillac Teddy for one. And the majority of people—at least those who have made their views known to me—have shared the view that Cadillac Teddy is a rather charming fellow. A rascal, to be sure, but nevertheless a charming fellow. But still, there have been a number of people who thought he was a blight on the body politic and the community social. Who's right? Well, neither one of us. Did you have a good time reading the story? That's what I want to do. Books cost a lot of money. You at least ought to have some fun reading. You don't have to agree with me.

MURPHY: *How do you rate* Defending Billy Ryan *among your many novels?*

HIGGINS: I know when I've been talking for publication, I've said every single one of my books is the best one I've ever done. But this is the truth. *Billy Ryan* really intimidated me. When I finally got—after six tries—into a story that I'm enjoying telling for next year's novel, I was very much relieved. As I tell all my students all the time—repeatedly until they get sick of hearing it—the writer is the captive of the story. The fact that the story you're writing this year isn't as good as the story you wrote last year doesn't mean you aren't as good. It just may mean your story isn't as good.

The example I like to use is Robert Penn Warren. Compare *All the King's Men* to *World Enough and Time. All the King's Men* is head and shoulders above the second book. There's a reason for it. It's a better story. It really frightened me with the prospect of trying to follow the act that *Billy Ryan* put out because I liked the book so much. Now was I right? Well, it was not reviewed by either the daily or the Sunday *New York Times;* it was not reviewed by either *Time* or *Newsweek.* Since I'm convinced I haven't lost my mind entirely, I have to think that in large part it was because of the competition for reviewing space—*Newsweek* and *Time* review what, three or four books a week—that's 208 books a year. The *New York Times* reviews six books a week. They don't review on Saturday, so that's 312 books a year plus however many they review on Sunday and that's usually now five or six novels times fifty is 250. So you've got a total number of books reviewed by the *New York Times* that could include fiction, of somewhere in the neighborhood of six hundred, say. There's fifty thousand books a year published. I don't know how many are novels, but probably at least forty percent. So there's twenty thousand of them and that means the *New York Times* is not going to review somewhere in the neighborhood of 19,500. But maybe these consoling numbers aren't the story. Maybe I was just wrong about *Billy.*

MURPHY: Billy Ryan *did get mentioned quite favorably, though, in a* New York Times Book Review *article by John Grisham.*

HIGGINS: Yes. A very generous mention and I appreciated that. But it didn't get reviewed. How that would influence sales I don't know. It also didn't hurt, obviously. But I also don't know what effect reviewers have. I've done a lot of book reviewing. Not having made enough enemies in the course of just walking around Boston, I like to recruit them from out of town, too. And I have seen quite often books that I have panned go immediately to the top of the bestseller list in the communities where I have panned them. Now, did that mean it was because "If Higgins doesn't like it, it must be good"?

Probably not. But there are those kinds of novels—say, the novels of Andrew Greeley. I don't think it really matters what reviewers say about Father Greeley's novels. I think it matters a great deal what they say about mine because I think my readers tend to be people who read book reviews and are influenced—not controlled, but certainly influenced—in their choices of reading material, by what they read in the reviews. I read the *Washington Post Book World* because I find it to be a very reliable source of guidance when I am making my visit to the bookstore. I can't read all the books that come out either. So I need some help in discriminating what books I can buy. And they cost too much, that's another thing. You start talking about twenty-two or twenty-three dollars for a novel, it had better be good.

MURPHY: *What is the state of your legal practice? Do you still have clients?*

HIGGINS: No. The last major case I had was 1978. It was a Murder One and I won it. Then I figured the clients would start beating a path to my door. You see, in Boston when they say that you've quit the practice of law to write full-time, you have. You may not know it yet, but you're not going to get any clients. Gradually I had to face up to the fact that I simply wasn't pulling in enough business to meet the overhead of running a law office. And then gradually the friends of my friends and my friends themselves all had children past the ages in which they got in trouble with the police—having too much to drink underage, or smoking marijuana or something like that. So I didn't have any more small cases on the hurry-up basis in the district court. I haven't been in court for years.

MURPHY: *Your résumé mentions that you represented Eldridge Cleaver and Gordon Liddy. Were those trials?*

HIGGINS: No. Liddy had exhausted all his legal avenues but I got him a presidential commutation. And Cleaver and I parted company because he was the most difficult client I ever had. I discovered, to my woe, that the surest way to get Eldridge Cleaver and his wife, Kathleen, to do something was to tell them to do the opposite. He just wouldn't follow my directions and, since I was trying to run my law office in Boston while representing him in Alameda County, I could only have done it if the client had been cooperative. Eldridge was not. And I really didn't want to sever the connection either, because I thought I could win that case. Whoever got it—I think a public defender—did win the case, for all practical purposes. He didn't do any more time. It was a weak case.

MURPHY: *What's next? Do you have another novel in the works?*
HIGGINS: Yeah, I'm working on another novel now. I can't tell you what it's about because I don't know myself yet. I won't know until I finish at least one draft, and even then I won't talk about it until I'm satisfied it's finished. I discovered, when I was in college, talking a novel is another form of publication and when I've published it once I don't have much interest in publishing it again, which means finishing the manuscript and going through all that agony. So I never discuss what I have in progress.

JONNIE JACOBS

Jonnie Jacobs's mystery, *Shadow of Doubt,* hit Bay Area bestseller lists in the summer of 1996. The book features San Francisco attorney Kali O'Brien, who travels home to the Sierra foothills for her father's funeral. During her stay, the husband of a high school friend is murdered, and her friend becomes the prime suspect. Convinced of her friend's innocence, Kali sets out to find the murderer. During her investigation, Kali discovers a missing teenage girl and an envelope of incriminating photos. Most of all, however, she rediscovers and confronts secrets from her own past.

In addition to the Kali O'Brien series, Jacobs writes a series featuring amateur sleuth Kate Austen, who lives with her young daughter, Anna, in an upscale suburb of San Francisco.

Jacobs earned her bachelor's degree from the University of California at Berkeley and her law degree from UC's Boalt Hall School of Law. She also holds graduate degrees from the University of Michigan in English, and from San Jose State in counseling. Before turning to writing, she worked as an attorney for Brobeck, Phleger, and Harrison in San Francisco.

This interview took place in 1996.

FICTION: Kali O'Brien novels: *Shadow of Doubt* (1996) ▪ *Evidence of Guilt* (1997) ▪ *Motion to Dismiss* (1999) ▪ *Witness for the Defense* (2001)

Kate Austen novels: *Murder Among Neighbors* (1994) ▪ *Murder Among Friends* (1995) ▪ *Murder Among Us* (1998) ▪ *Murder Among Strangers* (2000)

MURPHY: *Your latest book,* Shadow of Doubt, *is what I would call a classic-style mystery. What is so appealing about the classic-style whodunits that you've been writing?*

JACOBS: Classic-style whodunits in general are popular for a number of reasons. One is that they offer a sense of fairness in a world that is not always fair. In the real world the bad guy doesn't always get caught or "get it," and in mystery novels, he does. They also offer a sense of closure in that all the ends are wrapped up; in real life that never happens—there are a lot of loose ends, which is very frustrating. They have the elements of good, old-fashioned storytelling: a beginning, a middle, an end, and something that engages the reader, that makes them want to hopefully keep turning the pages. This is missing in what's called literary fiction, which I also enjoy reading. But you read that for a different reason than the story element in mysteries.

MURPHY: *Both your series feature female protagonists. Recently female protagonists and female mystery writers have become more and more popular. Why do you think that is?*

JACOBS: Women actually buy something like seventy percent of all books, so I'm sure that has a lot to do with it. For a long time male writers dominated the mystery field, so we are seeing a changeover where women are beginning to feel their muscle. They've also influenced the kinds of writing that men are doing. The traditional sleuth was the hard-boiled detective or PI, usually a hard-drinking loner whose investigation involved him, and therefore the reader, in the sleazier side of life. With women writers, you find sleuths who have family connections. Even if they're not married, they have fathers and mothers, they have friends. More and more male writers are drawing on these elements in developing and rounding out their characters. That's not to say there aren't still those hard-boiled PI guys out there, but a lot of male sleuths now have family ties and other personal concerns as well.

MURPHY: *The protagonist in* Shadow of Doubt, *Kali O'Brien, has some romantic involvement, beginning with a lawyer at her firm and then picking up* *with somebody in her hometown. I think you're right that male writers don't tend to write much about romance. Do you think that there's a crossover between readers who used to read romances and now are reading female mystery writers?*

JACOBS: There's a crossover of writers. There are a number of new mystery writers who were former romance writers and are switching over to mystery, believe it or not. It's relationships, not just romance but all kinds of relationships, which would interest women. My books are not legal thrillers, and there are a number of reasons for that. When I think about other female attorney-writers who write about attorney-sleuths, almost none of them are legal thrillers or legal procedurals either. They are stories about character and relationships, which is a different kind of approach.

MURPHY: *You have a lawyer protagonist, really an amateur sleuth, who doesn't get involved in courtroom activity. What kind of problems in writing did you have with an amateur sleuth in terms of her going out and investigating and doing things you really wouldn't expect a layperson to do?*

JACOBS: I like to think Kali actually is not quite an amateur sleuth. Having an amateur sleuth in my first series, I really wanted somebody who had a little more reason to get involved and pursue her investigation. I love to read courtroom dramas and would dearly love to be able to write one, but I don't have the kind of experience or background to be able to write it with the authenticity it takes to do the job well. So I decided to draw on my strengths, which are character and relationships.

MURPHY: *I was thinking about the scenes where she goes to the police station and tries to extract information from the clerk about the investigation of her client, Jannine. She's really doing what a detective would do. I guess she's not really an amateur sleuth, but as a lawyer, she's not somebody who should be detecting.*

JACOBS: That's true. Although, you know, it is set in a small town. And part of the reason for that is because the legal practice in small towns is not necessarily like it is in San Francisco. She's taken on this case as a favor to her friend, so she doesn't have the resources to draw on private investigators. It's also the town where she grew up. She has a relationship—the police chief was a family friend—so it would make sense that she would go and talk to him, perhaps, as opposed to hiring somebody. Things are done differently in small towns than in the urban setting.

MURPHY: *Why did you decide to set the book in a small town instead of a big city, like San Francisco?*

JACOBS: When I started out, what interested me about this book was going home, both literally and figuratively. Kali grew up in a small town. She was the kind of girl who, in high school, necked with the guys, drank beer out by the creek with her friends. When she left home, she vowed to put as much distance between herself and the town as possible. She got a law degree and is now very success-oriented. In the book, she comes back to her family, her roots. So she not only has to help a friend, who she thought she knew but isn't so sure after she gets into this investigation, but she confronts secrets from her family's past. She begins to see the change in herself, the contrast between who she was and what she's become and where she wanted to go.

And that interested me as much as the mystery. Plus, setting it in a small town does give her the opportunity to do things that, if it were a strict legal procedural in a big city, she probably might not do.

MURPHY: *You wrote the book in the first person, from Kali's perspective. There's always a problem in writing in first person since you have to be fair to the reader in terms of what clues Kali knows and what you divulge to the reader. It seemed to me, reading the book, that the murderer was a surprise. What kind of problems did you have in making the reader feel that you've been fair in terms of planting clues, but keeping the suspense alive?*

JACOBS: Actually there are two questions there. The first person is a problem in that everything the narrator knows—to be fair—the reader should know as well. But there are a lot of advantages to the first person also in terms of immediacy and the voice of the character coming through loud and clear.

In terms of the killer's identity, what I strive for anyway is that it is a surprise at the end. And the reader will say, "I never thought of that," but looking back can see things that make it a logical conclusion. There are some books where the killer just appears out of nowhere, and I find those very unsatisfactory. So I really do try to give the killer motivation throughout the story, which will hopefully be disguised so the reader doesn't pick up on it.

MURPHY: *The victim, Eddie Marrero, is a high school football coach and portrayed as a lying, cheating husband. So the reader's sympathy, at least through most of the book, is with the accused killer, his wife. Did you purposely portray him this way in order to manipulate the reader's sympathies toward the characters?*

JACOBS: No, I hadn't consciously thought of that, although reader sympathy in general is something you want to be aware of. I was more concerned about having the reader have sympathy for Jannine and yet wonder, as Kali does, whether Jannine is really guilty. One of the things that intrigues me is the way a given set of facts or given string of evidence can actually support two completely different, but both equally plausible, scenarios. And this was written way before O. J., but that's something that's always fascinated me. So I guess that was my bigger concern, making sure the readers had sympathy with Jannine but still questioned whether she was innocent.

As a writer, you sometimes want your victim to be someone that people hate and sometimes you want the victim to be someone that they really feel for, so that they want to find the murderer and have the case solved.

MURPHY: *In traditional mystery fiction there used to be a rule that the bad guy gets caught. Are there certain rules of the genre that you try to adhere to in your writing?*

JACOBS: Let me say first of all that I think mystery fiction has really changed in the last ten or fifteen years. It used to be there were very strict rules. Some of these rules are almost laughable now. For whatever reason, writers today are pushing what used to be limits of mystery fiction so that you have characters with relationships that aren't mere window dressing. You have personal stories that add to the mystery. So I'm not sure that there really are as many rules as there used to be. A good story is a good story regardless. There are mainstream writers who are incorporating mystery elements into their fiction. So where do you draw the line between what's a mystery and what's a mainstream novel? I think in general the reader wants to know who did it. I think you need to do that. If you can have sympathy for a killer who doesn't get caught, then you've got to leave your reader with a sense of being satisfied and some sense of closure. I think you need to play fair along the way. I think those are probably the only real "rules" you need to follow.

MURPHY: *One of the interesting things about the characters in* Shadow of Doubt *is that they're all real people. There are no politicians, no movie stars, no celebrities, the kind of people you see so much in popular fiction today. Have you purposely tried to deal with real people in your fiction?*
JACOBS: Yes, and I'm not sure that's a wise idea, actually, in terms of sales. The movie deals and the blockbuster novels often feature movie stars, politicians, people who are rich or famous. But I find what interests me is character, relationships, human nature. And actually I see all fiction, mystery fiction as well, as just basically a framework on which you hang human drama. Usually the personal kinds of things—the secrets, the personal tensions and relationships—interest me. I didn't intentionally set out to write about real people as opposed to celebrities; those are just the stories and situations that interest me. I may yet do one with a politician, a movie star, or whatever, just in the hopes of writing a blockbuster.

MURPHY: *I haven't had the good fortune to read your first two books. How does* Shadow of Doubt *differ from those two?*
JACOBS: My first two books are truly about an amateur sleuth: Kate Austen. She has a young daughter. They're set in the East Bay in the fictional town of Walnut Hills, which is through the tunnel, kind of a conglomeration of Lafayette, Moraga, Orinda. She has a rocky mar-

riage that has fallen apart, or is in the process of falling apart in the first book, so they're very different. I didn't know that I was writing a series when I started. I wrote the first Kate Austin book, sent that off, and sat down and wrote the first Kali O'Brien book. I thought I was writing books. I didn't realize how much mystery fiction is series-driven. Each of those sold and the publisher wanted me to continue with both characters, which is why I have two series. They're different, but not as different as they would have been if I had known from the beginning that I was going to be writing two series. I think I would have done one of them in third person, and I would probably have made the settings, which are both small towns, different as well.

MURPHY: *You've published two other novels already, and one about to be published next year. What motivated you to leave the law practice at Brobeck and start writing fiction full-time?*

JACOBS: Actually, I left Brobeck not to write fiction. I left because I had young children and it was just getting to be too much juggling. I was going to take a year at home, get to know my children again, and then find a job in the East Bay that was a little bit less demanding, that I could incorporate into being with my family. But when I was home I started writing and it just sort of went from there and I never actually went back to practice law.

MURPHY: *I know you've been writing off and on for over six years, even before you started publishing. What was the genesis of your interest in writing?*

JACOBS: A number of things. One was reading; I majored in English. While all my friends were either adding columns of numbers or dissecting frogs in labs, I sat there and read novels. I've always loved to read, and writing is just a continuation of that. You can lose yourself in the world. As wonderful as it is to sit and read a good novel, when the writing's going well, it's just as wonderful to sit there and create it yourself and make it happen. And I love language, so that's also a pleasure for me to work with.

GUS LEE

Gus Lee's first novel, *China Boy,* chronicles the coming-of-age of his alter ego, Kai Ting, the son of Chinese immigrants growing up on the streets of San Francisco's Panhandle. Through the devotion of his boxing coach at the YMCA, Kai learns to handle the bullies who enjoy using him as a human punching bag and to stand up to his controlling Caucasian stepmother.

In *Honor and Duty,* Lee's second novel, Kai Ting enters West Point's class of 1968. Lee vividly describes Kai's early meeting with a commanding officer with a heavy southern accent:

> "Whaat," *he drawled slowly at me, pulling the words like taffy on a cold day,* "inna name a good GOD hail *are* yeew?" . . .
>
> "SIR, I AM CHINESE-AMERICAN!" *I shouted* . . .
>
> "Waall . . . whup mah ever-lovin', long-livin', stand-up-straight *unit!* . . . "What's it lahk bein' *Chi-nese?*"
>
> "IT IS NOT VERY MERRY, SIR!" *I shouted.* . . .
>
> "WHY'D Y'ALL DECIDE TA BE A CHI-NESE?" *he roared.*
>
> "NO EXCUSE, SIR!" *I cried* . . .
>
> "Listen up, crothead. NEXT *TIME,* Y'ALL CHOOSE TA BE FRUM MISSIS-SIPPI, YOU HEAR ME?"

As Kai Ting struggles through three years of West Point, he becomes enmeshed in investigating a cheating scandal, forcing him to confront his own concept of honor and duty.

Gus Lee attended West Point before graduating from the University of California, Davis, with B.A. and J.D. degrees. He has had a varied career, including working as director of legal education for the state bar of California. Previously he worked for the California District Attorneys Association and as a deputy district attorney in Sacramento. Now retired from the practice of law, he writes full-time from his home in Colorado.

This interview took place in 1994.

FICTION: *China Boy* (1991) ▪ *Honor and Duty* (1994) ▪ *Tiger's Tail* (1996) ▪ *No Physical Evidence* (1998)

MURPHY: *Many people view their lives as uninteresting, yet you've now written two largely autobiographical books. When did you decide that your life would be interesting for others to read about?*

LEE: I never made a conscious decision; I found myself sliding into it. I was in the process of writing a family journal for my then seven-year-old daughter, answering her questions about her missing Bubu, my mother who had died when I was five. While I was preparing this journal—which had certain fictionalized narrative bridges to create a consistent story for a kid—I was hoping someday she would be interested in reading it. At no time was I thinking that it was my life that would be of interest to anyone besides my daughter and my son. In this process, through the recollections of my three older sisters, I ended up, inadvertently, sliding into my own life as a kid. I was the only American-born member of a Shanghai family, growing up in a black neighborhood in San Francisco, struggling culturally to become a successful black male youth.

Now, looking back at it, taking no credit for creating the various cosmic features of local neighborhoods—it wasn't my doing—I can say that my life was interesting, not because of me, but because of where I was and the people I knew and the circumstances in which I found myself. Almost everything I did represented a direct culture clash. Sort of a bowman from Sherwood Forest picking up an automatic grenade launcher, with the same sort of negative, explosive results. So I never had to decide that my life was interesting and worthy of print, because it just began as a journal for my daughter.

MURPHY: *It's interesting you say that it began as a journal because when I read* China Boy *it seemed to me you were writing* China Boy *for yourself: growing up as a boy and your fights with local bullies, boxing at the YMCA, and all that. When I read* Honor and Duty *it seemed to me you wrote that book for your classmates at West Point. Am I on target there at all?*

LEE: I think so. The first part of *China Boy,* which is really the genesis of the small amount of writing I've done, was for me to recover the memory of my mother for my daughter. I had gone forty years of life without having any active recollection of my mother. I had learned to live both without her in the physical world since I was five years old, and without any memory of her thereafter. But it was my daughter who really had a right to know about her missing grandmother. Who had a basic, pure, innocent curiosity about this missing, mysterious grandparent. And so what I had not achieved for myself—which was to uncover her memory—I very quickly did for my daughter. Now I had a legitimate purpose. When I asked my father about my mother, I was sort of breaking a rule. His second wife, my stepmother, my *chimu,* had decreed that there would be no discussion, and I learned to live with that. And I carried it with me even to the age of seventeen, after I left home.

So, the part of *China Boy* that was exclusively for me begins at the point in the narrative when the mother dies. See, at that point I had fulfilled my mission to Jena, my daughter. She had asked about her grandmother and I told her the stories I had heard from my sisters and I put them in writing for her. At the point at which my mother died, it was done. But I kept writing. I now remembered the neighborhood in which I had grown up. I remembered characters from that neighborhood. I remembered the bullies and the angels, the rogues, the larger-than-life characters both in that neighborhood and in the Tenderloin and the central YMCA, and I was off into the land of my own recollection. And when Jena asked, "What was life like for you when you were my age?" she was seven. I was seven when my American journey began, when I left the home, the Chinese apartment of my mother, to enter the streets of San Francisco and a black neighborhood. Living with a very articulate seven-year-old, whose only language was English, gave me the ability as an adult to look back at this haphazard, babble-mouthed, hybrid Chinese black American kid that was me. And that was for me to recover.

Honor and Duty is really more for West Point, first, and secondly for my classmates. West Point has played the role of, I think, another surrogate parent in my life. I mean, some people talk about their college and say *alma mater*. To a certain extent, it's *alma mater* and *alma pater* to me, and that relationship continues to this day. A very colorful, almost undecipherable connection, but it is still very vibrant. Both books, you're right, have been tributes—tributes to caring adults in *China Boy,* tributes to a school that strives, however imperfectly, for perfection, and for people who really enact a life committed to service, in *Honor and Duty.* That will always be admirable to me.

MURPHY: *The dialogue in both books is extraordinary. Particularly, for example, in* China Boy *the black accent is fantastic and right on point. Did you do all of this just from memory, or did you have to go back and talk to old friends, do anything like that, to bring it back?*

LEE: No, it's always been there. It's always been my second ear. My first was Chinese and my second was black English and my third is academic English, which is where I try to live, however inadequately now, but it was all there. And it wasn't so much that when I left that neighborhood as a teenager to enter a white neighborhood, and then from a white neighborhood to a very, very Anglo-driven West Point, I had to reach back that far. Because throughout my life I've naturally drifted toward the black caucus in whatever society I found myself in. Many of the members of that caucus didn't quite understand what I was doing there and wondered at my mimicry of expression. But throughout my years in the service, it's a voice that never leaves you.

I was concerned about this after writing the journal. I sent it to a couple friends of mine at UC Davis who have had even more years than I perfecting the black American experience by virtue of their not coming at it as outsiders. One of them is really an expert in vernacular black language and I really had this expectation that the manuscript would come back bleeding and dripping carnage from its corners. But she made no corrections. Just, "I think you've got the voice and I wouldn't change anything." So all those years of being a bad speaker and inadequate communicator had the payoff of making me really listen. I was struggling to listen because I knew in the listening, eventually I could own some of those words myself. And of course there's no way of knowing when you're a bumbling kid that this is going to end up in a journal that will become published throughout the world.

MURPHY: *Did you ever have occasion when you were growing up, or even at West Point, to use that black vernacular as sort of a defensive mechanism against bullies to avoid fights, that kind of thing?*

LEE: No, not so much defense. I think I used it more as an open hand. There weren't many people of color at the Academy in the sixties and it was very important to me, based on who I was, to ask black troops for permission to spend time with them. And language was the only way to do it because I wasn't going to do it by my face. I had a real, well-worked-out routine of how to do it, which was to say nothing. And you just sit down during chow and all the black troops are off in one corner and all the white troops in another and you've got this Chinese guy wandering around in between. And I would mosey toward the black troops. And I'd have to camp out near them. I couldn't just sit down in the middle and say, you know, "What's happening?" It would be like: "Not you." So I would just sit there until people got curious and not threatened and then we'd share food, water, whatever it was, and I'd be in their group. Eventually someone would ask, "What the hell you doing over here?" And I'd say, "Well, you know, I grew up in a black 'hood, those guys didn't, and I miss home."

But that's the whole irony in *China Boy,* what I need to remind myself and my son, and that is violence is in our world. It beats in the hearts of young boys, it's testosterone driven and culturally supported and inflamed by television. There it is. So what do we do with that? Boxing is a way of managing the violence. Giving it rules, giving it discipline, infusing a sort of native impulse towards confrontation with respect and discipline. If kids romanticize fighting—put him in the ring and this other kid is going to hit him in the face with a big glove, or in the gut, and it's going to go for nine minutes and then it's over. You shake hands before and you shake hands after and there are rules in between. When that kid leaves the ring—particularly after he's done it for a few months—he's not going to be hopping around, popping fists in the air, and looking for a fight because he knows what it means.

This is a big philosophic jump, but kids today in the inner cities are fascinated with guns, automatic weapons. Fine. Put them in the army. Make them clean it. Make them carry it on twenty-five-, fifty-mile marches. Make them live with those weapons, then the romance goes out very quickly. Teach them how to be proficient with it and to respect it, and then they won't want to shoot out of cars. It's not quite that simple because we're skipping the family role. But just in terms of specific management of violence, that's the way to go. In terms of bullies, once I—like Kai Ting—confronted my absolute, abject physical fear, my physical cowardice, of fighting—because I was compelled to learn boxing—I put up my dukes and fought. I boxed. I didn't have any more fights. Win, lose, or draw, it didn't matter. I was now too much work for bullies, a waste of time. There were easier pickings. I used to be the classic prototype "easy picking" but after I learned to defend myself—not to win, but to defend myself—then bullies left me alone. Once I lost my fear of fighting, and learned the skills that attached to it, I didn't fight anymore. But as long as I said I don't believe in fighting, I believe in pacifism, but I'm in a hard hood where the rule of blood is in charge, and I'm afraid of it, then it ruled me. It had me by the throat.

MURPHY: *That's when they would pound you.*

LEE: That's right. It's just a metaphor: whatever we confront, as adults or children, the thing that plagues us in our lives, we can go through it. As long as we get some help. I didn't go through this because I was a wonderfully courageous kid—quite the opposite— a screaming, weeping coward. But I was given help, and with that help and with some work on my part, I was able to get through my fear. So, bullies no longer were a theme in my life. They were when I was real little. I figured out what you do with a bully, which is you throw down on them and you say—when you're ready to throw up: "Do your best." I'll take your best now, rather than let you build up on me from my running on you. My balance is going to go down, your coin is going to go up, and when we meet each other, I'm going to know I already ran from you. And that will eat at me.

MURPHY: *You give a lot of credit in* **China Boy** *to the YMCA, particularly the boxing programs there. That's really changed now. The YMCA is more of a yuppie health club than it used to be.*

LEE: Absolutely. And it grieves me deeply. I really believe in people in organizations knowing what their missions are. And the mission of the YMCA, as I read it, as a YMCA alum, both as a student and as faculty, is to take care of poor, unguided, inner-city male youth. That's it. And I understand that after the big baby boom generation passed through the Y programs that they were empty and they had to bring adults in to keep the lights on. But the kids are back. They've been back for a long time. And now they're shooting cars, doing drugs, and rousting people and running drugs, and the YMCA is filled with lawyers and accountants—grown men and women, educated, earning a living, running on Exercycles and doing StairMasters and filling the weight room and taking the gym, while the kids outside the Central Y are dying in the street of neglect and it's wrong.

The adults in this city don't lack for health clubs. And the YMCA has become a marvelously successful yuppie health club with tax breaks because they take care of kids. But the boys' department, which saved my life, is a senior citizens center and the children have been kicked out of the building. They're on the corner on Turk. And I admire the staff at Turk, nothing against them, but they should be in the main building. Instead of pushing the kids out, they need to push the adults out, even though—guess what—they get more money for the adults. But that's why they get the tax break. They're supposed to be a mission—"Young Men's Christian Association," not adult men and women. If we keep not taking care of the kids, we have no right to say, "How come they shoot at people? How come they're so angry?"

MURPHY: *Let me get back to* China Boy. *The betrayal of Edna, the step-mother, is decidedly negative in the book. . . .*
LEE: There you go jumping to conclusions. [Laughter] Just because she looks like a monster, you think she's just portrayed negatively.

MURPHY: *Even though she did force you to learn English and adapt to Ameri-can culture, she's like the stepmother in Cinderella, if you want a parallel in fairy tales. How did your real stepmother react to this?*
LEE: There's no coincidence that I didn't write this until she had been dead for some time. My stepmother died in 1975, and I would not have written this if she were still living. But I would have told the story to my daughter and my son in oral form if she were still in the world.

On the other hand, in all honesty, I probably would not have married if she were still alive. I had incorporated her into my life and my psyche sufficiently to where I could not imagine bringing a daughter-in-law to her. I couldn't be sure of what she would do. She didn't have physical dominion anymore, but her ability to injure psychologically was quite profound. I was afraid that would become part of my married life, so I did not seriously consider marriage, and every time I did I found myself backing off because of this unspoken fear of somehow repeating history.

MURPHY: *How has your father reacted to the depiction of his wife?*

LEE: He hasn't said. He's reacted very generously, with a great deal of kindness really, to my doing what no truly honoring Chinese son would do, which is to write about his own family, particularly his parents. It would be one thing to write a book and criticize your children—you have license to do that—but not your before-borns, not your own parents. But he's been very generous about it. And he understands that this is a fictionalized account of a family's life and the reader can't know the degree of accuracy in the novel. That's part of its intrigue.

MURPHY: *Did you edit out parts of the book knowing your family would be reading it?*

LEE: Absolutely. Some of them appear in *Honor and Duty.* The most painful one, involving the sister, Janie, I took out of *China Boy,* and I did write about it in *Honor and Duty.*

MURPHY: *Right. The one who had been sent away by your stepmother.*

LEE: Yes.

MURPHY: *Do you still have contact with that sister?*

LEE: Oh, absolutely. I'm very happy to say that my three sisters are quite close to each other and they've accepted me as their sibling, and the four of us are a pretty powerful group.

MURPHY: *It's ironic that in Chinese culture women are treated essentially as second-class citizens, yet it was the American stepmother who banished your sister from the home.*

LEE: Yes. It is a terrible paradox that in coming to America my youngest sister had a chance of being enfranchised and legitimized, recognized, and an American woman cast her out. Disconnected her from her father and her baby brother—the two people to whom she owed a Chinese bond of loyalty. So she couldn't fulfill her mission by the dictatorship of another woman. It's a terrible irony.

MURPHY: *Getting back to* Honor and Duty: *There are some obvious ideas behind what is honor and what is duty in terms of West Point, but I assume you had several different concepts in that title. What were those?*

LEE: I think Chinese honor and duty are pretty easy. They're interchangeable. The rules attach to males—it's a sad but fundamental distinction. There are all kinds of esoteric refinements, but in the main, a Chinese son of a Chinese man honors his elders, honors his father, honors the emperor, honors his older brother, and honors his older friends. The top three are the *san gang,* the "three bonds." He is, by definition, a dutiful son. Or, putting it another way, because there is an interchangeability—if a Chinese son is dutiful to his father, the emperor, and the older brother, then he is an honorable.

Now, I made up something here—the true *san gang,* the true top three, are son to father, ruled subject to emperor, and wife to husband. But for a man, you would take out wife to husband because your wife is serving you, in a traditional way, and you bring up the next one, the fourth relationship, which is to the older brother. I'm editorializing to a certain extent.

So honor and duty become interchangeable. There is no question that doing your duty to those to whom you owe the bond—you would not lie, you would not cheat, you would not steal; you don't even have to say that. In American honor and duty, honor is a very individual thing. It seems to imply character, integrity, and honesty with liability: trust. Today, the connotation of the context changes about every ten years. Only thirty years ago Kennedy gave an extremely patriotic inaugural address, asking what you could do for your country. His concept of duty was quite clear: You serve the republic, you serve democracy, you fight the evils of Communism. Duty was a clean word. Honor spoke for itself. In the wake of Vietnam, there was no duty. If there was a duty, it was a duty to oppose existing order. To challenge, to question, to reinterpret patriotism in an individual rather than in a community sense—a big change. Kennedy believed in some American military involvement in Vietnam. If you heard the late sixties protests against it, it wouldn't have sounded as if that went with the 1961 inaugural address. So in less than ten years in America, duty went from a good word to a bad word. A good word "serve your country" in 1961; "resist the draft" in 1968.

Today, "duty"—what does that mean? Is it a tariff on goods, a duty-free shop? Clinton talks about a service corps. Well, there's a big, resounding response to that. Nothing. This country is not interested in doing that. And honor is just honesty. So Chinese honor is really honoring others, American honor is having integrity and not being a crook. Chinese duty is honoring others, and American duty is sort of an oxymoron. That's how I see it today. If we wonder why we are failing as a society, I think it's because we've failed relationally, in a way that Chinese tend not to, because they are trained not to fail at relationships.

MURPHY: *Also, it seemed another concept of honor in the book was when Kai Ting entered West Point in 1964, before the Gulf of Tonkin resolution, it was a big deal. People actually looked up to him. When he got out in sixty-eight, people from West Point were looked down on.*

LEE: Exactly. And it went from being one of the highest honors you could experience in America. There was a reader who asked a question of me at A Clean Well-Lighted Place for Books last night. She asked how can anyone even hope to teach honor using those brutal, militaristic methods at West Point. The answer apart, what's clear is the sense that the military is a mindless, savage, rather stupid beast that could do a Vietnam. That idea remains with us, despite the fact that West Point didn't decide to do Vietnam. It wasn't up to them. It was up to a president who decided that it was his duty to fight Communism wherever it appeared, and of course he had to use the military to do it. Somehow the military got stuck with the policy and manner of execution, and that is not altogether appropriate.

MURPHY: *A key part of the book is a cheating scandal that Kai Ting gets enmeshed in. In terms of the honor code at West Point, it does seem in a way paradoxical that you're not supposed to lie, cheat, and steal, but on the other* *hand you're supposed to turn in your friends. Do you think that's a good way to build character?*

LEE: I do. I think that West Point did not kid around in terms of pitching its lessons. It made them very clear, it had all the subtlety of cannonballs in spring. And when you take young men who have been successful in life and put them into the military academy and tell them, at the tender age of seventeen, eighteen, nineteen, that they have two guiding axia under which to live: one is a cadet does not like you to steal or tolerate someone who does, and secondly, you are nothing if you do not support your classmates. You must be a team player. You must be collegial; you must serve others; you're not here for yourself. And when those two come into conflict with each other, because a person you are pledged to support cheats, lies, or steals, then a young person must make an extremely difficult decision of character. And it is a decision of honor. He can pass it off as friendship by winking at it, he can call it loyalty by covering it up, he can call it fidelity by lying about it in order to cover the original offense, but he knows in his heart it's honor. And it will weigh on him fifty years later. Not that he was loyal to friends, but that he covered up a dishonor. And that's who we are. Not because they're West Point cadets, but because that's who we are as people. I can't think of a better or more painful way of teaching it than by making each person responsible for protecting something greater than himself. West Point attempted to maintain a perfect system of honor using human beings, and of course there's a paradox there, there's a native impossibility there, but I admire it, and continue to this day to admire it for the attempt. For the courageous and enduring commitment to that standard. As impossible as it seems, I do not blame West Point for the dishonesty of senior officers in Vietnam. Nor can I blame the government. It's those individuals' faults. They faced the honor trial in their own hearts and failed and brought down many with them. So whatever didn't work in Vietnam to me was not a failing of West Point, but a failing of individuals.

So it always bothers me whenever there is a suggestion that the honor code ought to be altered at West Point since there are people who cheat. Also, there are people who kill. Well, maybe we'll get rid of all the murder statutes. Obviously, they fail to work. You can't lose faith with a principle, you just have to see how you can maintain the spirit of the Academy in the active army following graduation. That's where character comes in. I like the idea of strenuously preparing idealists, knowing that everyone's not going to do it. But that's hardly a reason not to try.

MURPHY: *You make an interesting point in the book that America should have paid attention to the lessons of Chinese history. The Chinese went to Vietnam and spent a thousand years trying to beat the Vietnamese and were unsuccessful. Do they teach that kind of history in West Point?*
LEE: Actually, they do. But they don't teach it in all the state universities. They weren't teaching it in the schools of diplomacy. Because it didn't matter—what's Vietnam? Find Vietnam on the map. You're an American in 1961.

MURPHY: *A little country somewhere over there . . .*
LEE: That's right. We think Asia, Vietnam, Caribbean, Surinam? Vietnam? But ironically at West Point is where I and other cadets learned the history of warfare in Indochina and specifically the failures of the French. Less emphasis on the Chinese. The French were there for seventy years, 1884 to 1954. American national policy in Vietnam to a large extent, in my opinion, followed the French model. And we were being taught at West Point how not to do it and then there it was. And it does require a nice tango in my mind between a naive White House and unobservant Congress and a somewhat arrogant, self-inflated military to create the kind of experience that we achieved in Vietnam.

I know that there were many senior general officers in the army who voiced misgivings about methods of operation and commitment in Vietnam and of course were they selected for MACV commander? No. Lincoln had to find a man who was willing to fight for him—Grant. Johnson had to find a man who would agree to Johnson's type of war in Vietnam—Westmoreland. Because Westmoreland was a "Yes, sir," three-bags-full general officer. He did not believe in arguing; he believed in making his requests doing the best with what was given him. A good man in a battlefield environment. In my opinion, the wrong man for strategic planning in a cutting-edge area of American military experimentation in wars of national liberation.

If we had followed the advice of OSS officers from World War II, we never would have entered Vietnam. If we had, we'd have come in on the Ho Chi Minh side. He was the one we fought alongside in World War II. Not the French, who sided with the Japanese after the surrender of France. So we had a tremendous foil against Red Chinese expansion—Ho Chi Minh—whose traditional enemy was not America, not France, but China. And he was our Tito. He would have kept the Chinese at bay as he did after beating the Americans, beating the French, beating the Japanese—he beat the Chinese again.

It's militarily nothing but a gigantic juggernaut. American troops' land war in Asia? That's it. That's the formula you're supposed to avoid. The air lines of communication are stretched across the Pacific Ocean. Your troops are not defending Long Beach, Omaha, New York, the Statue of Liberty. Uh-uh. They're fighting against an indigenous military force which is antiforeign. Not because you're American, but because you're white. Not because exclusively you're white, but you look like colonials. You look like the kind of white men who went over here and ruled that country when no one asked the white man to come in and take it, and now Americans come over "to give you democracy."

And you have the two huge Communist superpowers on that side of the world in charge of the supply lines. These guys by tradition will fight to the death. Your troops will fight one-year rotations—six months in line; six months off. There's no continuity, no accretion of expertise; constant development of half-amateur, quick learning, quick dying, little military units waiting to serve their time to get out. Now, it doesn't take a rocket scientist to do the formula on that one, and that was the French formula.

MURPHY: *The book is very complimentary about General Schwarzkopf. Was he really a family friend?*
LEE: No. But he was a mentor to me at the Academy. Schwarzkopf was my mechanics of solids professor. He found me a miserable engineering student. He motivated me through abject fear and unique spiritual inspiration to become a better student in engineering, which I was for him. And when I had trouble there academically, he was the guy who clearly, by virtue of brains, courage, reputation, would have understandably spent all of his time with the Rhodes scholar candidates in my class, not with guys like me. But he spent his time with the goats. He worked with the guys who were in trouble, not the guys who had it all and had mastered West Point. I had mastered all of West Point except for engineering, which happened to be sixty percent of the curriculum.

MURPHY: *And which was your father's occupation, I understand.*
LEE: That's right. And I was very immature about how to handle it, which was, Well, I don't like it, so ignore it. A charging rhino—I don't like the charging rhino, so I'll ignore it. Good. Schwarzkopf was a very gifted officer who spent his time with the cellar dwellers instead of the stronger. And as a consequence, I remember many of my faculty from West Point, but twenty years later, the one guy who stayed in my life was Schwarzkopf.

MURPHY: *I noticed in the* **Contemporary Author's Directory** *your mother's occupation is listed as "storyteller." Was she really a storyteller?*
LEE: She was a storyteller. She would wake up in her bedroom in Shanghai, during the war years, with little kids in the household seated around her bed silently waiting for her to awaken. And I gather, before she did anything else that morning, while still in her bed, she would tell them a story. And they she'd say, "Go off and do

your duties," and she'd get on with her day, but it started with a story.

MURPHY: *I get the idea that this is the subject of another book—the prequel to* **China Boy?**

LEE: It could be. I don't know—I'm writing a third book right now, which is the capstone to the Kai Ting trilogy. This book will not be as agenda-driven as the first two, and will be more for the reader.

MURPHY: *Does Kai Ting get to law school?*

LEE: Kai Ting gets out of law school and becomes a trial lawyer. Becomes a criminal defense lawyer in the army in Korea. He finds himself in a nasty conflict-of-interest situation where he wants to serve a client who is an elder and he has *gang* with him, an unbreakable bond of obligation. When you're a lawyer you have *gang* with your clients. And all our failures as a profession—as far as I'm concerned—have arisen from the failure of that relationship. Not failure of the court, not failure with appellate work, not failure with trial preparation—failure with the relationship. Because we don't control all that other stuff, but we control that relationship. So he has this *gang* with an older man, an older American soldier who has been arrested for theft. He understands the propelling causation for the theft, and is invited to help resolve the situation. But that goes far beyond his role as a lawyer, and far beyond his role as an army officer. He does all of this in Asia, as an Asian American attempting to live as an Asian in Asia, for the first time.

MURPHY: *It sounds like, at least with the third one, you're going to be in the legal thriller genre. Maybe the bestseller list is on the horizon.*

LEE: These have made bestseller lists, but not the *New York Times,* which is the ultimate grading sheet in the industry. I'm learning the craft; I don't know how much I'll learn. At one level I am disturbed about the idea of trying to shape a book so it will sell. It's back to really who lawyers are. To make a story understandable to a jury—is that wrong? To make the story interesting to the jury—is that wrong? To make the story so interesting to the jury that they care about your client—is that wrong? No, clearly not.

MURPHY: *That's the essence of lawyering.*

LEE: It's certainly part of it. So, instead of thinking of it in crass terms and of merely generating sales, perhaps a bestseller is merely a better-told story. And that's now what I am trying to create.

JOHN MARTEL

John Martel's first novel, *Partners,* explores the fallout from a big corporate law firm taking on a plaintiff's personal injury case. Beneath its blue-chip veneer, San Francisco's Stafford, Parrish, and MacAllister faces financial ruin. Only managing partner Austin Barrington knows how bad things are. In a memo to his partners, he says:

> *An opportunity has arisen to represent a hundred or more personal injury plaintiffs suffering from various illnesses, including cancer, the result of ingestion of toxic chemicals in their drinking water. . . .*
>
> *I can anticipate your resistance to taking on these personal injury cases but I urge that you not be so concerned about tarnishing our image. I for one would prefer to be known as a viable firm that occasionally handles P.I. work than a bankrupt firm that once handled only the most glamorous, complex, and exacting business litigation. And after all, we're not exactly chasing ambulances here. This case could well result in the largest verdict in history.*

Martel is a partner with the San Francisco law firm of Farella, Braun, and Martel. He received his B.S. and L.L.B. degrees from the University of California at Berkeley.

Martel has been named by *The National Law Journal* as one of the top ten trial lawyers in the country. He served as a prosecution consultant in the O. J. Simpson murder trial.

The first interview took place in 1988 and the second in 1995.

FICTION: *Partners* (1988) ▪ *Conflicts of Interest* (1994) ▪ *The Alternate* (1999) ▪ *Billy Strobe* (2001)

───────────

MURPHY: *You've been in practice for twenty-eight years now. What made you decide to write a novel after all that time?*

MARTEL: I think everybody wants to write a novel, and since I started writing mine, I've learned that every person in the free world has a novel in them "dying to come out." I just decided to do it and I did it. I owe a lot to novels in my own life growing up . . . Jack London, Howard Pease, and people like that who took me on adventures I could never have gone on without their books. So, in a sense, it was fun to become a part of that teaching tradition, telling people about things that they may not be able to personally experience without *Partners.* So this was just a joy to me and also, there's just the plain fun of being an author. I've never known an author, so to really get to know one I had to become one. I think that we hold our authors in fairly high esteem in this culture, and I wanted to be a part of that tradition. And then there's, of course, the money. . . .

MURPHY: *Incidentals.*

MARTEL: [Laughter] Incidentals . . . fame, greed, all these motivations.

MURPHY: *Had you carried around the idea for* **Partners** *for a period of years before you actually sat down and wrote it?*

MARTEL: No. It popped into my mind one morning as I woke up. The basic plot idea popped into my head and I thought, "Shoot, I should write a book about this," and that's where it started. It was that simple.

MURPHY: *When was that?*

MARTEL: It was in late 1980, 1981.

MURPHY: *And did you start writing at that time?*

MARTEL: I roughed out a very crude ten-page outline, showed it to an agent who I got an appointment with through a friend of a friend. And this agent, Kathy Robbins, Robbins and Associates in New York, was very encouraging from the start even though now, as I look back, I see the draft was pretty crude. She told me to expand the outline and to write a couple of chapters and she'd take a second look at it. I did that and we were off and running. Within I guess about six months, she had sold the novel to Bantam, the very first publisher she took it to. So *Partners* was sold with embarrassing ease. When I look at trained professional authors like William Kennedy who had to go through the tortures of the damned to get *Ironweed* published (twelve publishers rejected it) and then think about how simple it was for me, it seems unjust.

MURPHY: *Did you work on it from the time you wrote the outline in 1981 until last year?*

MARTEL: I was about due for a sabbatical. Our firm has a three-month sabbatical program. My marriage was breaking up at the time so I had time on my hands. I just sat somewhere for three months and wrote. I finished a long outline and several chapters—I don't know how many, seven or eight—and then finished the book five years later during my next sabbatical. I also worked on it between sabbaticals on vacations; that's how it was written. I practiced law full-time and continue to do so.

MURPHY: *The plot of* Partners *revolves around a toxic tort case and several plaintiffs who suffered catastrophic injuries from toxic exposure. Did you base the plot on any particular case you had?*

MARTEL: No, it's entirely fictional although we do represent toxic tort plaintiffs at the present time. At that time I had done very little work in the field but I was interested in it, and as I did my research I became all the more interested in doing work in the field as I saw what we humans were doing to our planet. I researched it very carefully as you can perhaps tell from the book. Those facts I stand behind, and there would have been even more if the publisher hadn't had the good sense to curtail me, as I was really going crazy on the subject of environmental dangers and society's apathy. Don't get me started on that one. We will never get off it. Yeah, I'm very fascinated with the subject and I hope that, although the primary function of the book is to be entertaining, that it will also get through some of these social messages in a way that will not put people to sleep.

MURPHY: *In* **Partners,** *the firm of Stafford, Parrish, and MacAllister encountered a great deal of internal resistance taking plaintiffs' toxic tort cases. Did your firm, Farella, Braun, and Martel, have the same kind of resistance?*
MARTEL: No, although we did get invited into one major toxic tort case that we turned down, but not for the reasons that concerned Stafford, Parrish, and MacAllister. SP&M is a blue-blood, Brahmin-type firm that just didn't want to involve itself in the personal injury field.

MURPHY: *Kevin Stone is one of the main characters in* **Partners.** *Is there any part of John Martel in Kevin Stone?*
MARTEL: Only in his fierce desire to win and his somewhat obsessive need to succeed. I suppose there are also some similarities in the victory string that he had achieved, but I hope, without ruining the book for people who have not read it, that the similarity ends there. [Laughter]

MURPHY: *That's understandable.*
MARTEL: Although I have a great deal of sympathy for Kevin and it is through Kevin that I try to convey one of the most important themes of the book, which is that large law firms comprise a matrix for tough ethical decisions. And it seems to me that when people compromise in making ethical decisions, they rarely do so with an explosive nuclear suddenness. It's rather more like water on a rock and you'll notice that Kevin's compromises, while they may ultimately have been unthinkable, came in a graduated sequence. At any one time it was almost understandable perhaps, to some people, how he could have made those decisions, and of course, if he had taken the

time and had the prescience to see the end of the road, he wouldn't have made the decision he made the first time he was presented by Austin Barrington with an opportunity to compromise. But compromise he did, and I think this is important for lawyers and other people in the world of commerce to know that you can get yourself in a whole lot of trouble taking that first step. Once Kevin Stone took it he was hooked. I tried in *Partners* to create the ultimate ethical dilemma, one in which readers might be willing—despite themselves—to forgive patently outrageous behavior, at least in the early going.

MURPHY: *There are a lot of attorneys making compromises on ethical decisions in* Partners *and, of course, without revealing the end, some of them made the ultimate compromise. Did you consider how laypeople would view lawyers after reading* Partners?

MARTEL: Not really. I guess I feel that the smoke is out of that bottle on this issue. Laypeople already have a very poor impression of lawyers and there is little I can do in fiction to make it worse than the reality. If you look closely at the book you will notice that only four lawyers really compromised. The rest did not and were quite strong in their condemnation of what the other partners did. It is particularly to Rachel Cannon's character that I hope laypeople will look to see how younger lawyers are advocating a renewed sense of ethics, morality, and what a lawyer should be like. And it is Rachel Cannon who lifts this phoenix out of the ashes and, I think—I hope—justifies the book in terms of society's tarnished image of lawyers. I don't know much about laypeople's reactions, but the reaction of establishment-type lawyers has been remarkably favorable to the book. Naturally, people who oppose the direction I took on the book probably wouldn't be as vocal as those who approve it. I have addressed law schools, major law firms, and the Regional Conference of the American College of Trial Lawyers (which is quite, let's say, a sturdy establishment arm of our profession not generally known for its radical, youthful nature) about *Partners,* and they've all loved the book. I think it speaks well for the profession that they have been able to accept the book with a sense of its fictional intent—with a sense of humor—and I have been surprised and gratified by that.

MURPHY: *You mention that Rachel Cannon is the lawyer who rises above the ashes and takes the proper moral stance. Is it a coincidence that she happens to be a female attorney?*

MARTEL: Maybe not. I've learned a lot about the need for women in the law as I have observed our own four partners and numerous associates. Let's face it, women, thank God, are different from men. In a very positive way they possess, as has always been attributed to them, a high sense of intuition and morality that I see here in our firm and that I think will ultimately result in the betterment of the whole profession. It was a very natural thing for this book to have a heroine, not a hero. I don't know where it came from but it was inevitable. I enjoyed her character very much. So did other people. All my bachelor friends wanted to know where they could find her. [Laughter] I'm afraid I can't help them.

MURPHY: *Have you had any comments from the female lawyers in your own firm about Rachel Cannon's character?*

MARTEL: From my own firm and outside my own firm, women have enjoyed *Partners* even more than men. Women have not only liked the book, they've loved it and some have flattered me by doubting that I was able to write it without a woman's input. This is the ultimate compliment for me out of this entire process.

MURPHY: *It's interesting that you find that women liked the book more than men. I talked to a lot of women who were not lawyers and who did not like your portrayal of Denise Stone and thought you were very unsympathetic to her.*

MARTEL: That's true. I was very hard on Denise and all I can say is that I was equally hard on some of the men, too. I don't think anyone can say that the men suffered less than the women in this book. In fact, Denise was the only gender victim of this book and the fact is, that there are women like that. I can attest to it.

MURPHY: *Was the character of Denise Stone based on your own personal experience?*

MARTEL: No. No more than the other characters were. All the characters are composites of people stored in my unconscious and, like Malamud says, these characters spring from events with which I have been familiar but that doesn't make them events in my life. He favors the term *autobiographical essence* over *autobiographical history,* as do I. In that sense, these characters do spring from my consciousness and they are, therefore, part of me. But no, I have never known anyone as bad as Denise Stone and have never known anyone as bad as Barrington; I've never known anyone as good in the courtroom as Kevin Stone and I've never known anyone as morally strong and beautiful as Rachel Cannon but they're out there and they know who they are even if I don't. [Laughter]

MURPHY: *It's interesting that you refer to Denise Stone as being bad, because one impression a reader would get from the book is that she is a housewife with children and her major complaint is that she just wants her husband and he is never home.*

MARTEL: There's more to it than that. I'm not saying that Denise is not a victim. I think in a sense we are all potential victims and it's our job in life not to be. But Denise was spoiled and pampered from her youth and somehow it was inculcated in her program that she was entitled to anything she wanted. And what she wanted was the American dream: two children, a nice house, and a husband who looks like Robert Redford and is the greatest trial lawyer in the country. When she didn't get the full attention she felt she deserved, she became spiteful and when I say that she's bad, I mean she possesses and manifests a bad trait, being spiteful. Who knows? Denise might somehow turn her life around with Kevin out of it. But probably only with psychiatric help. She has a long way to go to be a whole person.

MURPHY: *Stafford, Parrish, and MacAllister, a staid old corporate law firm. Did you have any San Francisco firm in mind?*

MARTEL: No. I've had that question asked many times. The *S, P,* and *M* rang a bell with a lot of people as representing PM&S. If I had thought that through at the time I would have changed the name of the firm and the initials so as not to seem to be pointing to PM&S. SP&M is an entirely fictional law firm. We lawyers here in San Francisco know this because, for one thing, we know there are no firms as big as SP&M that have no women in their partnership. Some of my best friends are PM&S lawyers. [Laughter] There are some very nice people over there.

MURPHY: *You anticipated my next question about Pillsbury. There is a reference in the book to a Judge Weston's decision in* **Arnett v. Dow Chemical** *and, of course, that was actually Judge Weinstein.*

MARTEL: That was clearly a reference to Judge Dan Weinstein. I didn't feel like bugging him for permission and I didn't think he'd mind that I just changed the name. He called me after reading the book and asked me how I had acquired such knowledge about the factual underpinnings of *Arnett v. Dow* and cases like it and seemed quite pleased with the book. I'm sure that if I had had time and had asked him, he would have been happy to have me use his name. But I guess it's enough that lawyers know who "Judge Weston" really is, at least those lawyers who are in the field.

MURPHY: *Is that the only character in the book that you would relate to a natural person?*

MARTEL: [Pause] Yes. I do mention a lot of my partners in the book just for the fun of it. I think there was a breakup of a firm in the novel called Wolf and Anderson, which refers to Randy Wulf and Gary Anderson. I just took a lot of liberties in that regard, sticking friends' names in. I've always been a secret admirer of Deborah Norville—she's the anchorperson on the "News at Sunrise" show, NBC. She's quite attractive and very bright, and so I named a character "Delbert Norville," one of the minor characters, just for the fun of it. She wrote and told me she sometimes feels like a "Delbert." That's part of the pleasure in writing a book; you get to play God and create all these things, not only the plot but also the characters.

MURPHY: *I have a couple of technical questions for you. After the defendants have appeared in the action and the trial date has been set and depositions of plaintiffs have been taken, all of a sudden there is a demurrer and motion to strike the cancerphobia claim. It seems like that's not the proper procedure at that period in the litigation.*

MARTEL: Demurrer after an appearance—did I do that? [Laughter]

MURPHY: *Page 221.*

MARTEL: Steve, you're the first person to catch that and there should have been a motion to strike. . . . That's amazing. I have no alibi or defense. . . . It's wrong.

MURPHY: *Sorry to bring that up.*

MARTEL: Not as sorry as I am.

MURPHY: *Another question. As a person who does a lot of plaintiffs' personal injury work, my experience has always been that as soon as the complaint is served and the defendants answer, they subpoena the plaintiff's medical records. Right in the very beginning. And, in this case, it seems they wait to the very end before they even try to get them. I think it's six weeks before trial and Barrington still has them in his office and somehow he has the original records and the defense has never tried to subpoena them.*

MARTEL: Well, you can see how the plot might have come unraveled if I had followed that actual procedure. You are quite right, that's normally what happens but I had to have the action move along a time line quite some distance to allow the opportunity for a lot of events to take place. It was Kevin's job to stall discovery as long as possible and perhaps I could have made that more clear in the book. As you know very well, there are ways to stall almost anything and it would have been, I think, more accurate for me to use some of those techniques, burdensome, oppressive, blah, blah, blah.

MURPHY: *I can see where the plot would have suffered.*

MARTEL: Yeah, it's that part about being God again. You get to tamper, though I tried very hard not to tamper too much, because it's really important to me that lawyers read this book and don't find a lot of flaws and staging for dramatic purposes, as you find in almost all other books about the law and certainly in movies such as *Jagged Edge* and *The Verdict,* which were dramatically successful but technically insulting to the law profession. I guess I've taken small liberties as you have pointed out so I shouldn't complain about someone taking big liberties. But somehow, I think there is a difference and people, laypeople, should not have the myth perpetuated that judges are so corrupt they can get away with things like the judge was trying to do in *The Verdict.* Or that trial lawyers can bring opponents to their knees as Perry Mason always did. These caricatures create dangerous expectations on the part of the lay public and potentially interfere with the proper relationship between attorney and client. So that's why, for example, in the cross-examination scene where Rachel takes apart the psychologist, I used, almost verbatim, a cross-examination that I performed in an actual case with George Agnost, the city attorney of San Francisco, on the other side. All of her fears, all of her confusion, her ignorance of how to proceed—were my fears, confusion, and ignorance, all real. That witness was really sprung on us, and I had to react. And so I tried to be fairly accurate, and so far, no inaccuracies have been pointed out—until today. Congratulations.

MURPHY: *You mentioned a couple of authors, such as Jack London, whom you admired and read. Were there any particular authors upon whom you've modeled your own writing style?*

MARTEL: Not at all. It's funny. I don't know what my writing style is because I'm too close to it. It perhaps needs considerable maturing before it becomes a true voice in the literary sense. I've noticed that the authors I most admire write books quite unlike my book and that those authors are predominately women. Joan Didion, I think, is one of my favorite modern writers, followed closely by Anne Tyler, five of whose books I read back-to-back, and Doris Lessing. For adventure, I like le Carré and particularly his most obscure book, *The Honourable Schoolboy,* which bored a lot of my friends and

I thought was just a fantastic book. So I end up writing a book about sex and murder and romance, quite unlike those books I enjoy reading the most. I don't know how to explain that. Fortunately, I guess I don't have to as long as people enjoy the book and keep buying it.

MURPHY: *What kind of sales have you had?*

MARTEL: I should preface this by saying that it's hard to know what hardcover sales of a book are until the books have been returned to the publisher, an event which has not yet occurred. My agent, with whom I dined late last week, estimated that the book has sold around twenty-eight thousand hardcover so far. That's all I know. It will be published in paperback in the summer and I know they're looking for very large paperback sales. They are very pleased with the sales of the hardcover, given the fact that it is my first novel and that, outside the law profession, nobody has the slightest idea who I am.

MURPHY: *Have you got any plans for any promotional tours?*

MARTEL: I've actually done some promoting of the hardcover. Not a whole lot. I was on *People Are Talking* two weeks ago, a very interesting show with Richard Dysart, the actor who plays the senior partner on *L.A. Law*. I've been on *Ronn Owens,* many of the radio shows around town, *Frank and Mike in the Morning,* things like that. I've done a lot of obscure morning television shows in Portland, L.A., and San Diego. I literally followed a dog act, a dog psychiatrist. It's been a great experience and I suspect that when the paperback comes out I'll do some more. Hopefully some East Coast work. *Partners* was not publicized east of Modesto, my hometown. I understand that's pretty much the way publishers treat first novelists. They throw it out there and it's Darwinian survival from then on.

MURPHY: *Has there been any talk of making a movie out of the book?*

MARTEL: Yes. No one has read the book without commenting that it would be a great movie. My agent is talking to people in Hollywood

who are sort of caught up right now with the idea of *Presumed Innocent* being the big law movie right now and *L.A. Law* as being a free
option for people to tune in to. I think it's the expectation of my
agent that with the paperback coming out next spring, that will be
the appropriate time to strike a movie deal.

MURPHY: *You've written an article in the July issue of* **Trial** *magazine about
lawyer burnout. You've been in practice now twenty-eight years. Have you ever
felt like you burned out?*

MARTEL: I haven't burned out, but I sure see the symptoms. I see, for
example, a profound loss of interest in confronting a room of documents. A really able trial lawyer has to have a lot of energy for his or
her task and each year now I seem to be less enthusiastic about looking at that stack of depositions that have to be read before you can go
argue a major motion or go try a case, and that's a manifestation of
burnout. I think it's a psychological given that you can't keep doing
the same thing for twenty-eight years without it affecting you. The
human mind was not built for that kind of focus. I think that I work
best now when I can do a task until my mind begins to get tired of it
and then go do another task and then come back to that task. That's
why I like the idea of writing. Writing is reflective work done in a
quiet studio, whereas trial work, as you know, is done in a boiler
room, an emotional boiler room. It's high pressure and noisy, so the
contrast is marked and therefore stimulating. It's like hot and cold
contrast therapy for muscle tissue. It's good for you, but what we tend
to do as lawyers is get immersed solely in law and it's not good for us.
We forget to cool off.

MURPHY: *Did your writing* **Partners** *help you work through those symptoms?*

MARTEL: Absolutely. One of the things I recommended in my July article is to vary your regimen and do other things to allow your creative
impulses to come out. Barry Siegel's book *Love, Medicine, and Miracles* suggests that cancer can be caused by thwarted creative instincts.
It builds up and becomes a tumor. Whether that's true or not, it's cer-

tainly true in my own experience that music before and now writing have kept me going. People are sometimes surprised that I can be as enthusiastic about being a trial lawyer after twenty-eight years of doing it and that I haven't become an alcoholic or a pharmaceutical junkie, that I am in good health and like what I'm doing. I love my firm and everyone in it. So why is that? I think it's because of our sabbatical program and because I have been able to do other things and have had the freedom to do other things.

MURPHY: *I noticed from your biography in* **Martindale-Hubbell** *that you have written two law review comments, one you wrote in law school, one more recently, and currently the burnout article. Have you written any other articles?*

MARTEL: I've written a lot of articles, a lot of law pieces. I've edited PLI books but I hadn't done any fiction until *Partners* other than country music. I've written about seventy-five country music songs and I think that, while I haven't done it excessively well, those who do are the real masters of short story writing in our culture. They have to tell a whole story of life, death, love, incest, disappointed love, whatever, all the things that are important emotional triggers in our lives, and they have to do it in three minutes. That's very, very difficult and I think that in this process I learned a lot about writing that carried into the novel; for example, how to make a chapter concise and make the reader want to go on to the next one. I think writing briefs can also be a good background for writing fiction, if you know how to write a brief in a way that will hold the judge's interest. If you have a beginning, middle, and end, and if you are concentrating as you write on continuity from paragraph to paragraph, you keep the judge reading. After all, the judge is human just like you and me and any other lay reader. If they're not interested they're going to put it aside and watch television. So my training for writing *Partners* has been disciplined law writing and seventy-five country music lyrics.

MURPHY: *Have you been able to have any of your songs recorded?*

MARTEL: No. I've done many demos but have failed to get a record contract. One song has been published and I've won several American songwriting contest awards, just about every time I enter, which is about every other year. There's a big difference, however, between that and succeeding in the commercial world of music. It's highly competitive and one has to focus one's entire attention on writing. One probably should go down to Hollywood to live and I just can't do those things. But what I can do is take sabbaticals and write novels.

MURPHY: *Did writing the country music songs come out of your roots in Modesto?*

MARTEL: In part. When I was a kid I used to sneak into the Uptown Ballroom in downtown Modesto and watch the Maddox Brothers and Rose. That was very exciting to me. I'd stand there at the foot of the stage peering up in reverent awe at this thing called a steel guitar and I'd say to myself, That is a modern wonder. How did anyone ever build that thing and learn how to play it? I don't consider myself a real true, deep down Rose Maddox or Nashville fan. I prefer what is known as "L.A. country" epitomized by the Eagles. I don't even go as far as "Austin country," although I like Waylon Jennings and Willie Nelson. So I certainly don't see myself in the true country tradition but I like what they say. The stark truths delivered in country lyrics appeal to me. The simplicity of the chord structures makes it possible for me, without a lot of music background, to have been able to play with sufficient expertise my original material at places like the Palomino Club in Hollywood and the Troubadour in Los Angeles. That was enough for me.

MURPHY: *You've played your own songs there?*

MARTEL: Yes, I was a singer-songwriter.

MURPHY: *What instruments did you play?*

MARTEL: Guitar and piano.

MURPHY: *And you're still doing that?*

MARTEL: Just for my own joy and the joy or punishment of my family and dear friends. Actually, the last time I performed in a group was at our law firm party. Joe Silverhound in concert.

MURPHY: *That's your stage name, Joe Silverhound?*

MARTEL: Yeah. It has been a serious professional effort. I've been a member of the musicians' union now for some thirty years and I don't take it lightly even though I haven't had the commercial success I've had with *Partners* and in the field of writing.

MURPHY: *Now that you've had that success with* **Partners,** *do you plan on writing another novel?*

MARTEL: Yes, I've done an outline.

MURPHY: *Have you started it?*

MARTEL: Yes.

MURPHY: *Can you give us a glimpse of what the plot will be about?*

MARTEL: I can't, not because I'm being secretive but because I believe what other writers have written: that you've got to keep it bottled up. You've got to keep that pressure relief valve absolutely closed until you're ready to sit down and write, because even if you talk about it just a little bit it somehow diminishes the energy for writing. The next book will also be about a law firm. It will be a different kind of book and will involve a different kind of law firm. It brings into play some of my music background. The final tease is that I was also an air force pilot for four years and it will have some of that in it as well. It's going to be, I think, an interesting book.

MURPHY: Conflicts of Interest *involves ethics on several levels, from the individual lawyer to the large law firm. How would you compare the ethical problems that the large firm faced in* **Partners** *(and also in* **Conflicts of Interest)** *with the ethical problems that Seth faced in* **Conflicts?**

MARTEL: In *Partners,* it wasn't so much the ethics of the law firm as it was three people within the law firm. It was four bad eggs. I'm very much into the notion of bad eggs in the law firm, more than bad law firms necessarily. I've never known a bad law firm. In fact, I've never known anyone as bad as Barrington. What I'm trying to say is that there are—to my knowledge—no evil law firms, but there are, in all probability, unethical partners within law firms that stretch the limit of the law. Then in *Conflicts,* you really didn't have a firm with bad ethics. You had Anthony Treadwell, who is a son of a bitch. But it is unclear in the book whether he really knew anything about what was going on. He may have. It may be said about him that in the exercise of reasonable care he should have known what was going on. But I guess what you're asking is how would I compare the ethical dilemma facing Seth Cameron with the bad conduct of the four partners in *Partners* and possibly the ethics of Anthony Treadwell in *Conflicts of Interest.*

MURPHY: *Actually, I'm more interested in the broader picture in terms of the ethical problems faced by a small firm practitioner versus partners in large firms representing big-monied clients.*

MARTEL: I think there are very similar stresses on small firm lawyers as on big firm lawyers. Big firm lawyers, because there is never enough money, have to reckon with the pressures put upon them by major clients that they can't afford to lose. The small practitioner is faced with more primitive needs, such as three meals a day, and is therefore subject to his own temptations and might well yield to them, just as the large firm lawyer might yield to them because he wants to upgrade from a Lexus to a Mercedes.

MURPHY: *In* Conflicts of Interest, *Treadwell's firm defends a case against a woman who had actually consulted him first. Isn't that an obvious conflict?*

MARTEL: I tried to make it less of a conflict by having Seth file the complaint in his own name and limiting the contact between the firm and Elena.

MURPHY: *Conflicts also gives many details about airplanes, weapons. Why this emphasis on the military details?*

MARTEL: I tried not to make it as detailed as a Tom Clancy novel but I did want the reader to get some sense of the problems of the military attitude. Just recently we saw that Congress approved over a half billion dollars for more B-2 bombers. Exactly five hundred and fifty-three million. If you want to have the exact number. People are wondering, when it turns out that we are spending ninety-two cents post–cold war for every one dollar we spent during the cold war, where is the peace dividend?

MURPHY: *There's an overriding theme of the book, of Seth longing to work in a big firm and succeed there. Then when he leaves he longs to get back. What's so great about working for a big firm that makes Seth have these longings?*

MARTEL: Seth Cameron looked at life through a distorted point of view. He equates happiness with money, specifically the tenured wealth of partnership in a large firm with the kind of happiness that will fill the gap in his heart left when he suffered the abandonment of his mother at a young age. But it can only do so if it is achievement of a spectacular sort. And in his mind this can only be found in a large city in a large firm where large and complex cases are usually found.

MURPHY: *There're parts of the book in which you describe the angst of a plaintiff's lawyer starting a trial. I think these are very informative for both young and old lawyers. Were you putting in these kinds of trial practice tips to appeal to lawyer readers?*

MARTEL: Yeah. I found that lots of my mail after *Partners* came from lawyers, and because I have done a good deal of teaching, it's my nature to try to do that in any form I can. I hope there are some things in there that will show lawyers how to behave and certainly how not to behave.

MURPHY: *There are many references to Joe Silverhound in the book. Why did you put these in* Conflicts of Interest?

MARTEL: Two answers to that question: One, because I like the idea of combining art forms. I did a reading last night in which I sang those versions because I am Joe Silverhound. So that's my idea of a reading, where you can combine the different kinds of forms. And it makes for a really nice entertainment for an audience. And, also, I had written the lines. I liked the lines; they were appropriate for the feeling that I had at the time. I thought it was a different way to illustrate what was going on in his head.

STEVE MARTINI

In Steve Martini's second novel, *Compelling Evidence,* attorney Paul Madriani defends his ex-lover, Talia Potter, from charges she murdered her husband, a nominee to the U.S. Supreme Court and Madriani's former partner. Prosecutor Duane Nelson describes the crime in his opening statement:

> *Ladies and gentlemen, the state will produce evidence, testimony by expert witnesses, that the victim, Ben Potter, was brutally murdered at another location, shot in the back of the head, execution style, that his body was then transported to his law office in this city. Expert witnesses will tell you that a twelve-gauge shotgun was then used, inserted into the victim's mouth and discharged in an effort to deform the body, to conceal the earlier bullet wound, to make it appear as if the victim had taken his own life.*

The *San Francisco Chronicle* called *Compelling Evidence* a legal thriller in the tradition of *Presumed Innocent* and "one hot ticket."

A graduate of McGeorge School of Law, Steve Martini has practiced both private and public law, including as a staff attorney for the California Department of Consumer Affairs. Before admission to the bar, he worked as a reporter for the *Los Angeles Daily Journal* covering the state legislature and state agencies.

This interview took place in 1992.

FICTION: *The Simeon Chamber* (1987) ▪ *Compelling Evidence* (1992) ▪ *Prime Witness* (1993) ▪ *Undue Influence* (1994) ▪ *The Judge* (1995) ▪ *The List* (1997)

▪ *Critical Mass* (1998) ▪ *The Attorney* (2000) ▪ *The Jury* (2001) ▪ *The Arraignment* (2001)

MURPHY: Compelling Evidence *begins with a graphic description of an execution in the gas chamber, but the execution itself has nothing to do with the plot. Why did you begin the book this way?*

MARTINI: Actually, I've been criticized in some reviews for that. There were two reasons. In fiction, you have to have a "hook" to pull the reader in, and I felt that there was some nexus with the heart of the story, which is a death penalty trial. The stakes had to be made as clear as possible to the reader as to what was happening here.

I will admit, in the two novels I've written I've gone back and done either the prologue or the first chapter fairly late in the book. This is not something that I wrote in the early drafts of the manuscript, but something that I inserted later as I got toward the end of the book, actually. And I felt I needed some kind of a charge to get the book going, rather than just a bland opening, and I think it worked for that purpose. I do feel that it added something to the stakes of what the story was about, what risks were involved here. That's basically why I did it.

MURPHY: *Your book came out a few months before Robert Alton Harris was being executed. Was this purely coincidental?*

MARTINI: It came out in February, and it was in the hands of the publisher about five or six months before that. So, actually, while I was aware that Harris was moving forward, and in fact, had passed one execution date the previous year, I can't say that it had any real bearing on the story. A lot of lawyers were becoming increasingly aware that there was going to be an execution in California after that long period—the long hiatus—just based on the composition of the federal courts and the decisions that were coming down in that area. I think you could sense the time was running out. Whether it would have been Harris or someone else is hard to predict, but it was probable that California would restore the death penalty and actually carry it out at some point in the not too distant future at the time that I wrote the book. So there was some surmise on my part in that regard.

I did go to San Quentin. I did look at the gas chamber, and I took a tour of some of the facility there. I did not go on death row, which is generally closed, even to the writing public. But it was a rather chilling experience just to be in the room where the witnesses would stand. Basically, what I wanted in order to garner color for the story was to experience what a witness would have experienced, other than the actual thing that the execution carried out. But to see the buildings, the facilities, to enter through San Quentin in the same way that an official witness would enter on a prescribed date for execution. And that's basically what they did for me. Gave me a tour.

MURPHY: *Your book has received a lot of praise from some noted trial lawyers— including F. Lee Bailey and Melvin Belli—for the authenticity of the trial scenes. Yet, from your résumé it appears you haven't had any criminal trial experience.*

MARTINI: Not much. I had some criminal trial work back in the seventies; I was with a general practice firm in Sacramento for a little over a year. I did have somewhat of a baptism of fire there, because that firm did do a good deal of criminal work, mostly misdemeanors. There were a couple of felonies I handled but they were not death penalty cases or anything near it. Actually, I would say that I drew heavily on experiences from my background as a journalist. I had covered the courts in Los Angeles for a period of time back in the late sixties, and then again in Sacramento when I was a Capitol correspondent there. I covered the local courts for the *Los Angeles Daily Journal.* So I had a good deal of experience covering the courts, observing criminal proceedings and some rather good trial lawyers at work. I would say I probably drew more heavily on that than I did on my own experiences. My experiences probably resulted in the characterizations. Every character you use in a book is a composite. I think that I drew on my own life's experiences in crafting the characters, and probably what I observed others doing pretty much driving the story.

MURPHY: *The plot revolves around attorney Paul Madriani, who is defending his ex-lover, who is accused of murdering her husband, Ben Potter. Where did you get the inspiration for this story?*

MARTINI: You always start with a puzzle when you start plotting fiction. You start playing "what if" games—what if a character did this, and what if that happened—and when you write trial fiction, it takes on a life of its own because of the dynamics of the trial process or the legal process. In all honesty, I don't think I knew where this story was going when I started it. I had a rough outline, and that outline underwent probably twenty different major revisions during the course of the actual writing of the book. So it was a process where the book grew almost of its own accord as I wrote. Many of the things that are in the final book now were not there in the earlier versions of the outline.

So I can't say that it came from any single experience. It came from knowing some notable people who were driving forces in the community where I worked and lived and watching those people and wondering what would happen if a Supreme Court nominee had this kind of a skeleton in his closet, and how far it would go, what conceivably could happen from the dynamics of this whole thing. I would say that the story grew in that fashion. I guess the only thing that I wanted to do was make it a "whodunit." Both of the novels that I've written so far—*Compelling Evidence* and *The Simeon Chamber*—had that element of "whodunit" just to keep the reader turning pages. And the third book I'm working on now also has that in it as well. But I think to some extent they're classic mysteries, but they are woven in the fabric of a legal trial and a legal procedural, so that's sort of the difference.

MURPHY: *You mentioned your experience as a reporter. Did the transition from straight reporting, factual reporting, to fiction create any problems in your writing?*

MARTINI: No. Other than the fact that I had to struggle a little bit with dialogue. From doing news stories, when people are quoted, oftentimes it's unintelligible. You can look for a long time and not find a string of words that forms a sentence. So when you fashion dialogue in fiction, you have to clean it up. You've got to make it intelligible for the reader. But to me, anyway, it didn't take much for me to figure that out.

There was a little bit of trial and error in the first book, I would say. I probably rewrote the first four or five chapters several times to get it down right. But once I had mastered that technique for writing dialogue, the rest of the book came to me fairly easily, actually. I don't want to minimize it. It's a great deal of hard work and there are days when you just don't want to sit down and do it. But the actual technique of doing it is not something that I struggled with a great deal.

MURPHY: *Your book is both a trial novel and a mystery. Mysteries traditionally spend a lot of time describing the physical characteristics of the characters, yet there is no physical description of Paul Madriani in the book.*

MARTINI: Yeah. I've been criticized for that. I don't give one, and in fact in the next book I don't give one either. I pretty much decided early on that I was going to leave that to the reader's own imagination and they could each have their own Paul Madriani, if they wanted to, and form their own opinion of what this man would look like. I've seen other fiction that has done that successfully. Usually, mysteries will describe in minute detail what the character looks like. It is difficult when you are writing first person, I will tell you, because the only way you can describe what the character looks like is through devices or contrivances; like when he's looking in a mirror, or he looks at a picture of himself, you can, in an offhand way, describe what he looks like. But it is contrived, and I think that's why I left it out pretty much. I felt that the writing in the first person propels the story forward. It has a seductive quality that draws the reader in, but at the same time it has limitations. Your character always has to be onstage and it is a little self-critical, I guess, to have him describing himself. It just doesn't come across well in a book, so I think that's probably why I left it out.

MURPHY: Compelling Evidence *has been compared both favorably and unfavorably to* Presumed Innocent *by many reviewers. You have the attorney involved in an affair, a troubled marriage, the mysterious murder, a twist ending, and a lot of other plot similarities. As I understand it, you started writing the book around 1988, after* Presumed Innocent *came out.*

MARTINI: That's true. This book was written after *Presumed Innocent,* and I'll admit that I was impressed by its style, the way in which the story unfolded. I thought it was a magnificent style. Turow is a good writer; I give him credit for that. In my opinion, he's one of the best. I can't deny that I was influenced by that story, because obviously I was. I still think the story stands on its own two feet. I think it has some strengths and some weaknesses. And the reviews that I've read have been fairly accurate. He has been credited with being a better writer than I am in his descriptive abilities, and I think that's probably true. I've been given high marks for humor, which is probably one of my strong points. I do like to write a story that can turn on the human equation and find a humorous side to it. It's fun for me to set up characters and have them do things that make people laugh, sometimes to the characters' own embarrassment. But I think that is probably the strength of *Compelling Evidence*—it had a little more humor in it and caught that side of humanity a little more.

MURPHY: *What are the weaknesses of* Compelling Evidence *that you see now?*

MARTINI: One of the criticisms that I have heard—a question propounded to me by a critic—was that some lawyers felt the stakes really weren't high enough. That this wasn't really the kind of case that would have resulted in the death penalty had she been convicted, and the chances of a conviction were few. I felt that there were enough pitfalls in the story as it unfolded because of Madriani's relationship with the defendant, and the fear that that relationship would ultimately come out during the trial and that he would be discredited. What the effect of that would be on a jury—who knows? It's hard to say. If there was a major fault, that might have been it. You can always try and stack the stakes a little higher against your protagonist, in order to make him more of a hero as the story unfolds—more of a master of his own fate. The problem with that is that if you take it to too far of an extreme you end up with stick figures as your characters. You wind up with people like James Bond, who never do anything wrong.

MURPHY: *How important was it to you as a writer of fiction to make* **Compelling Evidence** *accurate in terms of criminal procedure, trial procedure, and that kind of thing?*
MARTINI: I would say that's probably where I spent most of my time.

MURPHY: *Why is that so important to a fiction writer?*
MARTINI: I've been criticized for it by some lay reviewers, although others found it fascinating. They got caught up in the voir dire, one of the areas that I dreaded writing, actually. In fact, you find early in the story that I was going to take the process through every step, through the preliminary hearing, voir dire. I was going to walk through all these steps, and then, as I approached each one of these, it became more daunting. Not because I couldn't write them, but because I was afraid they would turn out like a legal treatise.

So I had to find ways of trying to make this entertaining to a layman. I literally had to take the voir dire process and dissect it: What was it all about? What would go through the minds of jurors? What were the fears the lawyers would be feeling here? How easy it is to alienate jurors, how you want to save your peremptories, all of the strategies that go into this process. I want to admit that I did a great deal of research before I wrote that section. And personally, I think it is one of the best sections in the book because there's a lot of humanity. You have the older juror who is not up to dealing with the rigors of a long trial and the fears that that breeds in the minds of the attorneys who have to deal with that. Yet they don't want to get rid of this individual and alienate any of the other jurors. And you've got the judge who is sitting and deciding, I'm not going to let this guy go for cause, you're going to have to burn a peremptory and get rid of him.

So you've got all the dynamics of that whole process in there and it really is, I think, a fascinating process. You've got a love-hate relationship on the part of many people—the lay public out there—toward lawyers and the law. While many of them despise us, they are also fascinated by the whole process, and sometimes can't get enough of it. So, I felt that it was interesting to give them this insider's view. Using the first-person voice—I'm inside of Paul's head—you can listen to the ruminations that are going on there, the strategies that are being played out. It gives the reader a special view of this process from the lawyers' perspective.

MURPHY: *One problem that I saw with including the preliminary hearing was that you had some witnesses testify both in the preliminary hearing and in the trial, and it got somewhat redundant.*

MARTINI: Yeah. That might have been a weakness in the story. I thought about that. By the same token, I guess the easier way to handle that—and you learn technique with each story—would be to pass them off in a quick paragraph. If you go into detail in a preliminary hearing, when you get to the trial you just put this character up there, but he's off in one paragraph. You don't go through any detail with him. That could be a criticism of the way in which it was crafted.

MURPHY: *The book's written, of course, from Madriani's perspective as the defense lawyer. Did writing in the first person present any problems for you, particularly in terms of what evidence to reveal?*

MARTINI: Yes. That was tough. There are a number of problems that you have with first person. You are limited. The first book I wrote was written in the third person and the ability to move from scene to scene in the third person is much easier. You have more variation available to you. And you can have digression. You can have a scene that doesn't involve this character, involving somebody else when you are doing third person. When doing first person, that character, your protagonist, has to be onstage constantly and you've got to be very careful because a reader can get tired of that person unless there is something to keep the reader's attention.

And I think, as I said earlier, for me that's humor. If they keep reading for humor as well as excitement they will stay attached to your character. But the first-person style was something that took a little bit of time for me to master and to craft. It did not come that easily. And it is not something that I would recommend to someone who is writing a first novel. I'm not sure I could have mastered it in the first book that I wrote. I think I'd still be back there writing that first book.

MURPHY: *One of the difficulties you have in writing in the first person is that there is evidence that comes to your protagonist that you can't reveal.*
MARTINI: What I had to do basically is, if there was a defining piece of evidence or information that would follow the whodunit aspect of the story, ultimately, I had to keep that away from my protagonist until close to the end of the story. It was either that or, basically, violate the rules of fiction. That is, your protagonist would know something that he does not reveal to the reader, and that basically is viewed by most fiction writers as a no-no. You're not supposed to do that. So, what it boils down to is that your protagonist has to discover fairly late in the story what the ultimate outcome was.

In *Presumed Innocent,* you will recall that Rusty figured it out, but he goes back and explains that he figured it out late in the game. Toward the end of the trial he figures out what's going on by basically tripping over the evidence. Circumstances led him to it, totally fortuitous. And the same type of thing happens here. You're limited. I mean there are only so many things you can do when you're dealing with a formula fiction, and there are only so many ways you can get to the final outcome.

MURPHY: *One reviewer has criticized your portrayal of female characters. The defendant, Talia Potter, who is the glamorous, free-and-easy wife, and Nikki, the wife of Paul Madriani, are the main female characters. Do you think your female characters are poorly portrayed?*

MARTINI: I will say that I've become sensitized. Yeah. I think that that's probably true. And I will tell you that from the commercial perspective of writing fiction, women buy the books. That's where most books are sold, and there are an increasing number of writers out there, both male and female, who are well aware of that. For that reason you find an increasing number of protagonists in books are female and those books sell quite well.

In terms of the manner in which I crafted the women in this story, that's probably true. But they weren't major figures in the story. Even though one of them was the defendant in the case, her role was rather limited. It's something I'm working on in the next story. I don't know whether I'll actually overcome it or not. It's very difficult for me, and I suspect for many male writers, to write with a lot of insight into female characters. I find it difficult. I know there are guys out there who have written stories about women from the woman's perspective entirely. Their protagonists are women and they can do this. I have a tough time doing that. Whether based on life's experiences, I just don't have the background—I'm married, but maybe I don't have enough background to make a major character a woman. Now, this next story I have ideas on, but I haven't gotten to that portion of the book yet. But this may come about though; we'll have to wait and see.

MURPHY: Compelling Evidence *is set in Capitol City, which is obviously modeled after Sacramento. Why not just call it Sacramento?*

MARTINI: I guess I could have done that. Now I'm writing a series of books set in that area. I'm sort of relegated to not going back and changing the name of Capitol City to Sacramento. I don't know why I didn't. I felt it was better to fictionalize things. To some extent, I guess I was hiding a little bit. You want to make your characters as much as you can composites of people so that they are not any single individual. You want to make the locations also fictional. I could have used actual locations in Sacramento, and some people would argue that "Wong's" is "Frank Fat's." Obviously you've got some thinly veiled areas here that people will discover where you are going. I think I may have in fact used the name of one restaurant in town during the story.

I just chose not to. I thought it lent a little more credence to let people try and figure out where it is and where these places are. That's part of the fun of the game.

MURPHY: *You wrote an article for* **The Recorder** *called "Writing the Legal Novel" back in April, and commented on the cynicism that you found in covering state government as a reporter. Did the cynicism come across in* **Compelling Evidence?**
MARTINI: Yeah, I think it did. I think that some of the humor is created by that cynicism. It's difficult to cover, particularly government, for a long period of time—and for me it was about a decade—and not become cynical. The whole political process is one that I think increasing numbers of people out there become cynical about, and I think when you are so close to it, as I was, that sometimes you become very cynical. And I think it did come through.

MURPHY: *In addition to writing for purposes of a mystery or entertainment, do you try to make your novels have a theme, any kind of statement you want to make? Such as, trials are a crapshoot?*
MARTINI: That became the theme, probably. You can't predict the outcome of a trial. Who knows what that solid piece of evidence is that's going to turn the tide in any trial? Nobody knows what it is. Trials by and large are really a truth-finding process, or are they something else? I think they are something else. What else I'm not sure I'm ready to

explain yet. But the obvious factor that pulls this trial is the SODDI defense—some other dude did it. Madriani had what he felt was some evidence pointing in that direction but, in fact, it didn't bear out in the end. That tells you a lot about the trial process and that jurors can be distracted by it. The system is obviously not perfect, but then I never said it was.

LIA MATERA

Lia Matera is a graduate of the University of California, Santa Cruz, and Hastings College of the Law, where she served as editor in chief of the *Hastings Constitutional Law Quarterly.* She has served as an extern to the Honorable William W. Schwarzer of the United States District Court and as a teaching fellow at Stanford Law School.

She has been nominated many times for prestigious mystery writing awards, including a Mystery Readers International Macavity Award, the Bouchercon World Mystery Convention Anthony Award, the Mystery Writers of America's Edgar Allan Poe Award, and the Private Eye Writers of America Shamus Award. Matera has given up the practice of law and writes mystery novels at her home in Santa Cruz, California.

This interview took place in 1990.

FICTION: Willa Jansson novels: *Where Lawyers Fear to Tread* (1987) ▪ *Hidden Agenda* (1988) ▪ *A Radical Departure* (1988) ▪ *Prior Convictions* (1991) ▪ *Last Chants* (1996) ▪ *Star Witness* (1997) ▪ *Havana Twist* (1998)

Laura Di Palma novels: *The Smart Money* (1988) ▪ *The Good Fight* (1990) ▪ *A Hard Bargain* (1992) ▪ *Face Value* (1994) ▪ *Designer Crimes* (1995)

Anthology: *Irreconcilable Differences* (ed., 1999) ▪ *Counsel for the Defense and Other Stories* (2002)

MURPHY: *Your first hardcover book,* The Good Fight, *recently received a favorable plug from Herb Caen. Have your reviews generally been favorable?*

MATERA: Yes, I've gotten very good reviews with this book. The best of them was on National Public Radio; John Leonard really loved it, which boosted its sales, to the point where it went into a second printing. I've had good luck with this book. I've been very pleased.

MURPHY: *What is the good fight?*

MATERA: The good fight is any struggle of a continuing nature in which people have been engaged. In the context of this book, it refers both to the veterans of the war in Vietnam and the so-called war at home. It refers to people who fought to stop that war and then kept plugging away at one thing or another that was related politically or ethically to antiwar work. I have two parallel stories, really, one about a Vietnam War veteran who's having some problems and one about a veteran of the war at home who is having some problems. Both of them were or are engaged in the good fight.

MURPHY: *The plot revolves around a group called Clearinghouse for Peace, which is infiltrated by FBI agents. This is your war at home. Do you find that there is still interest in this country in what happened during the Vietnam War in the United States?*

MATERA: Yes, I think so. I just got through teaching a class at UC Santa Cruz on the sixties. I was teaching nineteen-year-olds, freshmen. Initially, their attitude was, This is ancient history, this is very square, this is the kind of stuff that our parents were doing and is therefore very boring and not at all cool. The trick was to make them understand the emotional response, make them understand why people hit the streets in the 1960s. But people of my generation remember why we hit the streets. It's very fresh in our minds, in fact. I think there is a resurgence of interest, which is good news, bad news. Some of the interest is for the wrong reason, I think. On the one hand there is a tendency to rewrite history, revise the war in Vietnam, turn it into a glorious but flawed thing that we did, something heroic because it meant a commitment to obedience and patriotism and a willingness to change someone else's life for the better. That's what I think they're trying to turn the war into.

But that's not what it was for the Vietnamese people, not at all. And that's not what it was for people who objected to it and were forced to take part in it, and that's not what it was for people who objected to it and were forced into exile or were clubbed by police batons or were tear-gassed. I think there is a renewed interest in the sixties because of movies like *Platoon, Full Metal Jacket, Incidents of War.* The war suddenly is a big thing in the movies, it's big screen, it's exciting. It seems that for some reason or another we've waited twenty years to discuss it and now we want to explore it but we want to put this golden wash on it.

I think there is also a resurgence of interest in activism. People who have been, for lack of a better word, yuppies for the last ten years are becoming nostalgic. They finally have all the things they want and now it's important to them to decide whether things are enough. Those people are trying to become active in a way that doesn't involve a huge outpouring of wasted energy. A lot of activism, unfortunately, is a bull-headed desire to believe that one person can make a difference, whereas in many cases one person can't. And frequently, meetings degenerate into a cannibalizing process of proving each other's views passé, proving each other's philosophies politically incorrect. I think they can actually be counterproductive. I think people are trying to find another way to be active; it's very much in the public consciousness now.

MURPHY: *All of your books involve the sixties in one way or another. The main character in three of the books, Willa Jansson, is the daughter of two leftist demonstrators who are running off to Nicaragua and doing other liberal-type activities. Is this a reflection of your own background in the sixties?*
MATERA: Yes, I think it is. I am trying very hard to come to grips with all the things that my characters are trying to come to grips with. I got married very young. I got married right out of high school, married to somebody who was wanted by the FBI for various draft-

related problems. So we crisscrossed the country, not actually fleeing from the FBI, because when we finally did land somewhere and stay there a while we put in a change of address. The FBI, had it been more savvy, could have gone downstairs from its office in the post office in Eureka and flipped through the change of address cards and found it instantly. Instead, it took them two years of opening our friends' mail, and various other circuitous acts, to find us.

During that time I thought a lot about symbolic action. My husband did not have to be in that position. He had a medical problem that would have earned him an instant 4-F but he chose instead to make a statement, to take a symbolic action, and I disapproved of that very strongly. I felt that it was foolish to deliver one's self into the hands of one's jailers. But to make a statement just to make a statement was not my style, certainly. And so I thought a lot about it at the time. I thought a lot about activism in general because I went to a lot of meetings. I felt that I had to be on the streets as long as the war in Vietnam was going on. I had to do something but it was clear to me that what I was doing was not really effective. Maybe the antiwar movement pulled the country a little more to the left for a while. I don't know. But I continued thinking about it over the years as I watched people I knew changing in various ways.

Interesting the way people changed with the times. I mean in the early sixties to mid sixties, there was a reaching out: We want to help people. We want to help the blacks. We want to register voters. We want to do good. A very Kennedy-era mentality, a real optimism: We can effect change, we really can. The president said so, by God, and now we're going to do it. As things heated up and Johnson and Nixon decided that they wanted to crush the movement under their heels, repression and violence triggered militarism in the movement. It was rather horrifying to watch. I did not like the movement's emphasis on bombs and guns, and I think in the early seventies many people couldn't handle it. They clicked off and decided to focus on inner consciousness, and that was not satisfying. So suddenly people were preppies and then suddenly people were yuppies and now they don't know who to be. I watched my ex-husband change from a radical firebrand to a very straitlaced corporate lawyer whose main client is the very bank people talked so heatedly about bombing in the early years of our marriage. It is an interesting transition that a lot of people made. It interests me very much thematically. There is a lot there to explore because, in a way, you can't blame people for turning away from something that was frustrating and painful and in many ways ineffective. And yet what they turned to is in some ways superficial, painfully superficial.

MURPHY: *Do you see yourself as the spokesperson for the liberal causes that originated in the sixties, in trying to keep these causes alive through your books?*
MATERA: No, I think I'm more interested in exploring how people try to deal with problems that cause society as a whole a lot of pain. Because I don't think there is an answer. It's not a math problem and I don't think that it's useful for a novelist to be preaching. I think the most useful thing a novelist can do is present a problem fairly and try to show the shades of gray and some of the subtleties so that people will think about it, just think about it. I don't have an answer so I don't feel I can get on a soapbox and offer anybody an answer. All I can do is explore the problem in an entertaining way so that people will be pulled along by the plot and think about things that maybe are not much fun to think about.

MURPHY: *You went to law school and now are not practicing law but writing full-time. Why did you make that choice?*
MATERA: I have always wanted to be a novelist. I was writing novels during the summers in college. Like every other field that really takes some practice, my first novels were not that good. When college ended I was very discouraged. I didn't know if I would ever get anything published and I felt that I needed to have some kind of career. I think a lot of people go to law school because they are verbal by nature and it seems like an interesting option. A lot of people go into law school but have some other higher aspiration. They really want to be something else but they just don't know how to go about it. They hope they can somehow fit their dream into their law practice, com-

bine them in some way; environmental law, constitutional law, the "sexy" kinds of law. But I knew in law school that if I could get a book published I would stop being a lawyer. I kept trying to find a job that would allow me enough time to write.

I externed for a federal court judge, thinking that I would apply for clerkships and that would be closer than most legal positions to a nine-to-five job. I could write in the evenings. I ended up taking a job as a teaching fellow at Stanford thinking that I could write summers. But somehow it just never was enough time to write. So when I had a baby I decided, This is it, I have got to stop writing "midlist" books, books that are not particularly marketable, don't fit into any category. I decided that I would try to write something I could sell. I was a lifelong mystery fan and mysteries seemed interesting and literate and fun and so I gave that a try. I wrote a lot when my son was very young because it seemed to me I had maybe two years and then I would have to go back to work. It really was publish or practice.

MURPHY: *The narrator of* **The Good Fight,** *Laura Di Palma, made her reputation defending the murderer of two congressmen whom she got off by using a defense called the "T.V. Syndrome" defense. Have you used actual cases in coming up with these details?*

MATERA: I have analogized, yes. The reason that I used the "T.V. Syndrome" defense in the book was because actually it was not the way that she got that murderer off. But it is what everybody thinks she used. So it's analogous to the Dan White case. Everybody thinks the "Twinkies" defense is what saved Dan White, whereas the jury found voluntary manslaughter based on a straight heat-of-passion defense. That interested me very much. I have heard homicide detectives praising Doug Schmidt, who was Dan White's lawyer. I have heard them praising the techniques that he pioneered, cross-examination techniques, courtroom techniques. The level of admiration that they feel for him is extraordinary. And what interested me, I am not sure if this is true or not, but a homicide detective told me that Schmidt's law practice suffered because of the brilliant job that he did in the Dan White case. He was held accountable for the sins of his client. That fascinated me and I wanted to use some of that. I have never met him. I have no idea what his feelings are about any of it but it was fun to put Laura Di Palma in a position similar to his.

MURPHY: *In the book, Laura is a sixth-year associate at a conservative San Francisco firm and still trying to defend leftist causes, which creates a lot of tension in the firm. Do you find that those two activities are contradictory?*

MATERA: Yes, I think so. That's a bell that goes off immediately for most lawyers. A lot of lawyers go into firms with the assurance that they will be able to do some kind of pro bono work and then they find that even if the law firm were to encourage them to do pro bono work there is so much competition for getting those billable hours up that they simply don't do it. Yes, it's unrealistic to think of an attorney taking on a big pro bono case. In *The Good Fight* I do stress that this is an old friend of Laura's and that it's her last fling with pro bono criminal defense.

MURPHY: *The client is Dan Crosetti, who lost his legs when he was run over by a National Guard truck in 1972. Sounds like you were using another recent incident for that example.*

MATERA: Yes, there are things I read about in the newspaper that fascinate me and that I know would be thematically interesting. I alter them to suit my needs so that I can explore the core issue. James D. Houston is an author I admire very much. He talks about using real-life experience and facts, just plain old newspaper facts, how to weave them into good fiction. What he says is that it's okay to change the facts in order to tell the truth. Dramatic license. I enjoy doing that. There are things I find irresistible and so I tailor them to illustrate my point.

MURPHY: *All five of your books are written in the first person. Three of them involving Willa Jansson and two with Laura Di Palma. But in* **The Good**

Fight *you change that a little bit in that you have a prologue and epilogue in the third person. Why did you do that?*

MATERA: It just felt right at the time. I'm not a planner. I don't outline. I sit down with something in mind. It varies, a voice sometimes, a theme sometimes, something I care about, something I want to think about, an opening line, whatever, and I go from there. That day I sat down and wrote a third-person prologue.

MURPHY: *Do you have in mind who the murderer is when you start writing?*

MATERA: I am lucky if I know who the murderer is three-quarters of the way through the book. This is why I love using a word processor. I can go back and change things. Put in the right clues and make sure that everything conforms. I like a book that grabs me, pulls me in, and drags me along. The kind of book that Dick Francis writes, very involving on a personal level. The narrator has something at stake, not the kind of puzzle where it's, with an amateur sleuth, "Oh, my goodness, what have we here, another dead body." I like to be personally involved and the first person helps me do that. I mean, as a writer I need the same thing. I need to get pulled into my story.

MURPHY: *The other book involving Laura Di Palma,* **The Smart Money,** *does not involve so much liberal causes as her return to her hometown to seek revenge against her ex-husband and try to investigate the death of her ex-lover. Why did you use a more personal motivation in that book as opposed to the liberal motivations of your characters in the other books?*

MATERA: When I sat down to write that book, what I cared about was family and hometown and what it does to people. How it boxes people up. I was also interested in the feeling people have that a certain incident, at a key moment, would have made all the difference. A certain lover wising up and saying, "Yes, you're the one," would have made all the difference. As happy as a person might be otherwise, there remains a nagging feeling that they might have been happier if something else had happened. I was interested in that, very interested in hometown and family.

MURPHY: *Your interest in family went so far as having Laura get involved with her second cousin, Hal Di Palma. Why did you have her romantic relationship involve a family member?*

MATERA: Because I wanted to contrast their situations while showing that their basic reaction to their family was the same. That it was constricting, that it was embarrassing, and they both wanted to flee. I think that's the reaction of many, many people to their families and their hometowns. But they did it in very different ways. At the opening of the book, they're standing talking in an abandoned house but she's an extremely successful and famous attorney and he is basically homeless, a transient. I think it happens a lot. The same family raises two people who in personality are quite alike and in their reactions to family and background are quite alike also, and yet they end up in completely different places because of different aspects of the same personality traits. It's a very nice, subtle thing that was fun to explore.

MURPHY: *The characters in your books reappear from book to book and even cross paths. You have two main characters, Laura Di Palma, who's a successful middle-class attorney with some liberal ideals, and Willa Jansson, who on the other hand is more committed to the liberal causes and her family has a liberal background. Why did you use two main protagonists in your books?*

MATERA: I had planned, initially, to write books that were not series books, like Dick Francis does where it's always the racing world, but it's a different narrator in each book. I wanted to do that with the legal world, but to take it a step farther and build a legal community, which is why I have characters crossing paths in the books. I think if you practice law in an area as small as the Bay Area, you tend to know people in different firms and find that all your friends know the same people and you gossip about the same people from firm to firm. It's an extended family.

But when I got a phone call from Bantam Books about my first book, the editor said basically, "We would like to buy this book if you can assure us that your intention from the very beginning was to create a series. We don't want to force you to write a series. We don't want something formulaic but we are only buying series books." It had never been my intention to do a series, not for a minute. But I had wanted to publish a book for years and so I told them that writing a series was my life's dream, that I had the next three books completely planned, and that writing a series had been my goal and my most precious aspiration always. So she bought the Willa book and the first Laura Di Palma book, *The Smart Money*. I had already written it and it was making the rounds in New York at the same time. So she saw that one and bought it, too, even though at the time I hadn't planned to turn it into a series book.

MURPHY: *In two of your books,* A Radical Departure *and* Hidden Agenda, *the method of murder is with hemlock. What inspired you to use hemlock?*
MATERA: I am an amateur naturalist and mycologist so I'm out tramping around looking at wildflowers and mushrooms a lot anyway. Of the things you can gather easily and find quickly, hemlock is certainly one of the most deadly, especially if you use the roots. It was as simple as that.

MURPHY: *In* Hidden Agenda *there is a change in the activities of Willa in that she goes from being a pot-smoking, leftist employee of a lawyer named Julian Warneke to a $90,000-a-year job with a major law firm. You use the technique of introducing a noncharacter named Bud Hopper to get her from her liberal background to this law firm. Why did you use that technique?*
MATERA: Bud Hopper. It was mostly to show that Willa does not trust the obvious. This Republican has supposedly interceded on her behalf and because she wants the $90,000-a-year job it would be very easy for her to say, "How nice. You know, some Republicans are really nice guys and it's wonderful that my law review article has such wide appeal that this magic thing could happen to me." But I think veterans of the war at home can be quite cynical about fate being kind and interceding on their behalf. Also, I think there is something Pollyannaish about too many first-person narrators. You know, it's part of that B-movie syndrome of the young, fresh, dewy-eyed woman saying, "Yes, I'll open the door," even though it might be the

murderer on the other side, or being alone in a room with a murderer and saying, "Yes, I'm the only one who knows it's you and now I'm going to go and tell the police." I wanted Willa to be less dewy-eyed, more cynical, and it was a way to show that.

MURPHY: *Despite her cynicism, she still falls in love with the police lieutenant Surgelato. Why did you include that romantic tension there?*

MATERA: Because it made a nice counterpoint, I thought. People who are trained to admire one thing, a certain attitude in people, often find they're attracted to something else on a gut level. It may be what they are attracted to is something one level deeper than the attitude, the thing that gives the attitude its legitimacy. In the first book she is attracted to someone who's conservative and she's attracted to him for his sense of humor. In later books, she is attracted to a police lieutenant because she can rely on him. As much as she loves her parents, in a certain sense they let her down over and over again as a child. They went off to jail. They did their symbolic actions. They hammered dents in missile nose cones. They poured blood on draft files. The result of that for her was abandonment for a cause. But this police lieutenant is willing to do the opposite, to put his moral principles aside a little bit. To do a personal favor for her at the end of that second book.

MURPHY: *Since your first book was published, have you changed your technique or method in writing the books?*

MATERA: I think my level of sophistication has changed, yes. In my first book, I was bewildered by mystery plotting. There is this old Raymond Chandler line: If you're stuck, have two men with a gun walk into a room. With me it was: I'm stuck, I'll kill someone else. So I have, I think, five dead bodies in my first book. And I actually unmurdered two characters or it would have been seven. But by the time I got around to the third or fourth rewrite, I had enough technical skills to propel the plot without so many corpses. There have been fewer murders in each of my books as I've learned how to maintain suspense without actually killing off my characters. But I still like a fast pace. I am the type of woman who sees all the *Nightmare on Elm Street* movies.

MURPHY: *Do you believe that your writing style has changed any of the standard mystery techniques? Does your style have any innovations in mystery writing?*

MATERA: I think my books show a greater disregard for what the public wants in some ways than some of the books that came before. I am conscious of when I have Willa smoking pot, when I have her worrying about herpes, when I have her making a lot of political comments, that I am cutting down my audience. And there used to be a feeling that that was suicide, that you can't do that. But I've been fairly successful and writers have told me that that's made them a little more willing to worry less about the audience, worry less about offending people.

CHRISTINE MCGUIRE

Santa Cruz prosecutor Christine McGuire's first book, *Perfect Victim,* sold over one million copies and reached number one on the *New York Times* bestseller list in 1989. *Perfect Victim* is the true story of the Red Bluff sex slave who was kept prisoner in a box for seven years by a man and his wife. McGuire prosecuted *People v. Hooker,* winning convictions against both defendants.

McGuire's first novel, *Until Proven Guilty,* features a serial killer who preys on young Hispanic women, a killer so gruesome he has been compared to Hannibal the Cannibal. More than a horror story, *Until Proven Guilty* depicts the efforts of assistant district attorney Kathryn Mackay as she visits the crime scenes, examines the victims' mutilated bodies, and battles the sexism of the media as well as her colleagues. McGuire sympathetically portrays Mackay's struggle to succeed in a male-dominated profession:

> *"Imagine," he said, smiling. "The Iron Maiden, making an offer."*
>
> *Kathryn didn't reply: there was no point. She'd learned the rules long ago. It was all part of being a woman in what was still perceived as a man's world. The funny names were little jibes thrown at you to point out you weren't being feminine enough. Come on strong, you were a pushy bitch. Fail to do so and they'd patronize you or, worse, ignore you.*

Christine McGuire received her law degree from Southwestern University in southern California. She has been a prosecutor since 1980 and has taught classes on sexual enslavement at the FBI Academy in Quantico, Virginia.

This interview took place in 1993.

FICTION: *Until Proven Guilty* (1993) ▪ *Until Death Do Us Part* (1995) ▪ *Until Justice Is Done* (1995) ▪ *Until the Bough Breaks* (1997) ▪ *Until We Meet Again* (1998) ▪ *Until the Day They Die* (2000) ▪ *Until the Final Verdict* (2002)

NONFICTION: *Perfect Victim* (1989)

MURPHY: *Your first book,* **Perfect Victim,** *is a true crime story. What made you change direction and write in the legal thriller genre?*

McGUIRE: The legal thriller genre is real popular. It's what I read, it's what I enjoy. The idea actually came from my agent for *Perfect Victim.* He drew out the idea one day and we talked it over and decided to have a go at it. He was pretty confident that he could get either William Morrow, which is the publishing house for *Perfect Victim,* or another publishing house to look seriously at it. He thought that the time was ripe for a legal thriller to be written by a female attorney, because he didn't see any novels out there written by female attorneys. Most of the thrillers in the genre of Turow and Grisham are all written from the defense perspective. It was time for the prosecutor's perspective. So, with that in mind, he encouraged me to begin to put together a novel that he eventually would convince Simon and Schuster to buy.

MURPHY: **Until Proven Guilty** *has been compared to* **The Silence of the Lambs.** *Was Thomas Harris an influence in your writing the novel?*

McGUIRE: Not necessarily; however, I, too, was fortunate to consult with a special agent from the Behavioral Science Unit of the FBI at Quantico, Virginia. I received material from the FBI on profiling which helped me to develop one of the characters in *Until Proven Guilty.*

MURPHY: *You're referring, of course, to Steve Giordano, the special investigator.*

McGUIRE: Correct.

MURPHY: *The book spends a lot of time on the psychological profile. Have you had occasion in your practice to consult experts on profiles such as this?*

McGUIRE: Personally, no. However, law enforcement has consulted with profilers in murder cases. The police agencies have brought in profilers as an investigative tool. Profiling proves useful to law enforcement to help narrow the field of suspects. When there are few clues, it gives law enforcement a direction to go in.

MURPHY: *I thought it ironic in the book that a lot of time and effort is spent on developing the profile, and yet the killer really is found because of some hard legwork by the DA's investigator, Dave Granz. Were you making a commentary there on the effectiveness of the profiles?*

McGUIRE: No. While there is nothing better than hard legwork by the police and while good old-fashioned police work is often what solves crimes, we have forensic tools available to us to help solve crimes as well. Profiling is one of them. Once Kate accessed information Dave had obtained during his unauthorized investigation, the profile Giordano had constructed was useful to narrow down the list of suspects. Hard legwork and profiling worked hand in hand. If I was making a commentary about anything, it was that good old-fashioned police work and profiling make for a good "marriage," so to speak.

MURPHY: *The killer, Lee Russell, is introduced at the very beginning and we learn of his childhood, which, while unhappy, wasn't really all that horrible.*

McGUIRE: I agree.

MURPHY: *Were you trying at all in the book to explain why people become such terrible killers?*

McGUIRE: How can one know why people become such terrible killers? There are people who have lived through terrible experiences as a child, yet they do not commit murders. And then there are those who do kill. Russell's childhood did impact or, rather, influence the kinds of crimes he committed throughout *Until Proven Guilty.* And while that's not so unusual, I was not trying to explain why people become such terrible killers. I don't know why.

MURPHY: *You focus in the book on Kathryn Mackay, the assistant district attorney, yet since the book is told in the third person, we get a lot of glimpses of the killer's life and how he commits the crimes. Do you think you were giving away a little bit of the suspense by disclosing so much of the killer?*

McGUIRE: No. And that's been borne out by the reviews. One of the first reviews of *Until Proven Guilty* was written by Patricia Holt of the *San Francisco Chronicle*. Ms. Holt comments that *Until Proven Guilty* "struggles valiantly to break away from some of the cheap formula that typically shapes the serial killer novel. . . . She brings the kind of inside knowledge of sexual pathology and its investigation to her second book (the first was the nonfiction bestseller *Perfect Victim*) that makes for compulsive page-turning."

MURPHY: *Patricia Holt also comments on the gruesomeness of the crime and the fact you describe in great detail how he skins and mutilates his victims and, basically, acts almost as bad as Hannibal the Cannibal. Why were you so graphic in your descriptions?*

McGUIRE: I disagree that *Until Proven Guilty* is gruesome. In fact, much is left to the imagination of the reader. In order to make the law enforcement characters' dedication understandable, there must be a criminal out there who is committing very bad crimes. Otherwise that dedication, almost to the point of obsession, on the part of Kate and Dave would be misplaced.

MURPHY: *So you wanted to make the crimes so heinous that the reader could understand why the DAs and other people were spending so much time on it?*

McGUIRE: It makes sense of their dedication. And as I have said, I disagree that the crimes are so heinous, although granted, my view is colored by thirteen years of work as a prosecutor. Much of that thirteen years has been spent trying crimes much like the kinds of crimes depicted in *Until Proven Guilty*.

MURPHY: *The killer also has an intellectual side. He sends notes to the press and the DA's office which contain ciphers and forces the recipient to decode* *them, with a drawing of a little gingerbread man, as well. Has it been your experience that a lot of these serial killers are quite intelligent?*

McGUIRE: We see that, yes, especially in what is described as the "organized" serial killer. It is not uncommon for that kind of a killer to be quite intelligent.

MURPHY: *There is a discussion in the book about the organized versus disorganized killer. Have you had occasion, in your practice, to try to differentiate between the types when prosecuting or investigating a case?*

McGUIRE: It can become quite important to differentiate between the two when examining the modus operandi of a serial killer or rapist, especially when you intend to introduce his "m.o." to prove identity during the trial.

MURPHY: *Kathryn Mackay spends a great deal of the book acting more as an investigator than a prosecutor. Do DAs really spend that much time in the field looking for criminals?*

McGUIRE: I took a bit of literary license, but not much. In my position as a team leader of the Special Prosecutions Unit, I carry a pager and I am available to law enforcement seven days a week, twenty-four hours a day. I get called out to murder scenes. I go to crime scenes involving violent crimes other than murders. When I am finished at a murder scene, I go to the morgue. I deal with the legal issues as they come up at the scene. I am to advise law enforcement on legal issues, to make recommendations to bring in forensics experts, to direct that certain pieces of physical evidence be seized. I might advise the police to seize a door that has a bloody print on it or a piece of flooring spattered with blood. So the way I have depicted Kathryn Mackay is very, very close to the way DAs who are assigned to murder cases work.

MURPHY: *There are a few subplots in the book—trials that are ongoing. One of them involves a man who killed his girlfriend with a tire iron. Were you using this crime as any kind of a comparison with the serial killer?*

McGUIRE: No. The purpose of the subplot was to show the reader that prosecutors and Kathryn deal with more than one case at a time. Prosecutors never have the luxury of being in trial to the exclusion of everything else. Typically, you're in trial prosecuting a murder and you're briefing motions for the murder case that is trailing and the one you are trying. For a number of years I tried murder cases back to back. Those years I recollect only by the murders I tried. You never have the luxury of dealing with one case at a time—everything becomes a juggle.

MURPHY: *There's a great scene in that trial where, in closing argument, Kathryn beats a deflated soccer ball with a tire iron. Do you think a judge would ever let a lawyer get away with that?*
McGUIRE: I know a judge would.

MURPHY: *Have you tried that?*
McGUIRE: Not that scene in particular, but similar. In my final argument, I move away from the podium and do something physical to drive home the act of murder to the jury. I've never had a judge complain. However, I may have had a defense attorney object.

MURPHY: *What kinds of things have you done?*
McGUIRE: In a recent trial, I got down on the floor and took on the part of one of the victims who had been beaten and stabbed by a butcher knife in order to drive home to the jury how the crime was committed. I have used a bat to show how it was used to kill the victim. I have used rifles, knives. I use the actual murder weapon, if possible, to demonstrate how the murder occurred. And I save the demonstration for my final argument.

MURPHY: *Have you had any jurors complain about that after the trial?*
McGUIRE: Never.

MURPHY: *A lot of the book involves Richard Sanchez, the TV newsman, and how he gets inside information and then broadcasts and in a way undermines the investigation. Does the news media play, in reality, that big a role in high-profile crimes?*

McGUIRE: In high-profile cases, the media is there for most of the court proceedings and throughout the trial. However, the reporters in Santa Cruz County are unlike Richard Sanchez. They are low-key and to some extent that's because Santa Cruz is a small county. Reporters know they will most likely see the same prosecutor again and vice versa, so there develops a sense of trust that cuts both ways. For instance, when you agree to go "off the record" a piece of information remains "off the record." However, *Until Proven Guilty* needed a bad guy so along came Richard Sanchez.

MURPHY: *He certainly does come across as even worse than Geraldo.*
McGUIRE: Some of the reviews compared Sanchez to Geraldo; however, I did not have Geraldo, or anyone for that matter, in mind when I created Sanchez.

MURPHY: *Have you found that you have to learn to deal with the media as a prosecutor?*
McGUIRE: Yes. It is a very important function of the prosecutor's job because of the public's right to know.

MURPHY: *I have a plot question to ask you. The first two murders, the body is left in a public place and then the third murder, the body is left in a high school . . .*
McGUIRE: Right.

MURPHY: *. . . and one thing that struck me was that nobody bothered to find out why the body happened to be left in that particular high school. And it just seemed that the logical thing to do would be to question employees of the high school, where of course the murderer was working. Did you ever consider that as a loose end in the plot?*
McGUIRE: Only a lawyer would ask that question.

MURPHY: *Sorry.*
McGUIRE: Sure. That was considered. However, it was too soon to

reveal the killer to law enforcement. I took some literary license and did not have Granz question the employees of the high school.

MURPHY: *You had to change style, I would guess, in going from true crime to fiction. What particular problems did you encounter in doing that?*
McGUIRE: First, there were tons of them.

MURPHY: *Was this your first fictional effort?*
McGUIRE: Yes. It's not like true crime. And it's not like anything we do as lawyers except for trial work. I have found, however, that there is a natural progression from trial work to writing a novel. As a trial lawyer, you take hundreds of pages of police reports and give them shape and meaning. Then you put on a kind of production for the jury. That's what you do with a novel. I like to think I am writing for a jury—and in many instances my jury panel is as diverse as I hope my reading audience is. I write like I talk to jurors—straightforward, no fancy words.

MURPHY: *A lot of writers say that one of the biggest problems they first encounter when writing fiction is dialogue.*
McGUIRE: Dialogue is difficult. Male dialogue, or cop dialogue, is very difficult because I am neither. Fortunately, my husband is an ex-cop. He hasn't forgotten how they speak or think. He is able to help me write dialogue for many of the male law enforcement characters.

MURPHY: *How are sales of* Until Proven Guilty?
McGUIRE: Terrific, but it's too soon for actual numbers. I hear in California it's selling incredibly well. As for the rest of the nation, it's too soon to know.

MURPHY: *How did you get involved in writing in the first place? Was it just circumstance that you were prosecuting the* Hooker *case?*
McGUIRE: I fell into it. And because *Perfect Victim* was a bestseller, it enabled my agent to obtain a two-book contract to write fiction.

And I don't kid myself that it's because I'm an outstanding writer—there are writers out there who are outstanding but will never be published. That's a sad fact. I've been lucky—real fortunate.

MURPHY: *You talked about the fact that* Until Proven Guilty *tells the story from a woman's perspective and also a prosecutor's perspective.*

McGUIRE: Yet it's not a "woman's novel." There is a hint of feminism in Kate and some of the issues she faces because she is a female prosecutor in a traditionally male environment, but no reader of *Until Proven Guilty* will come away from having read it thinking it is a woman's book—it is written to appeal to women and men alike.

MURPHY: *If you had to pick out one theme of the book that you believe is its dominant theme, or the main reason you wanted to write the book, what would that be?*

McGUIRE: Let me start with the dedication. *Until Proven Guilty* is dedicated to prosecutors everywhere, the true public defenders. My thirteen years as a prosecutor has convinced me that prosecutors are overworked and underpaid and the public knows little about what prosecutors do. I just recently completed a national tour to promote *Until Proven Guilty,* and that experience confirmed my feelings. *Until Proven Guilty* for me is a way to educate the reading public about the world of prosecutors and do it in a very entertaining way.

MURPHY: *Do you have a second novel in the works?*

McGUIRE: I do. The sequel to *Until Proven Guilty.*

MURPHY: *How far along are you?*

McGUIRE: I have submitted an outline to my editor at Simon and Schuster. It is different from *Until Proven Guilty.* You will, however, see Kathryn Mackay, Dave Granz, Dr. Nelson, and Emma again.

MURPHY: *I would suspect there would be more of a love affair between Kathryn and Dave Granz?*

McGUIRE: I can't give anything away; however, they will certainly have their ups and downs.

MURPHY: *Do you have a title for the new book?*

McGUIRE: I have a couple of working titles. The one I like best is *Fatal Justice.* Ultimately, it's the publisher that names the novel.

JOHN MORTIMER

Former English barrister John Mortimer is best known in America for his Rumpole stories. A public television hit for decades, the Rumpole stories combine wit, suspense, and astute lawyering. When not defending murderers and other criminals at the Old Bailey, Rumpole enjoys sipping a glass of claret at Pommeroy's Wine Bar. He skewers his colleagues at the Inn and suffers barbs from his wife, Hilda, whom he calls "She Who Must Be Obeyed."

A graduate of Oxford University, Mortimer received an honorary doctorate in law from Exeter University. He became a barrister in 1948 and in 1966 was named to the Queen's Counsel. He has won numerous literary awards: the Italia Prize in 1957 for his play *The Dock Brief*; the Writers Guild of Great Britain's award for Best Original Teleplay in 1969 for *A Voyage Round My Father*; a Golden Globe award nomination in 1970 for his screenplay *John and Mary*; and the British Film and Television Academy's award for Writer of the Year in 1980.

A prolific and versatile writer, Mortimer has tried nearly every literary type, including novels, short stories, plays, biographies, autobiographies, interviews, translations, adaptations, and screenplays. A sampling of his life's work appears below.

This interview took place in 1988.

FICTION: *Charade* (1948) ▪ *Rumming Park* (1949) ▪ *Answers Yes or No* (1950) ▪ *Like Men Betrayed* (1953) ▪ *Three Winters* (1956) ▪ *Narrowing Stream* (1956) ▪ *Will Shakespeare* (1977) ▪ *Paradise Postponed* (1985) ▪ *Summer's Lease* (1988) ▪ *Titmuss Regained* (1990) ▪ *Dunster* (1992) ▪ *Great Law and Order Stories* (ed., 1992) ▪ *Murder Under the Mistletoe and Other Stories* (1992) ▪

Under the Hammer (1995) ▪ *Felix in the Underworld* (1997) ▪ *The Sound of Trumpets* (1999)

Rumpole story collections: *Rumpole of the Bailey* (1978) ▪ *Trials of Rumpole* (1979) ▪ *Rumpole's Return* (1980) ▪ *Regina v. Rumpole* [later published as *Rumpole for the Defence*] (1984) ▪ *Rumpole and the Golden Thread* (1983) ▪ *Rumpole's Last Case* (1987) ▪ *Rumpole at the Bar* (1988) ▪ *Rumpole and the Age of Miracles* (1988) ▪ *Rumpole a la Carte* (1990) ▪ *Rumpole on Trial* (1992) ▪ *Rumpole and the Angel of Death* (1995)

Plays: *The Dock Brief* (1957) ▪ *What Shall We Tell Caroline?* (1960) ▪ *The Wrong Side of the Park* (1960) ▪ *I Spy* (1960) ▪ *The Wrong Side of the Park* (three acts) (1960) ▪ *Lunch Hour, and Other Plays* (contains *Collect Your Hand Baggage, David and Broccoli*, and *Call Me a Liar*) (1960) ▪ *What Shall We Tell Caroline?* (three acts) (1960) ▪ *Collect Your Hand Baggage* (one act) (1960) ▪ *Two Stars for Comfort* (1962) ▪ *The Judge* (1967) ▪ *A Voyage Round My Father* (1969) ▪ *Come As You Are!* (contains four one-act comedies, *Mill Hill, Bermondsey, Gloucester Road*, and *Marble Arch*) (1970) ▪ *I, Claudius* (two acts; adapted from Robert Graves's novels *I, Claudius* and *Claudius the God*) (1972) ▪ *Knightsbridge* (1973) ▪ *Collaborators* (1973) ▪ *Heaven and Hell* (includes one-act plays *The Fear of Heaven* and *The Prince of Darkness*) (1976) ▪ *The Fear of Heaven* (1978) ▪ *When That I Was* (1982)

NONFICTION: *With Love and Lizards* (with Penelope Mortimer) (1957) ▪ *Clinging to the Wreckage: A Part of Life* (autobiography, 1982) ▪ *In Character* (1983) ▪ *Famous Trials* (1986) ▪ *Character Parts* (1988) ▪ *The Oxford Book of Villains* (1992) ▪ *Murderers and Other Friends: Another Part of Life* (1995) ▪ *The Summer of a Dormouse: Another Part of Life* (2001)

MURPHY: *A lot of American lawyers know very little about you except that you're a barrister and you've written the Rumpole series. I was curious as to what your practice was as a barrister.*

Mortimer: I'm not a barrister anymore. I don't practice as a barrister anymore. I haven't practiced as a barrister for about four or five years. My father was a divorce barrister. There's a thing called a probate, divorce, and admiralty division, and he did probate and divorce. So that's what I did. I did probate and divorce for a long time . . . divorced a lot of people. Practically everyone I knew was someone I'd divorced. Then I became a Q.C. And so I became a sort of more important type of barrister, which is one who does rather large trials. That's divorce cases on the whole that require that sort of advocacy. I did crime and I did a lot of cases about free speech, books, and sort of what you might call civil rights issues, I suppose, and crime and defamation. A sort of mixed practice, like that. And then I stopped about five years ago.

MURPHY: *Are you retired now?*
MORTIMER: Yeah. I mean I stopped practicing and I just write.

MURPHY: *Were you practicing out of an Inn of Court?*
MORTIMER: Yes. You know that we don't have anything like your firm or partnerships. We're not allowed to form alliances [laughing] with other barristers. So we're like freelance actors, really. But I still have my chambers. I mean I could go and do a case tomorrow. You can't stop being a barrister in that sense. But I won't.

MURPHY: *Did you practice out of London?*
MORTIMER: Yes, I practiced in London, mainly. You know, I'd go anywhere. I'd do cases in Singapore, in the Far East, all over the place.

MURPHY: *You mentioned you did a little bit of criminal practice.*
MORTIMER: I did quite a lot of criminal. Yes, I did. But I was always a writer. I'd written my first novel before I became a barrister. And so I was always writing. I wrote novels, plays, poems, everything, throughout my life as a barrister. Which was much easier to do in England because, I mean, it would have been impossible for me if I'd had to go to a law office or have partners who would ask me what I was doing. If I wanted to go to court, I went to court. If I wanted to write, I stayed at home. So, in a sense I think that it would be much more difficult to be a writer and be an American. Because they'd

expect you to turn up every day. [Laughter] I never really went to my chambers. I was either in court or I was at home.

MURPHY: *Now Rumpole is, of course, a defense lawyer. Were you a defense lawyer?*

We really don't have such a thing. English criminal barristers can be prosecuting one day and defending the next, which on the whole I think is quite a good idea. But Rumpole has a sort of a conscientious objection to prosecuting. I did, too, so I didn't prosecute. I only prosecuted one case, which I prosecuted the police. [Laughter] They all got off. My talents weren't for prosecuting. So that's what I did.

MURPHY: *There's a line in the* **Rumpole for the Defence** *book I thought was very interesting, and I want to read it to you: "It is not, happily, very often that you get a client cursed with the possibility of innocence."*
MORTIMER: Yes! [Laughter]

MURPHY: *I wondered if that was your experience, too?*
MORTIMER: I don't think you make up your mind totally about whether your client's guilty or innocent because you feel that's not your business. But I think the most difficult person to defend is someone who you're absolutely convinced that they were innocent because you lose your critical faculties. I mean the great thing about certain people is to be able to see every point against them very clearly. And if you have a passionate belief in them, I think you might not do that. I mean the worst people to defend are friends, and [laughter] then the really worst people to defend are innocent friends. But if you think, "Oh, he's probably guilty," at least you see all the points against you, you're dispassionate, and you'll probably get him off. I know some lawyers who don't practice criminal defense and find it difficult to understand how lawyers can defend somebody who's guilty.

We never get to that position, do we. A criminal trial in our system isn't an investigation to discover the truth. It's an exercise to see whether the prosecution can prove guilt beyond reasonable doubt. So the fact that they fail to prove guilt beyond reasonable doubt doesn't mean that your client is innocent. It just means he hasn't been proved to be guilty. So you're never trying to establish innocence. And, on the whole, I think that that's why the things I didn't like to do are sort of professional crime. You know, big bank robbers and drug traders and things. But an ordinary citizen who may stumble into murdering his wife [laughter] in a fit of passion or something, I think it's quite, quite different.

MURPHY: *Have you ever had any second thoughts about representing somebody you knew was guilty and getting them off?*
MORTIMER: You never know that they're guilty, and if they tell you they're guilty then you can't defend them. If they tell you any story which is consistent with their innocence, then you'll have to put that forward. But if they tell you they're guilty, you can't call them to tell a different story. You've got to say, "Plead guilty or else I leave the case." You can't defend someone who's told you they're guilty.

MURPHY: *Are you required in England to put your defendant on the stand?*
MORTIMER: No, no.

MURPHY: *Because even if he's guilty, you could avoid calling him?*
MORTIMER: That's right. You could cross-examine the prosecution witnesses. But you couldn't do anything else.

MURPHY: *But you've never yourself looked back and said, "I wish I hadn't done that"?*
MORTIMER: No. Because I think the prison system in England is so appalling that anybody who can get out of it . . . [laughter] it's worth saving someone.

MURPHY: *You mention one of the interesting things about the English system that's different from ours. And that is that you have private prosecutors as well as the private defense counsel, and the same barrister can be both positions.*

MORTIMER: Yeah. We don't have any official prosecutors except at the Old Bailey, where there's a very small collection of people who always prosecute, but they can defend also.

MURPHY: *I know when I first watched the Rumpole series it was sort of disconcerting from the American lawyer's point of view that you'd have the prosecutor and the defense lawyer from the same Inn.*
MORTIMER: See, we're collected in chambers, which is one building and we share a clerk and we share the telephone, we share the bills, but we don't share our earnings and we don't have any other connection with each other. But I think in a way that's a good thing because you don't become sort of a prosecution-minded person. You can see the defense side of things. You can see both sides. And you don't become a sort of lawyer who's always thought of as the defense lawyer and the judge says, "Oh, Christ, there's that old defense lawyer getting up again."

MURPHY: *You get more credibility with the judge?*
MORTIMER: Yeah.

MURPHY: *Do you think the lay public would see any potential conflict of interest having the prosecutor and the defense lawyer in the same chambers?*
MORTIMER: No, because they don't have any financial connection with each other. The public doesn't like barristers being so friendly with each other, do they. All that, you know, "How are you, old chap?" and you meet outside court and things like that. But that whole system is not particularly well understood in England apart from at the Inns. [Laughter] It may well change. There's a lot of discussion about changing things.

MURPHY: *You've probably been asked this question a million times, but I have to ask you myself. Who or what was the inspiration for Rumpole?*
MORTIMER: It's partly my father. . . . I wrote a play about my father called *A Voyage Round My Father.* My father was a barrister who

quoted poetry all the time, like Rumpole. There's a quite a lot found in my father, quite a lot of various barristers around the Old Bailey who always called the judge "Old Dear." And really partly because I wanted a character to keep me alive in my old age, you know. Everybody hates lawyers so much; they think they're the absolute scum of the earth. And I just wanted to have a fairly good lawyer who doesn't make a lot of money out of it and stands for principles of liberty and justice, freedom, suchlike old-fashioned ideas!

MURPHY: *Rumpole has some other idiosyncracies that I suppose are peculiar to trial lawyers. He, of course, loves his Pommeroy's Claret.*
MORTIMER: Yes. [Laughter] That's right.

MURPHY: *Is there any significance in the "rum" in the Rumpole?*
MORTIMER: Well, not really. He had a different name when I first started out, then I found that somebody had that name and so I changed. I don't know, it's just a good sound.

MURPHY: *What name had you originally thought of?*
MORTIMER: Something slightly different, like Rumbler. Just a little bit different. Something like that, just a little tiny bit different, and I discovered there was one, so I changed it.

MURPHY: *I was curious as to whether you were using the Dickens technique of describing a character by his name.*
MORTIMER: I do that, yes, all the time.

MURPHY: *With Bullingham, Judge Bullingham, certainly.*
MORTIMER: Yes. Finding names of people is terribly important to me. I can't start writing about them until I know what their names are. And it takes a long, long time to think of names. And I think of a lot of peculiar names. But you have to find a name which is the character.

MURPHY: *Another part of the British system that I think American lawyers find interesting is the way the judge takes such an active role in the trial, questioning the witnesses, commenting on the evidence.*

MORTIMER: Yes, and of course the judge sums up the facts in a criminal trial, which he doesn't do in America. I mean, that's not altogether a very healthy thing, I think. The trouble is, the judges have spent their lives being advocates until they get made judges, which they do around their forties to fifties. So they find that habit is hard to drop. They find it very hard to sit quietly and not interrupt. And they find it hard not to take sides, because they are so used to that adversarial system. So the good advocates who are successful often don't make successful judges. The thing about judges taking sides is that if you can get them really to take sides against you, you'd probably win because the jurors don't like that. The most deadly judge is one who's absolutely fair. Sums up terribly fairly. See, often if you get the feeling the judge is going to take sides, it's quite a good thing to make him be more prejudiced against you to lure him into saying something actually stupid against you [laughter] and then the jury can react against him.

MURPHY: *Judge Bullingham seems to do that quite a bit.*

MORTIMER: He does that all the time, yes. The actor who played Judge Bullingham is dead, so we've lost Judge Bullingham now. We'll have to find substitute horrible judges. [Laughter]

MURPHY: *Would you say that the way Judge Bullingham acts in the courtroom is typical?*

MORTIMER: Well, it's typical of a certain sort of judge, particularly at the Old Bailey. The Old Bailey judges aren't the top layer of judges. The top layer of judges in England are Queen's Bench judges, who don't do crime all the time. And they're superior sort of judges. They're more elegant and polite and generally civilized, not the sort of decided backward judges at the Old Bailey. But I always get this thing from judges and they say why is it that all the judges in Rumpole are rather twits or malignant or malignant twits? And I say that's the dramatic necessity, because you can't have Rumpole getting up in court and the judge says, "Pardon me, Mr. Rumpole, your client can go now. Have a pound from the poor box." So you've got to have a conflict, so that's what makes all these judges so stupid. That's what I tell judges.

MURPHY: *Are you involved in writing the television series?*
MORTIMER: Oh, yes! I write it, organize it, boss it around, cast it, quite a lot.

MURPHY: *I understand there's going to be new programs coming out this year.*
MORTIMER: Yes, well, it's just started in England, and there's a new book, a new Rumpole book, a new Rumpole program.

MURPHY: *Are you still writing the Rumpole stories?*
MORTIMER: Well, I shall do it again, probably in about a year's time.

MURPHY: *I know you wrote about Rumpole's last case.*
MORTIMER: Yes! It isn't Rumpole's last case at all. I think Sherlock Holmes's last case comes right in the middle of his career. But I think it's best to leave about two years between them.

MURPHY: *One of the interesting issues raised by the Rumpole books is the way female barristers are accepted in the chambers.*
MORTIMER: It's a bit better now, but there's a terrific amount of prejudice against them. They weren't allowed the key to the lavatory and all sorts of things. And still there's about, I don't know, I think there are about twenty-two barristers in our chambers and there are about four women, but it's becoming much better. And they also are sort of segregated. I mean they tend to do certain types of work—they do family law, crime mostly. So to find a good woman in commercial chambers or libel chambers is rare. Very chauvinistic.

MURPHY: *Is the same true for the female solicitors?*
MORTIMER: I think it's less true, although they perhaps do that sort of work. Women doctors have difficulty in England. Certain jobs . . .

even in films, even in American films. There are a number of women cameramen; they can be producers; there are very few women directors.

MURPHY: *The major woman, of course, in Rumpole is . . .*
MORTIMER: She Who Must Be Obeyed. [Laughter]

MURPHY: *Right. And one thing I've been asking a lot of the other lawyer-authors is their treatment of the trial lawyer's wife, who often is not portrayed very favorably. Do you find that that is in fact the trend among trial lawyers in England—that their wives are not looked upon very favorably?*
MORTIMER: [Laughter] I don't think so. The reason why She's so awful is I need to make life hard for Rumpole. You know, like Philip Marlowe, he has to have a bad time, so you have to have nasty judges and a terrifying wife. His colleagues are all against him, so he has to sort of have pressure put on him. I think it's quite difficult to be a barrister's wife and particularly in England if you're a busy barrister you're just working all the time. And it's quite difficult for barristers' marriages. In fact, like anybody who works a lot, and they work in the evenings—it's sort of an occupational hazard of being a barrister. You get very boring and you talk about your cases all the time. [Laughter] You become boring and pompous until you get boring and pompous enough to be a judge. [Laughter] It's difficult to be married to one, I would think.

MURPHY: *What would you describe as the major theme, if there is one, of the Rumpole series?*
MORTIMER: Of the whole thing, I suppose the major theme is that all our liberties which we have fought for, bled for, down the centuries, in both of our countries, are under attack by politicians who don't want the fair trial particularly, and also the public are pretty inert about it and don't care very much. They think anybody who's arrested is probably guilty. And so the people who have to keep these lamps of freedom glowing are the poor old criminal barristers who have to get out and chat about it and fuss about it and are disrespected

for doing it. In a way, that's the sort of basic theme. And in every Rumpole story I try and give it a theme, you know, that it's about something, some contemporary problem or whatever. So even though it's a comedy, certainly, it's a comedy about something that's important and necessary.

MURPHY: *Have you been influenced by any particular authors in your writing style?*
MORTIMER: Oh, well, yes, Dickens no doubt, P. G. Wodehouse and Sherlock Holmes. The sort of shape of Rumpole stories is very much like Sherlock Holmes, you know. Evelyn Waugh's dialogue . . . Graham Greene.

MURPHY: *So it's an eclectic group?*
MORTIMER: Yeah. [Laughter]

MURPHY: *I understand in England there's no such thing as the lawyer's contingent fee, which we have here in America. What are your views on the contingent fee?*
MORTIMER: I think it's a terrible institution because, you know, it creates litigation when it's not necessary. And it also could, I think, be a temptation for dishonesty in various ways. So I would be all against that. And I suppose it's been responsible for all these cases against doctors getting more and more proliferating. I mean, well, I'm against it. [Laughter]

MURPHY: *Do you think it is at all useful in allowing poor people access to the courts?*
MORTIMER: The poor people should have access to the courts from legal aid, which they do in England. I mean, you get legal aid and you can do anything. If anything, the limits of legal aid are a bit too low. But practically every criminal trial in England is defended on legal aid. And you get the best barristers, the top barristers that there are, for nothing.

MURPHY: *And legal aid would cover civil cases as well?*

MORTIMER: It does, yes. Except for libel; it's funny, they haven't introduced it for libel, which is wrong. But it does cover civil cases. The only problem with legal aid is that if you're a person who has just too much money not to get it, your opponent who's got it could go on to the House of Lords, you know, and go forever, and you could bankrupt. So I think it needs to be a higher level. And the law is much too expensive, and I don't know why that is. I don't understand why it's so expensive. Nobody seems to be getting terribly richer.

MURPHY: *The English have the barrister/solicitor division of lawyers. The Americans don't have that. Do you think it's good to have that separation?*

MORTIMER: I do, but I think it'll go. I don't think it's going to survive. To me, it's good for really two reasons. One is that if you did a murder anywhere in England, you know, at the end of Cornwall, you would get the best barrister, the top barrister to defend you. Whereas if you didn't have that divided bar, you might be stuck with the person in the firm that you happen to go to who would think that they'd like to do your murder for you. And the other thing is that when you have that division, the solicitors prepare the cases and see the witnesses and get the witnesses' statements and prepare all the evidence. The barrister has nothing whatever to do with that. And you're not even allowed to talk to witnesses if you're a barrister except when they're in the witness box. So that you're very aloof.

I mean it would be impossible to be a corrupt barrister. Maybe you could be a corrupt solicitor, but you wouldn't know what was going on if you were a barrister. [Laughter] But if you thought that your solicitor was behaving dishonestly, you could tell him to go and get lost or that he mustn't do it, and there are plenty of other solicitors who'd bring you work. Whereas, if you were a member of a firm which was behaving dishonestly, it might be much more difficult for you to tell them, you know, how to behave properly. And so I think it makes it some safeguard against dishonesty. It also means that the judges have an enormous confidence in barristers. If you tell a judge something if you're a barrister, the judge accepts it without any hesitation. And there's a terrific trust between them, judges and barristers, all of which might go if they were part of a firm that got the cases. Also, my life would have been impossible if I'd been a member of a law firm. I just couldn't have lived as I lived. But I don't think it'll last. I think it's one of those good things that will end.

MURPHY: *To wrap up, I see you've got your book* Paradise Postponed.
MORTIMER: Yes, yes.

MURPHY: *Is that your latest?*
MORTIMER: Well, no. It isn't. No. My latest book's called *Summer's Lease.* But I'm doing a sort of sequel to it.

MURPHY: *To* Paradise Postponed?
MORTIMER: Yeah.

MURPHY: *Do you have any other present plans as far as your writing goes?*
MORTIMER: Well, this book, *Summer's Lease,* which is my latest novel, which goes on in Italy. It's being filmed in England, so I've done the script for that. But I have to write this novel. Then I have to write another Rumpole series. Then it'll be two years' time. [Laughter] And I'll come back to San Francisco.

MICHAEL NAVA

San Francisco criminal defense attorney Michael Nava has carved out a unique niche in the ever-expanding legion of lawyer-authors. Nava has written several mysteries featuring Los Angeles attorney Henry Rios, who happens to be gay. In a refined and introspective style, these first-person narratives explore the vagaries of gay life.

In *The Burning Plain,* Rios becomes embroiled in a case involving a gay serial killer who has murdered three gay men, leaving graphic antigay messages at each crime scene. Rios passes through the criminal justice system in several roles, first as acquaintance of a victim, then as suspect, and finally as attorney for the accused. With each new role for Rios, Nava manages to create renewed reader empathy for his protagonist while fashioning a solid and satisfying mystery.

In addition to Rios, Nava introduces some intriguing minor characters, including Rios's friend Richie Florentino: "Tall and thin, his long face was framed by a luxuriance of thick, wavy dark hair and he had the square-jawed glamour of a forties movie star, a look he carefully cultivated." Florentino introduces Rios to Alex Amerian: "His skin was olive-colored, his hair was a toss of damp, black curls and his face had a delicate, Mediterranean masculinity, like the face of an archaic Apollo."

A native of the Sacramento barrio of Gardenland, Nava received his bachelor's degree from Colorado College and his law degree from Stanford University. He has practiced in Los Angeles as a deputy city attorney, research attorney for the California Court of Appeals, and appellate attorney. He works as a staff attorney for the California Supreme Court in San Francisco.

This interview took place in 1998.

FICTION: *The Little Death* (1986) ▪ *Goldenboy* (1988) ▪ *How Town* (1990) ▪ *The Hidden Law* (1992) ▪ *The Death of Friends* (1996) ▪ *The Burning Plain* (1997) ▪ *Rag and Bone* (2001)

NONFICTION: *Created Equal: Why Gay Rights Matter in America* (coauthor, 1994)

MURPHY: *You have written a number of mysteries that put a human face on the gay experience. Why did you choose the mystery genre to do this?*
NAVA: I didn't intend to become a mystery writer, actually. I tried to be a poet until I was in my midtwenties in law school. Something about going to law school dried up my interest in poetry. So I decided to start writing fiction, but I didn't want to write that sort of turgid autobiographical first novel that every young novelist writes. The one that ends up in your drawer. I was looking for something that would force me to create a plot and develop characters and not just write narcissistically about a thinly veiled me. I like mysteries, and so I thought I would write my first book as a mystery. Publishers kept asking for more. So that is how I became a mystery writer.

MURPHY: *Were you an avid mystery reader before you started writing mysteries?*
NAVA: Not really, and I got a wrong impression of mysteries because I only read the best writers. I read Ross MacDonald and Raymond Chandler and some of the English writers—Josephine Tey and Ruth Rendell. So I didn't know that mysteries were trash. I thought that they were just good novels. It was only later that I found out that they were considered pulp.

MURPHY: *I think you're right. Not all mysteries are trash, but that is kind of the public perception. Your background in poetry does come through in your writing, in that you take great care in your language, your use of words and description. Do you find sometimes you get a little too poetic when you're writing mysteries?*
NAVA: Yeah. Some writer once said, "When I come across a passage that I think is particularly fine, I strike it out." I try to do that, too.

When I go back and revise and I come across something I think is really beautiful, I know that's generally a sign that it should go. I try not to write prose that calls attention to itself.

MURPHY: *Your books focus on what really are universal gay themes: AIDS, gay bashing, tension between a gay man and his lover's parents. Certainly* **The Burning Plain** *focuses on all those things. Have you been concerned in writing with these kind of themes that you might be writing the same story over and over?*

NAVA: No. It's true that Rios is a gay man but he actually lives on the peripheries of the gay world. But the deep underlying theme I'm writing about is being different. Standing outside of society and what that looks like to an outsider, how he experiences his life on the outside. Rios embodies all those virtues that society purports to admire, like perseverance and loyalty and compassion, but seldom demonstrates. To me that paradox is a very rich field for writing, as are the specifics of his experience as a gay man. It's very compelling, but the larger theme is about being on the outside of things. There's a lot to say about that.

MURPHY: *As a Hispanic man, Rios is caught in the tension of his culture and his sexuality. In* **The Burning Plain,** *of course, the detective Gaitan seems to have extra hatred for him because he's not only gay but Hispanic gay. Is that a tension that you've encountered in your own life?*

NAVA: Yes, when I was a kid. I don't actually know how different things are now. I suspect they're a little different. I lived in a very poor Mexican neighborhood, and family was really the focal point. It was a very traditional sense of family: mother, father, children. That's what we were all expected to do—get married and have kids. And it was also Catholic. And there was very little room to be "different." I mean, one couldn't even be heterosexual and unmarried in that culture, much less homosexual. And there's a great deal of hostility toward homosexuality and a great deal of ignorance about it in Latino culture. I had to leave home in order to be who I knew I was when I was twelve years old. I think that's probably still more the case than not among working-class Latinos. Maybe those attitudes are different among middle-class Latinos. I don't really know, I don't have much connection to my ethnicity at this point.

MURPHY: The Burning Plain *features a serial killer who is focusing on gay men. I don't think it's giving away the plot to say the killer is also gay, since all the suspects are gay and there are antigay carvings on the victims' chests. Why did you decide to focus in this book on how badly gays treat other gays?*

NAVA: Because it's true and because it illustrates a larger point, which has to do not just with gay people but with minority people generally, which is that the exposure to hatred turns you into someone who hates. The poet Auden has this great line in one of his poems: "Those to whom evil are done do evil in return." That's really the theme of the book and that's why I chose to make the murderer a very conflicted gay man, someone who responds to the hatred of gay people by internalizing it and acting it out on other gay people.

MURPHY: *You chose as the title a reference to Dante's* Inferno—*The burning plain. Maybe you could explain for those who haven't read the book what the reference means.*

NAVA: In Dante's *Inferno,* which is a wonderful book, there are different levels or circles where he places sinners. The deeper you go, the more serious the sin. There are nine levels, I think, and homosexuals are pretty much down there. I think in the seventh circle. The seventh circle is where he puts the violent, and homosexuals are the violent against nature, because in Dante's medieval view homosexuality was a sin against nature. They occupy this plain of burning sand where they run around the perimeter for eternity while fire constantly rains down on them. That's their punishment. When I wrote the book, I thought, This sounds like Los Angeles to me.

MURPHY: *You have a number of different archetype gay characters: Richie Florentino is kind of the sarcastic queen with the biting wit, and can't be trusted;*

Duke Asuras is a manipulator, the amoral producer for Parnassus Studios; and then you've got the victim, at least the first victim, Alex Amerian, who's a gay hustler. I don't mean to say these are stereotypes, but they do seem to be archetypes. Were you consciously trying to convey different aspects of gay life with these characters?

NAVA: Yes. Each of them is actually rooted in a real person. The thing about stereotypes is of course they reflect a reality and the world is filled with stereotypical people. It's actually hard to find that kernel of individuality and be yourself. It's much easier to be a stereotype. But the book is an allegory of sorts. To carry it off I needed these kinds of archetypical characters.

MURPHY: *One thing I noticed with all these gay characters—including Henry Rios, who is a recovered alcoholic; the victim Alex Amerian; the movie producer Duke Asuras; the other lawyer in the book, Nick Donati—have this intense sense of self-loathing. Is that something that all your gay characters have?*

NAVA: No. I wouldn't say that Rios, actually, has an intense sense of self-loathing. What he has is a critical sense of what the gay subculture has become. I would agree with your assessment about the other three. I would also point out that there are a couple of other gay characters. There's a lesbian DA who is happily married to her lover and they're raising a child. This work particularly is about the destructive effects of being hated. One of my other books deals with child sexual abuse; another one deals with dangers of being in the closet, involving a married judge who is gay and conceals it from his wife, and so forth. But that whole theme of self-loathing in these characters is not really representative of characters in my other books.

MURPHY: *Your characters all have very descriptive names, like Rios, Florentino, Gaitan, whose first name is Montezuma. Were you consciously using a Dickensian device in naming your characters?*

NAVA: No, those are all actual names, including Montezuma Gaitan.

MURPHY: *Are you concerned about lawsuits, especially from Gaitan?*

NAVA: We'll take them as they come. Actually, in my last book there's a character of a judge, a closeted married judge, whose name is Christopher Chandler, which I thought was a pretty safe name. In fact there's a Superior Court judge somewhere in northern California named Chris Chandler, which I found out about when they did a front-page profile of him in the *Daily Journal*. Obviously, the character in my book is entirely fictional.

MURPHY: *I want to ask you about this homicide detective, Montezuma Gaitan. He really epitomizes a lot of people's view of L.A. police, especially after Mark Furman in the Simpson trial. But he's even worse. He plants evidence, he commits other crimes, and he has intense hatred for Henry Rios and other gay people. Why did you portray him in such a one-sided way, as such a hateful character?*

NAVA: I needed a heavy and he fit the bill. I was a prosecutor in L.A., that's how I began my legal career, and I met a lot of cops. He is not unrepresentative of many of the cops that I met. To balance him out, I created another cop in the book, Odell, to illustrate that not all police officers are so corrupt and hateful. Gaitan is a bit overdrawn but not that overdrawn. Lots of L.A.P.D. officers are very scary people.

MURPHY: *Did you find that you had any difficulty in obtaining the police officers' cooperation while you were prosecuting?*

NAVA: Only the same trouble that all prosecutors have. They're sort of lazy and many of them have contempt for lawyers of all stripes. Sometimes you can't predict what they're going to remember when they get on the stand. It's a little embarrassing when they suddenly start remembering details that they didn't tell you about in the interview. But no, I didn't have any special problems. Of course, I never came out to any of them. That would have made it very difficult for me.

MURPHY: *Sergeant Odell is actually a very unusual character in the sense that he appears to be a typical cop, just his physical features, until you get to know* *him. His daughter is a lesbian so he has a particular sensitivity to the gay lifestyle. That kind of blends in with the theme, at the beginning of the book, of Rios's lover's parents still not accepting the fact that his lover, Josh, was gay. Is the acceptance by parents of a gay lifestyle a theme that you've explored in other books?*

NAVA: Not really. I've dealt with Josh's parents before in a couple of other books because he's close to them, but I haven't actually dealt very much with that issue. There's a third character in the book whose parents have trouble with his homosexuality; in fact, they institutionalize him.

MURPHY: *Rod Morse. You introduce him pretty much in the middle of the book. Was that an afterthought to get the plot going in a different direction or was that something you planned from the very beginning?*

NAVA: I planned the character from the very beginning but that sub-plot just sort of evolved as I was writing the book.

MURPHY: *It's a rather horrific story. His parents want to send him to Utah to a psychiatric hospital to treat him for gender identification disorder, for which of course he doesn't fit the technical diagnosis. What was it about this charac-ter that made you want to introduce him into the plot of the book?*

NAVA: As I've said, the book is about the destructive effects of hate. In the end, Rod rejects his own homosexuality because his experience of the gay subculture is more frightening to him than the thought of being institutionalized. That's kind of an over-the-top statement I wanted to make, so I brought him into the book. I got some nasty letters from gay readers about this book who thought that I was pan-dering to the worst heterosexual stereotypes about gays and about self-loathing and the dysfunction of the gay subculture. You can cer-tainly read the book on that level if you want to. But again, what I'm trying to write about is how people who are hated internalize hatred and how they act it out on each other.

MURPHY: *I had a sense of disappointment at the end of the book, when Rod decided he wasn't going to be gay, that he wasn't being true to himself.*

NAVA: No, he's not being true to himself. It's not something you can just put aside.

MURPHY: *I found that more tragic than anything. I don't know if other readers had the same reaction. Do you find that you have a lot of heterosexual readers?*

NAVA: No. And those I have tend to be women. In fact, some of my most avid readers are women who own mystery bookstores and who push my books. I think they're too scary for most straight men.

MURPHY: *In* The Burning Plain *you do have a number of sex scenes, but I found that you describe them with some restraint. Was that purposeful to make sure you didn't turn off straight readers?*

NAVA: I'm not interested in writing about sex for its own sake and it bores me when I read sex scenes, whether they're straight or gay. Sex is the easiest thing in the world to throw into your novel when things get slow, so I only use them to show something about a character or develop a plot point. When I use them, it's not necessary to be that graphic. The object is not to describe a sexual encounter, it's to describe a kind of intimacy or something about a character or to move the plot along. To do that, I don't have to give a blow-by-blow, no pun intended.

MURPHY: *I don't think straight people would be turned off by your descriptions of sex scenes in this book.*

NAVA: You'd be amazed. This book has more sex than any of my other books, but I got a review in the *L.A. Times* of one of my earlier books, in which I have one sexual encounter between Rios and Josh to illustrate the tenderness between them. In his review, the reviewer singled this out to warn straight readers that there was trouble ahead. It was a favorable review but he felt compelled to issue this advisory—sort of odd.

MURPHY: *As you mentioned,* The Burning Plain *does contain a number of characters who are lawyers, both gay men and lesbians. Most are portrayed favorably; perhaps Nick Donati is the least favorably portrayed. Are you* *concerned at all in writing a book of this type as to the way you portray lawyers?*

NAVA: No, because I think I portray lawyers in this book and my other books generally realistically. I like most lawyers. In fact, I prefer the company of lawyers to writers, especially in criminal law. I find that most people on both sides are sort of idealistic and they're not in it for the money and I admire that.

MURPHY: *Have you found it more difficult succeeding as a writer of gay mysteries as opposed to being a lawyer who happened to be gay?*

NAVA: Sure, because professionally, my homosexuality doesn't really enter into it. We're just lawyers. I've been out wherever I worked just because it's easier that way. I don't have to hide my personal life when I'm talking with coworkers at the water cooler. Being a writer who writes about gay subjects cuts both ways. The *New York Times* reviewed this book and suggested I was one of the best mystery writers writing, and that's great. I still don't sell very many books and I think that's because I'm gay. So being gay gets me review attention but also limits my audience.

MURPHY: *You've gotten quite a few favorable reviews.*

NAVA: Yeah. I was *People*'s Book of the Week for my last two books actually. I get the kind of reviews that most writers kill for.

MURPHY: *You've won several awards, but they're all Lambda Awards for gay literature. Any nominations for mainstream mystery awards?*

NAVA: No. Organizations that give away those awards tend to be extremely conservative. Now, it's also true that I'm not involved in the mystery establishment. I don't go to conferences, I'm not a member of Mystery Writers of America. They reward their own. I think that's the bottom line.

MURPHY: The Burning Plain *has quite a number of scenes that poke fun at Hollywood and the movie industry. One in particular where Henry Rios runs into a director at a restaurant. He wants to make a movie of one of his cases* involving a gay man and change it into a heterosexual relationship. Did you have much exposure to Hollywood while you were working down in L.A.?

NAVA: I knew a couple of entertainment lawyers and, of course, inevitably there were all those actor-waiters one runs into when you're down there. It's a company town and the business is unavoidable. The *L.A. Times* is basically a shill for the movie industry. It has a very bad, corrupting influence on the cultural climate of the city. When I decided to write about Hollywood in this book, I did some research and I read a number of books by insiders about Hollywood. Most of what I say in the book about Hollywood I took from my research.

MURPHY: *You'll never eat lunch in this town again?*

NAVA: I read that one. And there's *The Devil's Candy,* which was about the making of *The Bonfire of the Vanities.* And there was a book about the making of *Heaven's Gate,* and there was a book called *Indecent Exposure* about David Begelman, the movie executive who forged his client's signature on checks, which is where I get that episode in the book. I discovered there is nothing you can say about Hollywood that is actually as bad as what really happens. There's no end to the greed; that's what runs Hollywood.

MURPHY: *Have you ever toyed with the idea of writing books with heterosexuals as main characters?*

NAVA: I would never set out to write a book with heterosexual main characters simply because I thought that that book would be more successful. But if I had in mind writing a book about a character and it was part of that character's identity that he or she was heterosexual, that's legitimate. Writing for the marketplace is suicide. Now, I will say that in six books in this series, and probably another one, I have pretty much exhausted my interest in writing about the experience of being gay. So I'm thinking about writing about the experience of being poor. I grew up in a poor family; no one writes about poor people. There are a lot of very good Latino writers, I've been reading them, and I'm getting interested in that. I'll always be writing about people who are on the margins, because that's really where the action is as far as I can see.

RICHARD NORTH PATTERSON

Since the release of *Degree of Guilt* in 1993, Richard North Patterson has had a steady stream of novels on local and national bestseller lists. Inspired by the William Kennedy Smith trial and the Clarence Thomas/Anita Hill controversy, the book is a courtroom thriller that evinces a rare sensitivity to women's issues.

When television broadcaster Mary Cirelli is charged with murdering Mark Ranson, a nationally known novelist obsessed with a glamorous—and long deceased—movie star, she claims he tried to rape her. She asks Christopher Paget, her former lover and father of her son, to defend her. Like many characters in this novel, Paget and Cirelli are celebrities, having reached national prominence fifteen years earlier when their testimony before a congressional committee brought down the president. As Paget prepares the defense, he learns that Cirelli has not been completely honest with him and risks exposing secrets from their past, secrets that he desperately wants to keep from their son.

Patterson, who studied creative writing with Jesse Hill Ford at the University of Alabama, won an Edgar Award from the Mystery Writers of America for his first novel, *The Lasko Tangent*. A graduate of Ohio Wesleyan University and Case Western Reserve School of Law, Patterson has had a varied career as a securities litigator, including work with the Securities and Exchange Commission in Washington, D.C. That experience resulted in his working with the Watergate special prosecutor and formed the basis for his first novel. At the time of this interview, Patterson was a securities litigation partner at McCutchen, Doyle, Brown, and Enersen in San Francisco. He is now retired from the practice of law and writes full-time.

This interview took place in 1993.

FICTION: *The Lasko Tangent* (1979) ▪ *Outside Man* (1981) ▪ *Escape the Night* (1983) ▪ *Private Screening* (1985) ▪ *Degree of Guilt* (1992) ▪ *Eyes of a Child* (1994) ▪ *The Final Judgment* (1995) ▪ *Silent Witness* (1996) ▪ *No Safe Place* (1998) ▪ *Dark Lady* (1999) ▪ *Protect and Defend* (2000)

MURPHY: *When John Grisham made a ton of money from* **The Firm,** *he stopped practicing law. You reportedly got $1.6 million for* **Degree of Guilt,** *but you're still practicing. Why is that?*

PATTERSON: There are two reasons: One, I didn't get $1.6 million for *Degree of Guilt.* There's a reason for that figure, but my advance was in the high six figures and the rest reflects foreign advances that went to the publisher. But, aside from that, I want to continue to practice law. There are really two models: there's Grisham, who said upon quitting that he didn't even turn around to shut the lights off; and there's Scott Turow, who has maintained a practice at the Sonnenshein firm in Chicago. I think he works half-time, and maintains a vigorous practice. It's really much more the model I would like to have. I think but for being a lawyer, I wouldn't be a writer. I've had some fascinating experiences. You get some terrific revelations of character, and you see people at their best and worst.

MURPHY: **Degree of Guilt** *is peopled with celebrities: the defendant is the country's best-known female broadcaster, the victim is a famous writer, and there are movie stars and politicians who play a role in the book. Why did you put so many celebrities in the book, or people who could be identified with celebrities? Was this to boost sales potential?*

PATTERSON: No. Actually it wasn't, although I really have a hard time finding anybody who now believes it. Because if you sell books, and this book has become a bestseller now, there is the assumption that you cleverly set out to do it all along and everything you did must have been for that purpose. The thing that some people are fixed upon is the presence of certain high-profile characters in the book. That wasn't my reason.

I think the first reason why I wrote about characters who have achieved is that people who—for whatever reason—are successful, or starting to be successful, fascinate me. I'm interested in the unusual in people, the exceptional in people. I like writing about people who in some way or another are extraordinary. I don't know what writer it was who said he didn't want to write a novel about somebody's second divorce, but I sympathize with him, because I really prefer writing about unusual people, unusual situations.

The second thing that I was doing in the book was to deal with the way Americans tend to mythologize certain public figures. I'm thinking particularly of Marilyn Monroe and the Kennedys, who have mythic properties that a couple of the characters in the book really share. What I mean is this: Americans have a preoccupation with certain public figures and we project on them what we need them to be. We built around Kennedy this picture of intellect, moral perfection, idealistic aspiration, which to some extent was at odds with his true and more complex character. We now know, for example, that he was not always terribly noble in his dealings with women, which is an interesting aspect of his character. We built around Marilyn Monroe this incredible aura of glamour and sexuality, where in fact we now know that she was a fairly miserable and tormented person with limited individual resources; to a great extent a prisoner of the myth that was built around her. And, I might add, a pretty terrible role model for women, which has now become obvious. Yet, we have this retro Monroe revival. She's been dead for thirty years and we have kind of a Marilyn Monroe revival . . .

MURPHY: *And now we have Madonna. . . .*

PATTERSON: Right, which to me is in a way part of an antifeminist backlash. Everything I write is to some extent political: in *Degree of Guilt* I was trying to deal with the gap between the way we mythologize public figures and their reality, and by doing this suggesting that a mature society would look more closely at people we tend to idolize. Having said all that, it's very difficult for me now to persuade anybody that that wasn't a way of selling books—even though, if you look at the book jacket and you look at our promotion, that aspect of the novel really is not emphasized, hasn't been emphasized by the publisher, hasn't been emphasized by me unless somebody asked me about it. But I guess one of the curious aspects of having had a commercial success is that people tend to look at it through the retrospectoscope. Having known how the book ended as a business proposition, they assume that everything you did leading up to it was also a business proposition, cleverly calculated to lead to that result. And I guess there's really nothing I can do about that.

MURPHY: *If it were that easy I'm sure you'd do it over and over again.*
PATTERSON: If it were that easy, I would have done it the first four times. Somebody asked me if a first printing of 250,000 was a lot. I said, I'll put it this way, it's 241,500 higher than my previous record. And yet my last novel, *Private Screening,* also dealt with high-profile political issues, including the link between terrorism and television, whether televised trials are a good idea, the Vietnam stress syndrome as a defense, a political assassination, a lot of other things that could be called "commercial." But actually I think of them as political, because I tend to use fiction partially as a vehicle to write about ideas that interest me. And although *Private Screening* was extremely well reviewed, it did not have big sales in hardback. I can't totally explain why one book works commercially in hardback and another doesn't.

MURPHY: Degree of Guilt *has been called a women's book—the defendant, the prosecutor, one of the defense attorneys, and the judge are all women. Was it a conscious choice on your part to put so many women in the book so you could appeal to female readers?*
PATTERSON: I think that sort of evolved. I started out with an idea and then the idea took a certain direction in favor of presenting more characters who represented different aspects of the experiences of women of the 1990s. For example, I got halfway through the book and I needed a judge. Caroline Masters just appeared, but before the

day I needed a judge I never even reflected on gender. The Caroline Masters character was just a logical outgrowth of the book as I was writing more and more about women and women's experiences and became more caught up in it as a writer.

The subject matter that I started with, rape, obviously treats an experience which is, if not peculiar to women, certainly largely suffered by them. And I dealt with that in terms of the experience both of rape victims and of people who attempt to follow those cases through the legal system. But as a consequence, when the book became more and more about women's concerns, I became interested in other aspects of women's experiences. For example, the codefense counsel, who is a working mother and is the primary support of her family, reflects the experience of a lot of professional women that I know. And that role can be a very difficult one because even though we have now—in some sense—opened up the workplace, there still are assumptions that women are going to be the primary caretaking parent. And there's the guilt about departing from traditional roles that many working women still seem to have and society seems to inflict on them. I got more and more caught up in that as I went along. I think what happens when you write a novel is that you get swept up in a world and the novel starts to take you in different directions, and to some extent you start working for the characters, instead of your characters being your employees. And when that happens, it becomes a better book.

MURPHY: *The sex in the book is indirect and brutal—it's either rape, bondage, or voyeurism. There are no scenes of sex that are in the present time. All the sex is described by characters relating to past experiences. Did you consciously avoid present depictions of sex?*

PATTERSON: I didn't think, in terms of the plot, that there was any relationship in which a romantic experience on that level would be appropriate, or wouldn't be a distraction. So it was a relatively simple decision for me because the book wasn't a romance in that sense.

As for the depictions of sex that you describe, they stem largely from an exploration of the past life of the murder victim, whom the defendant accuses of rape, an exploration of whether there was something in his psychology which would suggest that he had a predilection to rape or sexual pathology and, in turn, an exploration of how much of this evidence could be presented in court under the rules of evidence as they now stand. Certainly there are depictions of sex and sexual subjects, but I think that the underlying point is that rape and sexual pathology are not about sexual desires as we understand them, but instead are crimes of violence or of anger. And that's the point that I was making. Although there's a fair amount of sex in the book, very little of it reflects very well upon the murder victim. People describe this as a sexy book; I find that sort of puzzling, really.

MURPHY: *The primary instigator of the brutal sex acts, of course, is the victim, Mark Ranson, but also Senator James Colt, the John F. Kennedy figure. In view of the overwhelming brutality of the sex by these two men, do you really think you were being fair to men?*

PATTERSON: I never set out to portray the totality of male behavior or human sexual behavior, so I didn't ever think it was a question of fairness. I did set out to portray sexual pathology, and I think with a fair amount of accuracy. So I'm not suggesting that all men are like this, or this is male sexual behavior across the board. I don't feel I have any apology to make, because that was never the premise of the book.

MURPHY: *A lot of legal thrillers have trial scenes, yet you decided to forgo the trial and just go with the preliminary hearing. Why was that?*

PATTERSON: A few reasons. First of all, I think it's an interesting legal proposition. It has been done, but it's rare. So I think in and of itself it's interesting. Second, it enabled me to present the legal issues in sharper relief because it made the judge a more active figure and the judge's legal decisions more clearly articulated. The third reason was simply for dramatic purposes. To me Judge Carolyn Masters is an interesting character, and concentrating the decision-making power in the hands of one compelling figure, whom the reader knows, rather than twelve figures, whom the reader can't possibly know, gives the trial scenes a dramatic focus that very often trial scenes and novels don't have.

MURPHY: *The focus of the hearing was primarily whether the three past victims of Mark Ranson will testify—Melissa Rappaport, his ex-wife; Marcy Linton, an author he had raped; and Lindsey Caldwell, an actress who had had an affair with Laura Chase and who was being blackmailed by Ranson. Do you really think that any of these witnesses' testimonies would ever be admitted in court?*

PATTERSON: Let's put it this way. Without talking about which experience is ultimately found to be admissible, I think that the one experience that is ruled admissible in this case is the most likely to be admitted. What I did is present a spectrum of different experiences which reflected upon Mark Ransom's personal psychology and then ask which of these is fair to present at trial. In the William Kennedy Smith case—which was on my mind at the time that I wrote this— three women came forward to testify that they had been assaulted by Smith and none was allowed to testify. My outcome is a little bit different. What I was doing was presenting one woman who was raped, another who was subject to consensual activities which reflected a certain perverse psychology on Ransom's part, and a third who was subject to sexual blackmail. I was presenting a range of experience and saying, Okay, which of these do you as the reader feel the courts should actually consider? And I certainly was raising the question of whether the rule that prevailed in the Smith case is a reasonable rule of evidence.

MURPHY: *It's been reported that you wrote the first draft of* **Degree of Guilt** *in three months, working twelve-hour days.*

PATTERSON: Yeah. That's pretty much right. I got through 750 out of 900 pages in three months. I wrote seven days a week, twelve hours a day; I really got swept up in it. After that I finished the book before work by getting up at 4:30 in the morning.

MURPHY: *Two of the main characters, Christopher Paget and Mary Cirelli, were characters you introduced in other books. Do you think your familiarity with these characters made it easier for you to write at such a pace?*

PATTERSON: Yes. That was a conscious choice that I made with that in mind. We have a wonderful program here, a three-month sabbatical that people who've been with the firm a certain number of years can take every five years. I had about a month of vacation to tag onto that and I wanted to try to write a novel. And it was in many ways an ambitious novel, and so I thought about what breaks I could give myself. One of them was to write about characters that I knew.

I never wanted to write a series, and don't consider that I ever will. But to take characters that I have written about literally thirteen, fourteen years before—my first novel was published in 1979—and then pick up their lives fifteen years later, was fascinating. It was like revisiting characters that I had known at twenty-nine, like seeing old college friends, and finding out what happened to them. They're different but they're the same, since character is fate. But it's interesting to see how character takes you along a certain road.

MURPHY: *You mention you hadn't written a novel in eight years, but I would imagine you had been thinking during that time about your next book, and the plots were germinating in your mind. Is that what actually happened?*

PATTERSON: I think you dredge up a lot of stuff on a subconscious level. Until a few months before I wrote this book, I had no plan to write it because I didn't see how my schedule as a lawyer was going to unfold. When a big case—to which I would have dedicated three or four months of trial—settled, I found I would have time to take a sabbatical that I might otherwise not have had. I went for eight years thinking, Maybe I'll write when I retire, and not really having a clear idea when that might be, so I didn't ever plot out a novel.

I think what happens when you sit down and actually write a book is you tap into what has made an impression for the past eight years, or whatever it is since you last wrote. One thing that made an impression on me, I realized, was that several women with whom I was friendly had told me about experiences with sexual assault. Although the experiences were peculiar to each of those women, they seemed to have certain things in common: the sense of isolation at the moment that they were assaulted, the sense of isolation afterwards, and the feeling that family and friends might not really understand, the sense of guilt that they might be responsible for what happened to them, the anger, shame—one person didn't even tell her husband. And then the sense of isolation within the legal system.

It's funny, although we all hear a lot of remarkable things, we tend to deal with our normal lives, and it's only when you sit down to fill up empty pages that you really take inventory of what it was that really impressed you on a subconscious level. And that's what I came up with.

MURPHY: Degree of Guilt *has gotten mostly good reviews, with a few mixed reviews. The* Chronicle *called it overwritten, too ambitious, self-aggrandizing, pompous, full of narrative problems; yet impossible to put down. This is your chance to respond to the critics.*

PATTERSON: That was a very odd review. As it happens, the reviewer and I know each other and long ago had profound disagreements about the role of literature, and what writers ought to aspire to. Without reopening that gratuitously, I had a sense of that being present in the review. I thought it was a review that liked the book and hated itself for liking it. People have a right to be offended by books they read, but I thought that there was kind of an undisclosed argument running through the *Chronicle* review that, had the reader known about it, he or she might have been able to make more sense of the review.

Generally, the reviews have been quite nice, and I'm very grateful. What I try to do is to go through the reviews I've gotten, and see if there is some thread that runs through them that's really instructive to me, that I ought to carry away and really think about. I don't think, and I hope I never reach the point, where I believe I've done the best I can do. So reviews can be helpful. But what has been odd about the handful of adverse reviews that I've read—particularly those written when it became clear that I had a commercial success—was the level of vituperation that I had not experienced before. You can attribute that to a number of things, I suppose, but I think when you are a commercial success, you're no longer a figure of sympathy. You're not the reviewer's private discovery—this wonderful writer I'd like to share with you. What distinguishes a reviewer then is to say that people may be reading this book, but here's what's wrong with it. So I think as a commercial success you command less sympathy and more criticism. If that's the price you pay for reaching an audience, then I'm certainly happy to pay it.

I must have read thirty, forty reviews of this book by now. And I've been struck by the diversity of the quibbles and how wildly different and contradictory they are. I happen to write with a lot of semi-colons, and I read a review from somewhere which said that it was clear that the book must have been edited quite heavily because of the presence of all those semicolons. Well, it's nonsense; it's total insanity. As it happens, the manuscript was pretty clean, and the editing had much more to do with whether a scene ought to be there. So this reviewer's enormous insight was, in fact, gobbledygook.

MURPHY: *Speaking of odd reviews, the* **New York Times** *book review, by a lawyer named Sidney Zion, referred to the book as a "post-yuppie saga of touchy-feely boredom and betrayal." Do you have any comments about that characterization?*

PATTERSON: Somebody asked me how I felt about it when I was in a particularly nasty mood, and I said that Sidney's biggest moment of 1993 will be panning my book. But that was one of those reviews that you have to put aside. It starts out with an inexplicable reference to Roy Cohn, which comes from nowhere, unless you know—as someone told me—that Sidney's written a book on Roy Cohn and is fascinated by him. He then proceeds to accuse me of thinking I know more than I do, a reference which is not otherwise explained. Then he goes on to talk about which sex acts in the book, in his view, would be most likely to lead to procreation. At the end of all this, you feel not like you've read a review, but like you're peeking at somebody's Rorschach test that hasn't turned out so well.

It is never pleasant to have somebody not like your book. But what is the most telling is when you feel as if the review is more revealing not of the contents of the book, but of the psyche of the reviewer. I've reviewed books and one thing that I never did was view this as an occasion for self-expression and self-preening, because, after all, you're writing about somebody else's work. The purpose of a review is to inform an audience, not to use it as some sort of self-exposition. But again, reviewers are people just like anyone else and they are no better and no worse. And there are some very conscientious ones. But when you write a book you throw yourself off to all those people. You don't get to choose who reviews your book, you don't get to screen their qualifications, you just leave yourself open. And if you're not prepared for the consequences of that, then writing is going to be an even more painful experience than it is.

MURPHY: *You mentioned earlier, with regard to the* Chronicle *review, some disagreement with the reviewer about the purpose of fiction. Is fiction to you for entertainment or is it for art?*

PATTERSON: I don't think they're exclusive. I don't think they should be. The first level of fiction writing that one has to deal with is to engage the reader, to make the reader want to turn the pages. That's the level of storytelling at which I think any writer should try to succeed. And then there's the deeper level of characterization, setting, meaning, and ideas. And if you succeed in adding those then you've taken it from a story, in my view, to a novel. I don't see any reason why something that is entertaining ought not aspire to deeper values. You know why *Presumed Innocent* worked? Not simply because it was a good courtroom novel—although it certainly was— but because Scott Turow is a very talented writer in any setting. And he brought the values of a novel of good characterization and the totally convincing depiction of a world to the courtroom novel. And that's why that worked, and deservedly so. And what Turow showed at his best is that the courtroom novel and commercial fiction needn't be some sort of literary parlor trick, but can really have lasting value and content. One of the things that really warms me about the success of Turow is that he is a fine novelist by any standard. In any event, I don't think art and entertainment are exclusive.

MURPHY: *I know you're going to write another novel and I would guess it's going to be a love affair between Christopher Paget and Teresa Peralta. Is that where you're going?*

PATTERSON: You're not a lawyer for nothing.

MURPHY: *Would you care to divulge any more plans, or is it too early in the creative process?*

PATTERSON: It certainly will deal with the terms and difficulties of their relationship, but there will be other plot devices involving a murder, among other things, and a criminal trial and the subject of parents and children and battered women. To some extent it will be generational and will involve not only Teresa Peralta but her mother, who is an offstage character in *Degree of Guilt*. She will be very much an onstage character in this book. I said once there were three great themes: parents, and children, and how they made their way in this world. I'm doing my best to write about all three in this next book.

JOHN PEAK

John Peak's third novel, *Mortal Judgments,* is a legal thriller based on a medical malpractice case. After ten hours of spinal surgery, a prominent businesswoman begins to ooze blood out of her pores. The code blue team is unable to stop the flow of blood and she dies on the operating table. The orthopedic surgeon consults defense attorney Vicki Shea, a former physician who lost her only child to cerebral palsy years earlier. As Vicki gets closer to solving what happened in the operating room, her expert witnesses suddenly die violent deaths. Vicki's own life is then threatened. As trial approaches, Vicki finds herself fighting for her own survival while trying to prevent a multimillion-dollar verdict against her client.

Peak graduated from the University of Nebraska and the University of Colorado School of Law. After a tour as a JAG officer in the air force, he came to San Francisco and joined the City Attorney's Office, primarily defending San Francisco General Hospital and other health agencies from malpractice claims. He has practiced in southern California, where he opened a private practice defending medical malpractice cases, and in San Jose, where he works for a workers' compensation defense firm.

This interview took place in 1999.

FICTION: *Spare Change* (1994) ▪ *Blood Relations* (1997) ▪ *Mortal Judgments* (1999)

MURPHY: *Your new book is entitled* Mortal Judgments, *but the original title was* Blood Lines. *How did the title get changed?*

PEAK: I came up with the title because it was a play on words. It was not *Bloodlines*—one word, like genealogy—but two words, like an arterial blood line, or a venous blood line that you'd have in a hospital setting. I was also playing on the fact that this woman's progeny—the protagonist child who died—is so important to her, her blood lines. I liked that, but unfortunately some very famous novelist whose name escapes me right now came out with a novel called *Blood Lines* a few years ago. I was aware of that before my publisher bought this book and when they bought it I told them of course that's got to be changed. I was in full agreement with them this time, but they didn't necessarily agree with me. They thought maybe nobody's going to confuse it and they sort of left it like that for about a year and two months. Then they called me and said, "We need another name by tomorrow." And so I called my agent and I called my editor and we went back and forth with some pretty outrageous ideas and hit on *Mortal Judgments.* I kind of like it.

MURPHY: *You write about a medical malpractice case, which is relatively unusual in the legal thriller genre; in fact, only Barry Reed comes to mind as somebody who has done that. Did you think you'd encounter any difficulty in explaining to the reader complex medical terms and keeping them enthralled with the story?*

PEAK: Actually, that's my field—medical malpractice. I try a lot of cases and that's what I have to do every time I have a jury trial; I have to explain it to laypeople. I start off in opening statement being as detailed and technical as I can. I know they're not going to get it all. But with any luck they'll get the general backbone of what this is about and then they'll get it again in the evidence as each expert comes up. Each expert thinks that the jury has never heard of any of this and they go over it again. So by the time we get to final argument I can give a pretty detailed technical argument and the jury will follow right with it. You watch their faces and they don't glaze over; they're right with it. I felt most laypeople—especially literate laypeople that are going to read books—will get it, if I do it right. If they don't get it, then I haven't done it right.

MURPHY: *In this book you decided not to keep the book focused solely on medical malpractice since it turns into a murder mystery as well. Was that in part to keep the readership interested?*

PEAK: I think I started off wanting to do a mystery. My first two books were both categorized as mysteries, although when I wrote them I didn't really think I was writing mysteries, but St. Martin's put them in that market and they did okay. They were looking for another mystery. By that point, I was thinking, Okay, let's sit down and deliberately write one. I knew of an incident where a patient died of DIC on the table after a back surgery, and nobody could figure out what caused the DIC. For the lawyers, and I'm certain for the defendant, it was a very frustrating experience. Not being able to figure out why this patient got such a complicated and macabre outcome.

MURPHY: *What is DIC?*

PEAK: That's disseminated intravascular coagulopathy.

MURPHY: *Which is what the patient in your book died of.*

PEAK: Yeah. And what it means in essence is all of the coagulating factors—the fibrins and the elements in your blood that cause it to form clots—for some reason get used up. And when they're used up you no longer have the clotting mechanism that you need all the time. It's not just when you have a cut. You have little leaks all the time in your system and if you don't have any clotting factor, it begins to come right through the pores. It will come right through the skin creases and through the gums and the nose and the membranes. Everywhere there is a blood supply close to the surface. So it's a macabre event. It usually happens when somebody's got a large hemorrhage and the clotting factors get consumed rapidly in trying to stop the hemorrhage. But this wasn't true of the real-life case that I was aware of. Nobody's got a real reason why this occurred. As far as I know nobody ever did figure out why that patient got DIC. So I solved the problem. I just murdered her.

MURPHY: *I want to ask you about the structure of the book. You start off with an incident in 1976 in which a baby dies of a congenital defect and the mother* *turns out to be the protagonist in the story, Vicki Shea. But the second chapter is really the only chapter that's not from her point of view. It deals with the operation and the catastrophe that takes place. Were you concerned about shifting the point of view in that one chapter?*

PEAK: I was. Because in the first book I had two protagonists, alternating chapters from point of view. The second book, *Blood Relations,* was entirely from one person's point of view, the retired police sergeant who is stumbling through trying to figure out what's going on. I liked that because when things occur, they gradually unfold as the person finds out more information, unless you have somebody sit down and reveal the whole damn thing, which ruins the book. You can't write a book that way. But if someone is going along trying to figure out a puzzle or circumstances or a case or anything you're involved in, a single character would get input from all over. But you don't have the input whenever you want. You just get it as it comes in. So I like that as a structure.

But I wanted to show right from the outset that there was no doubt that this surgeon was not a bad guy; that the surgeon had done everything that he could and that everybody was legitimately mystified. As lawyers, we're never quite sure. We get a client in our office and he's not only mystified by what happened to the patient, but he's outraged that the patient would ever sue him about it. And you're never quite sure if—before the lawsuit came up—he felt like that. The doctor may have had some lingering doubts: Maybe I should have done this, or should have done that. Of course, when the lawsuit comes in, the tendency of all of us is to dig our trenches and give battle and not to admit to anything. But I wanted it to be perfectly clear from the outset that this was an innocent man that we were dealing with, at least from a moral sense. I think there's legitimate suspicion that he may have done something wrong that he wasn't aware of. As all the physicians came pouring in on the code blue and were trying to solve this problem—the hematologist, the pulmonologist, the emergency doctors, the anesthesiologist—each one was equally puzzled as to what happened. They looked to the surgeon in the last line of that chapter because he's the captain of the ship. He's the guy in charge and so he's got to bear the brunt of this thing, and he knows it, but nobody's blaming him at that point. And I wanted to make it real clear that he is not a bad guy. But it was risky, you're right, to shift the ground like that.

MURPHY: *Another thing I found curious: from the first chapter, where the baby dies until we learn that Vicki Shea has become an attorney, my original thought was she's probably going to be a plaintiff's medical malpractice attorney motivated perhaps by the death of her baby while under medical care. And yet she first becomes a physician and then a defense lawyer. Why did you decide to have the protagonist make these choices?*

PEAK: She was already aimed at medical school when this baby died. She had just turned twenty years old, so she would have been a sophomore or junior in college. But she was already premed and so was her husband, so they were already headed that way when she had the baby with cerebral palsy. The baby died as she was starting her residency and that's when she dropped out. So her orientation was to medicine. She was a physician before she was anything else professionally. She gives up medicine because she doesn't ever have the confidence that she's got enough answers. It all goes back to this child with cerebral palsy. She never had a reason for it, never had an explanation that would make any sense to her. Because of that she felt like she could never have confidence to make decisions that doctors make all the time. She did well in school, she placed high in her class. But even when she compared herself to people who were at the bottom of the class—walking around like arrogant jerks—they could do it, she couldn't. And she dropped out at that point. Law school was then the logical next step for her and since I'm a defense lawyer I made her a defense lawyer. I know that side better.

MURPHY: *She's portrayed as vulnerable, she's looking for a mate in life, she's respected in her profession though she doesn't think she's respected enough. Did you find it difficult as a male writer to write from the female perspective?*

PEAK: I've got a wife, three daughters, a mare—yeah, it was a challenge. One of the things that led to this book was that I'd been thinking for a long time that the real story in these bad baby cases is the mother. A lot of them never bring a lawsuit so we don't see them, but the ones we see in litigation almost always wind up divorced, on their own. If the child survives, they struggle through getting help where they can, to get by day to day, do all the things they can do. A very high percentage of them wind up not being able to do it. They have to give that baby up, to go to a home. Sometimes it's a selfless act on the mother's part to do that because the baby simply gets better care, especially with real severe cases like Vicki's baby. They're going to get better care in a live-in facility than they are at home. But it's a wreck for the mother. It's a horrible thing for somebody to go through.

As parents, all of us, our biggest nightmare is for something to happen to that child. I can only imagine, having seen it from the outside, what it must be like when the child is born so severely injured right from the beginning. So the parent is not just anticipating something's going to go wrong and the kid will die because it's so fragile. But the parent knows something went wrong in the past and then keeps thinking, What'd I do, what'd I do, what was it that I could have done that would have solved this? What could I have changed? What could I go back and fix? What a burden that is for a person, especially a thinking person like Vicki Shea, to live with. And so that was an intriguing theme to me to get her through that. And I figured it would take her about twenty years.

MURPHY: *You give her a gay male secretary who is a former San Francisco cop. Why that combination?*
PEAK: This character was a central character in the first novel I ever wrote, which hasn't been published and never will. It's not a good book. But I liked that character and a part of the impetus for him was I wanted to write a San Francisco cop book. And how can you write a book about San Francisco without including somebody who's gay? But they're all cops, and so I just had to do it. But I liked it. He's certainly not someone you could say he's like anything. He's not like all cops; he's not like all secretaries; he's not like all gay people. He's just who he is. He's a decent guy.

MURPHY: *I have one bone to pick with you on the plot. While Vicki's driving a car on Highway 101, a concrete building block comes through her window, nearly killing her. It's obviously not an accident, but it's barely mentioned for about a hundred pages thereafter. She forgot about it, didn't call the cops, didn't tell her partner. She doesn't do anything about it.*

PEAK: She's not convinced it's not an accident. She doesn't know why anybody would do anything like that deliberately; or if it was something malicious, she doesn't think it was personal. She thinks somebody did it not caring that they might hurt somebody. But until the time her first expert witness is killed, she thinks that that was just a freak thing, that it must have fallen off a truck or something and hit her. I probably wasn't very clear about that. But in her discussion with the other lawyer, which is in the chapter following, they talk about that briefly. I sort of put a spotlight on the lawyer for the Haemosal blood salvage machine. He turns to her and says something like, "Well, that's just storm warnings." She's real suspicious. Why would he say anything like this? An odd thing to say. The other lawyer sitting with her raises her eyebrows: What an odd thing. It's meant to be subtle, but you should catch it as a reader that maybe this could have been something done deliberately.

MURPHY: *My only question was why didn't she tell the cops or be a little more concerned about a brick going through her window than she seemed to be.*

PEAK: I wonder if you would think that if it weren't a murder mystery. If you knew somebody that that happened to at ten o'clock at night, heading for the bridge down the Waldo Grade and here comes this building block through the windshield, you might not think that was a murder attempt if you weren't reading a book that is classified as a murder mystery.

MURPHY: *That's probably true. Certainly her suspicion rises when her expert's found dead of a cocaine overdose.*

PEAK: She starts putting it together and the cops are the ones saying, "Well, wait a minute." The cops are the ones that are skeptical.

MURPHY: *You name a lot of the characters after San Francisco lawyers.*

PEAK: I do. That's true.

MURPHY: *Did you get their permission to put them in your book?*

PEAK: No, for the most part I didn't. I do that mainly to keep track of who the characters are. With one or two exceptions, they are people who know me and I know them real well. The characters are nothing like the name character, the real-life person. I'll give you an example: In *Blood Relations* Dorsey Redlands is a major character. She's an economist. When I named that character I liked the name and I like Dorsey, the real Dorsey Redlands who is a practicing lawyer. People who have met with her and worked with her universally admire and like her. When that book sold I thought, "Uh-oh," because that was the first novel that I sold. I got the galley proofs and started thinking, I could have a problem with this. Not that there's a legal problem because clearly the character is not Dorsey Redlands the lawyer, but I called her up and she said, "Send me the book." So I sent her an actual manuscript and I think I signed the book and sent it when it actually came out. Never heard anything back from her.

MURPHY: *She never sued you, so you're safe.*

PEAK: Even if it depicted her, she wouldn't. But I wouldn't put a name of someone in a book of mine that I didn't get along with. But I don't always know the people real well. They're not always people that I've gone to lunch with or had dinner with or seen outside of just a professional capacity. If they're real villains, I try to make sure that the person's name I use is somebody I get along with just fine.

MURPHY: *I've read there's been some interest in making a movie of this book. The decedent's company, Adeline's Closet, is Victoria's Secret in disguise and would make a great part of a movie. Did you have that in mind when you chose that type of company for the decedent?*

PEAK: I wanted to make her someone who had enormous earnings potential. That was the bottom line. I just needed somebody who really had money. . . .

MURPHY: *You needed some economic damages.*
PEAK: Economic damages, exactly. Making her a banker was too dull. Although Dorsey Redlands wasn't dull, she was an economist. For one thing, I don't know anything about banking. I don't know anything about the lingerie business either, but at least that's a sexy topic. I've known one woman who is a fashion designer and has her own house and her own line. So I had a rough idea of how that might work in terms of one person being responsible for an enormous share of the income from a going enterprise. If I made her both a designer and a moving creative force in this business, then I could convincingly write it. In the sense that it wouldn't do very well without her, and yet still be worth lots of money.

MURPHY: *I do some plaintiffs' medical malpractice and, reading the book, one gets the impression that these are easy cases for plaintiffs to win, which of course is far divorced from reality.*
PEAK: Yes!

MURPHY: *I was hoping to see something in there about ninety percent of the verdicts are defense and you've got limitations on damages and attorneys' fees and everything else.*
PEAK: I've thought about that because there are a couple of snide remarks in terms of Vicki's thinking and taking slaps at the plaintiffs' bar. The thing you have to realize is that that's really how defense lawyers think. When I was in the City Attorney's Office, we would get people who were relatively new out of law school. Louise likes to get people with at least a few years' experience just like all the firms downtown, but George would occasionally bring in somebody right out of school. We get a lot of interns from Hastings in the summertime. They come over and they're idealistic and think, "Oh, these poor, injured people." But you're in a defense setting and

within a matter of weeks you get a new case in and the attitude is, "Oh, God, what's this fraud want?" It's just a defense attitude that you begin to see.

Among defense lawyers there's a great deal of concern about having juries decide cases that maybe shouldn't be decided by them. The case is really too technical or too complicated. You're limited in California to one expert to a side on a given issue. Now, we've all figured out ways to get around that but you're not going to just run away. You can't come in there, for instance, and prove that this is what the literature says, this is what the majority of doctors say, you can't do it. That's not an admissible thing to put in evidence. So you're stuck. You've got an expert, they've got an expert. If their expert is a better showman, he's more convincing, or she's more convincing and just seems to have more confidence, the jury may very well go with that. My feeling is that if the plaintiff is sympathetic, there's an arguable case on liability, and the jury wants to give them money, the jury will do that. They may not give them much; they may compromise it. But they will figure out a way to do it. Defense lawyers are afraid of that. All of us think about that; "Oh, man, you've got this case where there really shouldn't be any liability, but on the other hand look at this poor plaintiff left as a C-5 quad or something. Oh, my God, this guy was on his way to the major leagues and now look at him—settle it!" Because Vicki's a defense lawyer, I went with that attitude. I didn't try to do both sides.

MURPHY: *It seems, at least from the description in the book, that this is a tough case because nobody knows what caused the DIC and nobody's even articulated a breach of the standard of care. So I look at this as a case heading for a defense verdict. But that's not how the defense lawyers are looking at it.*
PEAK: No, they don't. From our viewpoint, especially prior to expert disclosure, you look at it as you know the plaintiff's lawyer is going to get an expert, the plaintiff's lawyer is pretty good. Vicki knows Stephen Sears, the plaintiff's attorney, will not only get somebody, he'll have a pretty convincing argument. She just can't figure out what it is. And yet as she's refining her own theories on the case, she

hits it pretty well. She's real close to it. And as you read further in the book you'll see she's thinking to herself, "Well, lots of things go wrong in surgery and the longer something lasts the more likely it is that you can have a problem. Why did this surgery take ten hours, for chrissake? The doctor is just a slow, meticulous doctor; he's doing a very complicated procedure." The jury is not going to appreciate that. Ten hours for a slow meticulous process; it might take an hour, or it might take two hours depending on how the jury is willing to look at it. But to take ten hours, it's hard to imagine that if you've never been in an operating room and watched somebody adjust something, look at the films, bring in the portable, look at it again, try this, take another look, stop, look at it. . . . All those things that go on in surgery take a lot of time. But ten hours is a long time to be in surgery and so she's focusing on that even before expert disclosure and she's hit it right on. That's exactly what the experts go after. They say with this machine to filter the blood, if you let something go on that long you're asking for problems. It might not have been the machine; it might have been some other problem such as pulmonary embolism. This guy should never have been operating for ten hours. That's the theory. Nobody's really said why this killed the patient but it's enough to get to a jury.

MURPHY: *There's a chapter in* **Mortal Judgments** *where Vicki goes home to her father and her brother's family. She rides her horse and has a pleasant time with her family. It sounds like a similar theme as* **Blood Relations:** *the importance of the parent/adult child's relationship. Is that a theme you're especially interested in?*

PEAK: It's something that I think is central to the way people view themselves. That's true personally, and for most people I know. First of all, they are their parents' children and then they are the parents of their own children. That's their definition of self and that's very important. These other things may have tremendous significance: how your standing is in the profession or how well you look to the juries and the judges and so forth. But still the core being of who you are is where you stand in relationship to those closest to you. That's more important to some people than it is to others, obviously. But the most important thing to me in writing a book is how the protagonist, the central person, defines him- or herself—period. And that includes relational family relationships. So the old man in *Blood Relations* had a family that was much closer to him than his parental family; his wife and his children were much more significant to him as an individual than his own parents were.

In this book Vicki never can do anything about that child. Her goal is to get over it. She doesn't know it. But she has been completely unable to get past the dead child and that's why, twenty years out, she is still struggling. She may be one of the best trial lawyers in the city; nobody ever says that but she could be. The lawyers respect her, the judges obviously respect her, she's got some credibility when she talks, the experts know who she is. But she doesn't think of herself as a success. She's struggling; she's hustling. She says, "Why am I doing this? Why haven't I arrived?" She won't step out and look at herself as someone else might and say, "She's got it made. She's not even forty years old but she's established, she's done it all, and she's well liked and respected." But internally the way you see it as a reader Vicki never can think of herself that way. She can't do it. And she keeps saying, because of this baby, "What could I have done?" She goes back and back in a circle like that. "What should I have done? What should I have done differently that I would have this daughter instead of just a picture and a graveside?" Well, the question is unanswerable. What the book's about is having Vicki deal with that.

MURPHY: *While she's solving the mystery of this patient's death.*
PEAK: You force her through the sieve. You just push her into a life-and-death situation where again it's not her fault. It's nothing she's done to cause this but she does have the opportunity to retreat, to get out of it. It's just another case. She's not the defendant. She could abandon ship and her partner begs her to do that. He tells her it is too dangerous, but she won't do it. When Vicki is put through this trauma where there's real danger, real fear, she's got to confront some things. I think she comes through it successfully. I'm not giving away the

ending again. She never solves the mystery. She also doesn't solve the mystery about her own child. She can't solve it. She doesn't have enough information.

MURPHY: *That's certainly not the typical ending you find in murder mysteries. One of the rules you always hear is that the protagonist is supposed to solve the crime.*

PEAK: Yes. And that's why I keep saying I don't really write mysteries. There's an element of mystery to it, but if there weren't why would you read it. If it were all obvious from the beginning, you wouldn't bother to read anything. There's got to be some element of it. The criminal aspect is just a convenient way to do it, but it's just a way to make a book interesting. I certainly wouldn't say that I write genre mysteries; I don't think I do.

BARRY REED

Barry Reed's first novel, *The Verdict,* was published in 1980 and became an international bestseller. The movie version of the novel starred Paul Newman and was nominated for an Academy Award.

In *The Verdict,* Frank Galvin, a down-on-his-luck plaintiffs' lawyer, confronts the Archdiocese of Boston over a medical malpractice case against St. Catherine Laboure Hospital. His client, a young mother, was rendered comatose when her heart stopped during a routine C-section. Galvin alleges the anesthesiologist was negligent. After turning down a $300,000 settlement offer, Galvin encounters one setback after another. Just when trial is set to start, his expert disappears. Galvin must decide whether to give up and return to the bottle or fight back against the Church and its high-powered lawyers.

Reed received his undergraduate degree at the College of the Holy Cross in Worcester, Massachusetts, and his law degree from Boston College. He practices with the Boston law firm of Reed, O'Reilly, and Brett, representing plaintiffs primarily in medical malpractice cases, and also served as president of the Massachusetts Trial Lawyers Association.

The first interview took place in 1990 and the second in 1994.

FICTION: *The Verdict* (1980) ▪ *The Choice* (1991) ▪ *The Indictment* (1994) ▪ *The Deception* (1997)

———————

MURPHY: *It's been ten years since* The Verdict *was published. What took you so long to write another novel?*

REED: Unfortunately, I have to make a living. I have a law firm in Boston. I have to meet a payroll on Friday night and we try mainly medical malpractice cases. Although I have written a lot of articles, you're right, it's been ten years since the next novel's coming out.

MURPHY: *What is your next novel?*

REED: It's called *The Choice.* It deals with Frank Galvin again, the protagonist in *The Verdict.* Frank hasn't had a drink in five years. It's going to be a very dull book, a lawyer who doesn't drink. He is with the largest law firm in Boston, kind of a Brahmin law firm. He's running with the Harvards and the Yales and kind of enjoys it. Keep in mind he went to Boston College . . .

MURPHY: *Not unlike the author.*

REED: . . . so he heads up the litigation department. He is the chief trial lawyer. *The Choice* emphasizes a problem that all lawyers are having today. Approximately five or six years ago I was trying a permanent and total workers' compensation case where my client was clobbered and was disabled. I am bringing a neurosurgeon to testify against the insurance company that he is permanently and totally disabled. On the eve of the trial my client tells me he has been working under the table for three years. Now what do you do? This is the issue, the choice, when your client isn't leveling with you and you learn the eve of the trial that your client has committed fraud on the court, that your client is lying to you. You've got a two-million-dollar offer, what do you do? You take the offer? [Laughter] Or do you blow the whistle on the client and tell him he has committed a fraud on the court, or do you withdraw, or what do you do? Under the code of ethics, the American Bar Association says (1) you are supposed to withdraw, (2) blow the whistle on the client. I don't know what the rule in California is but in Massachusetts you just withdraw, you don't have to give a reason. Let me say this. I took the $80,000 offer and settled the case. But that's the issue in *The Choice.*

MURPHY: *I imagine the issue in that book involves a lot more than $80,000 at stake.*

REED: Oh, yes. He is a defense lawyer and he is defending a large British conglomerate pharmaceutical house in London and Amsterdam and through a series of interrogatories and discovery and so forth he learns that the clients have been lying. Unfortunately, he waited too long. If he makes a moral choice he is not only going to bring himself down but he is going to bring his law firm down, a lot of good people down, including his client. Now, what does he do?

MURPHY: *There is a famous scene in the movie of* **The Verdict** *where the defense attorneys are all sitting in a long conference table and the lead defense attorney, Concannon, is at one end. It sounds like in* **The Choice** *we see Frank Galvin at the end of that long conference table. Has he sold out that far?*

REED: Well, he never has sold out. He is vulnerable, he is loaded with concupiscence, if I can use that term. He doesn't know what the hell to do. In fact, the femme fatale in the book meets him on a ferry to Belfast. Most of it takes place in London. He says, "I haven't got a good goddamned notion of what I intend to do." He doesn't know what he's going to do. You've got to be believable and you can't have all the answers. I won't tell you how it ends.

MURPHY: *In* **The Verdict** *Frank Galvin is really not a hero in the sense that he does anything heroic. He sort of bungles his way into winning that case. He does no discovery before the trial. He has not met with his expert witness. He has avoided meeting with his client. The guy's a walking malpractice suit!*

REED: No question about that. Everyone said, this is ridiculous. Any lawyer in a big malpractice case involving a comatose patient certainly would send out some interrogatories; certainly would know who the experts are on the other side, certainly would have met with his own experts. Frank Galvin isn't your typical hero. Frank Galvin is an accident waiting to happen. He lied to his clients; he didn't convey the offer to his clients; he broke into the U.S. Mails; he cheated on his girlfriend; and yet you kind of liked the guy. But he did everything wrong.

And I take issue with a lot of lawyers that took issue with me. In a malpractice suit, I would rather not have discovery. I would rather just show up for trial and get all my goodies together and all of a sudden, bang, here I am. No one sends me an interrogatory, I won't sent an interrogatory. I take issue with a lot of defense lawyers and a lot of plaintiff's lawyers that you got to have $400,000 worth of discovery in a case. It all depends, but some defense firms aren't that smart and I never send out even a letter sometimes and all of a sudden I show up for trial. But I don't think Frank Galvin was that smart. [Laughter]

MURPHY: *In the book, why did you choose to have Galvin be that kind of character, sort of the bungler who wins out in the end?*

REED: Frank Galvin was a coward playing a hero's role really. He didn't have too many redeeming qualities but what I tried to show is that these are ninety percent of the private practitioners in the United States. Not alcoholics, not liars and cheaters, but these are the guys that are just getting by. Can't pay the orthodontist's bills, trying to put the kids through college, drink too much, and do pull some sharp ones when they have to. But still good, moral individuals, they wouldn't step on a half dollar if you dropped it right here. They are fighting for survival. This was my hero and fortunately for me Simon and Schuster, who bought the book, never saw a hero like this. Twentieth Century Fox, who bought the movie, never saw a hero like this. This wasn't Gregory Peck in *To Kill a Mockingbird*. He had all the answers. He was smarter then everyone else. Frank Galvin wasn't smart. He survived just on the gut, primordial; he dipped down into some reserve he never knew he had. When he was being outnumbered and outgunned he just did a 180 and fought.

MURPHY: *In* The Choice *we know he is not going to be drinking but has he become more of the typical hero?*

REED: He really isn't a hero in *The Choice*. He is loaded with doubt. When he finally realizes what is happening, he tries to extricate everybody. He tries to extricate himself, tries to extricate the law, and he only worsens it. He should have cut his losses right off the bat when he first heard there was a fraud being committed. And he doesn't. He just waited too long. Now he's in a worse dilemma; now what does he do? As I say, he can get out of this very easily but if he makes the right moral judgment he is going to bring not only himself down but everyone else.

MURPHY: *There are a few scenes in* **The Verdict** *which—I am sure attorneys have told you—are totally unrealistic. For example, the defense associate who seduces Galvin to get information about his expert, the fact that the defense attorneys don't even know the identity of the plaintiff's expert, the judge being as biased as he is, I'm sure that's an exaggeration.*

REED: No, let me just correct you on that. I have seen many judges that are biased against me and biased against the plaintiff. I have seen that in real life; I am sure you have. It's unfortunate to get a judge like that. I agree with you, Steve, that I did take liberties with a lot of the factual situations and legal situations. The best evidence rule was my invention. A lot of law professors said, "That's crazy, where did Reed go to law school, he invented this crazy rule of law." Of course we knew all this but you have to have a little panache. A movie has got to do just that: move. There is nothing more boring than watching a murder trial in real life. So we had to invent a lot of stuff. I always said that doctors don't watch *M*A*S*H* to get tips in surgery. At least, I hope they don't! If I can answer my antagonists, and there are a lot of them, I always remember John Ford, the director. He said between fact and legend, give me the legend.

MURPHY: *It's interesting in* **The Verdict** *the villain is the Catholic Church. Is this a reflection of your own experiences with Jesuits at Holy Cross and Boston College?*

REED: I hope not. [Laughter] Some of my best years were at Holy Cross and Boston College. Especially Holy Cross. The Jesuits always took issue with the Cardinal, even today. Jesuits are Jesuits and they're not ecclesiastical yes-men. I really didn't take issue with the

Catholic Church. It was a big metaphor, if I can use that expression. The cardinal was depicted in satanic red and black. It was a scene from Pontius Pilot and we were speaking metaphorically. The cardinal, he didn't pay people off to secrete the truth. In fact, he asked Frank Galvin, "What is the truth?" And he was Pontius Pilot. And Frank Galvin said, "The truth is that you and me murdered that girl, we're being bought off. And I intend to try the case." So, I wasn't regaling against the church or the medical elite or the legal establishment. I think what I was trying to show was a redemption of a human being, Frank Galvin.

MURPHY: *The* Verdict *was solved when a nurse came virtually out of nowhere testifying that the medical records had been altered. Have you had a case where you've been able to prove the medical records had been altered?*
REED: No, wouldn't you like this to happen to you, Steve?

MURPHY: *That's what you always dream of. [Laughter]*
REED: The nurse comes forward after four years and said, "Everyone lied." In real life, I have seen medical records altered. I have seen a lot of these nurses and a lot of these librarians can lie very idly. I mean, they are believable. They can lie but they are believable. After four years the nurse in *The Verdict* didn't even come forward, she didn't bang on his door. It took a lot of contrivances. Moe Katz went down and they finally find this girl and have her come forward. You don't cross the medical mafia very easily, I'll tell you that.

MURPHY: *I understand your practice is about ninety percent medical malpractice. Does* The Choice *also involve medical malpractice issues?*
REED: In a way it does, but Frank Galvin is now defending a product liability case. The defendant is a large Dutch–English corporation that manufactures a product called Lyesin, which dissolves blood clots in the coronary arteries. We always say this is fiction and unfortunately, like Thalidomide or like some of the other drugs, ten to twenty years later some dire results come that no one can anticipate. It involves a

lawsuit in Fall River, Mass, where eight Portuguese families came up with birth defects and the mothers were taking Lyesin. Now, why Portuguese, why in Fall River? Frank Galvin is defending this multi-megabuck corporation and he learns on the eve of the trial that his own clients haven't been leveling with him.

MURPHY: *You had the incredible fortune of having Paul Newman play the lead in the movie version of* **The Verdict.** *Have you ever compared the sales of the book before and after the movie was released?*
REED: Yes. I am sure if it wasn't sold to Twentieth Century Fox, if Paul Newman didn't play it, I probably would have sold ten thousand copies and that would have been the end of it. I would have been writing poetry or love letters here and there. I am sure of that. But as a result of Twentieth Century Fox and Newman—we had Robert Redford for a whole year before we had Newman, and that is another story—it sold in twelve countries. The biggest seller was in Japan; I think it sold about two million copies in Japan.

MURPHY: *What happened to Redford? I hadn't heard that before.*
REED: The original star was Robert Redford. The original director was James Bridges, who did *The Paper Chase, Urban Cowboy,* and *The China Syndrome.* We showed up in Boston about a year before it actually came out, in 1983, to shoot with Redford and James Bridges, and the thing fell apart. So, Redford was the first choice. Not that Newman was the second choice but the producers, Zanuck and Brown, wouldn't let the project die. Then Newman was available and Newman was Frank Galvin.

MURPHY: *Have you had discussions about* The Choice *being made into a movie?*
REED: Yes, David Brown has the option on it. He called my agent last week; he's talking to Newman. There are only three or four stars in Hollywood: Barbra Streisand, Redford, and Newman; only about three or four. If you're a star you don't play a sequel, you don't play

television. They never played *The Sting* or *Butch Cassidy and the Sundance Kid II*. But David Brown has been talking to Paul Newman. I don't know what his decision is but he has been talking to him.

MURPHY: *When is the book scheduled to be released?*

REED: I'd say in September. Actually, I am working on the last three chapters. It takes place mainly in London and, unfortunately, when you are writing about a foreign city you have to be correct in your topography and also your legality. I take a poke at the British two-tier system of barristers and solicitors. I think it's double-dipping. I am sure I'm going to hear from the British Bar Association. In other words, a solicitor gets the case and gives it to the barrister to try. They both get a fee. But I suppose that's like in the United States where we have our referral system. Someone will get the case and give it to someone else to try it.

MURPHY: *You are presently the president of the Massachusetts Trial Lawyers Association. What do you think of the chances of plaintiffs in medical malpractice cases prevailing in trial in view of tort reform?*

REED: I hate to use that word, "reform." That's a word that the insurance industry has invented. It's kind of got a pietistical ring erroneously. Why use the word *reform?* Why not use the words *going backward?* Unfortunately, the reforms that the plaintiffs' bar have made in victims' rights over the past forty years are now beginning to erode. A victim is a victim. God, I watched *The McLaughlin Report* the other night and the attack on the contingency fee was absolutely unbelievable. The problem is that we have no spokesman to rebut these people. They get the Dan Rather types on to show how ridiculous the contingency fee agreement is when in fact it isn't. Pure sophistry but they're getting away with it. So it's erosion of human rights. What has happened in California on victims' rights? On joint and several liability? We are going back to the way the law was at the turn of the century, caveat emptor. I am sure that's going to be the next thing. President Bush is committed to do away with products liability. Florida is trying to put a $100,000 cap on everything. And I think it's Armageddon right now. If we lose here we lose. And it's going to be back where we were, suing the railroads back in the twenties.

MURPHY: *You have a high-level position, not only as president of the Massa-chusetts Trial Lawyers, but as a popular writer. Have you thought of using your fiction as a way to promote plaintiffs' rights in these kinds of cases?*
REED: Absolutely. I do that in *The Verdict*. I'm doing that in *The Choice*. I am giving a talk with defense lawyers tomorrow. I was crit-icized in *The Verdict* because eighteen Ivy League lawyers on the defense were all looking over depositions. Eighteen in one case. I always say to defense lawyers: What are you guys kicking about? Look at all those billable hours out there. We go down, they go down. I see the insurance industry getting on the media. It's pure sophistry and yet, it's effective. No question about it, we are losing all along the line. We are in retreat. I think it's a war we can't win, unfortunately. I would hate to be a young lawyer coming along now and think I'm going to show the world in products liability and medical malpractice. You're going to go bankrupt in a year, that's what you're going to do. Then you'll be back at the registry of deeds checking titles.

MURPHY: *You'd been in practice a number of years before you first came out with your first novel,* **The Verdict.** *What inspired you to begin creative writing?*
REED: Steve, I think it's in all of us. We all have a great novel in us. All of us, especially lawyers. Lawyers have human experiences you can't equal in fiction. Just crying out to be a novel. That's the grist of human emotions that a great novel is made of. *The Verdict* was an amalgam of my own experiences and things that people would tell me. And I'd jot them down. I'd take a notebook with me all the time and I would jot everything down. You might tell me something and I would jot it down. You may see it in the next novel. It's yours, but I'll steal it. Someone will tell you something and at night you'll say, "Jesus, that was great but what was it?" Jot it down. So I write from

five o'clock in the morning to seven o'clock every morning on a yellow scratch pad. I can't type, can't use a computer, so I write it down in longhand. And then I take it to my secretaries and they transcribe it. The next five to seven I get a cup of coffee and go at it again. The writing is my Walden Pond, it's therapy. I love it, I mean, it's certainly different from practicing law.

MURPHY: *Now that* The Choice *has been nearly finished, do you plan on regularly writing fiction?*
REED: No, I think it's my last novel. I love to write pieces. I wrote a couple of pieces for the *Los Angeles Times* and they pay rather well. I wrote for the *Boston Globe*. I wrote for travel magazines. That's what I'm going to do. I think this is the last novel. First of all, it's too hard. It takes too long. It takes too much out of your time. If you can't enjoy it then it's not worth it. Trying cases is the hardest job in the world and I don't get a kick out of it. I get ulcers when I try a case and I get holed up. You can't do this all the time or you're not going to survive. So this is my last novel.

MURPHY: *In* The Indictment, *why did you decide to use a different protagonist than Frank Galvin?*
REED: Frank Galvin's getting pretty old; he's like an aging fastball pitcher. He was fairly old in *The Verdict*—and that was fourteen years ago. Then there's something I have in my contract with Orion—*The Choice* is tied up with Orion—that I couldn't use the same character. So for those two reasons I thought I would use a brand-new character. In his forties, and a criminal rather than a civil lawyer.

MURPHY: *But why a criminal case? Your other cases focused on medical malpractice and products liability, which is your area of practice. Why did you decide to focus on a criminal case in this book?*
REED: I had decided here on the cause of death and time of death, which is very crucial to this story. It's a whole lot like the O. J. Simpson case.

The pathologist is going to testify on the time of death. So I studied pathology—as you have to, being a civil lawyer, even in malpractice cases. We always have death cases against anesthesiologists so I thought that would be very interesting to the reader. Time and cause of death. But criminal law always intrigued me although I never did go in for it.

MURPHY: *You portray the FBI quite negatively. They're sort of running around chasing their tails for most of the book. . . .*

REED: And they're all Jesuit products, as you know. . . . I have utmost respect for the FBI. My roommate went into the FBI. What Holy Cross or Georgetown grad didn't go into the FBI? But I've had some bad experiences with the FBI. I had an agent call me on the phone once, wanting information on my client. And I said, "Look, I don't know who you are. You say you're an agent. But even if you came and presented a gold badge to me, I wouldn't give you any information on one of my clients." But from past experiences—back to the days of J. Edgar Hoover—they cut a few corners. So I wouldn't give them any information one way or the other. But they are not pictured in the best light. Nor is the attorney general of the United States, although he's not a bad fellow. Nor is the U.S. attorney or district attorney. I do think they cut corners. I've been criticized that district attorneys wouldn't do this sort of stuff. Well, from Dick Nixon on down he was taping his adversaries. I know this happens and you've got to be naive to say it doesn't happen. I think we've all had experiences where the police cut corners and sometimes justice is held in abeyance.

MURPHY: *You mention tape recordings. In* The Indictment *there's a wiretap and bugging in Sheraton's office. In* The Choice *you also use tape recordings with regard to Moe Katz tape-recording some conversations. Is this something that you have come across in your practice? That is, people tape-recording each other?*

REED: There is one little scene in the book where I knew a client was taping me. Of course when you're aware of it you've got an advantage—at least you're aware of it.

MURPHY: *But the client didn't know you were aware of it.*

REED: He knew I was aware of it after a while because I talked like Dick Nixon waving the American flag. In other words it was all self-serving information. As you notice in *The Indictment,* they were always taking kids to the Red Sox game, and saving the rain forest, and writing wills for nothing. The trouble is when you are unaware of it you are in deep trouble. The tape recordings the FBI did in this case were all judicially approved. But then they were toying with the idea of claiming that they don't have to get judicial approval. I think we have to be naive to think that law enforcement agencies get judicial approval in every case.

MURPHY: *The IRA features prominently in the second half of* The Choice *and you use them again in* The Indictment. *I noticed there seems to be some parallel in* The Indictment *between you and John Grisham, who uses the Mafia and FBI frequently in his books and portrays them both in a bad light. Were you at all influenced by Grisham's success?*

REED: No. In fact I must confess that I've never read any of Grisham's books. So I never was influenced by what Grisham wrote. Some people call the IRA terrorist groups, some people call them freedom fighters. The line is very thin. Of course, events have indicated that my premise might be outdated. My sister said to me, "Are you a member of the IRA?" I said no. The Irish language comes from my old grandmother. She could speak Gaelic and I still remember some of her sayings, one of which is, Success is seldom forgiven among the Irish. She could say that in Gaelic.

MURPHY: *Any bites on* The Indictment *becoming a movie?*

REED: I think so. I think this would make a better movie than even *The Verdict.*

MURPHY: *Why is that?*

REED: It's got some chilling scenes in it. For example, the initial autopsy scene is a great way to open. It's got a lot more intrigue than *The Choice* and *The Verdict. The Verdict* was kind of a simple read. No one's all good or all bad in *The Indictment*. Even Dan Sheridan's no boy scout, stealing the district attorney's file through the aid of an accomplice who is the indictment clerk for the district attorney. In *The Verdict* everyone criticizes me and says, "This wouldn't happen." But you remember the guy broke into the U.S. Mails. That would get you twenty years, so even Frank Galvin wasn't a boy scout. He was doing everything wrong. He was a flawed but indomitable hero.

MURPHY: *Sheraton seems to be much the same. . . .*

REED: Yes. I think I've carried that flawed character into Dan Sheraton. They want me to do another book but I'm kind of reluctant. I want to play a little golf, after this hip gets better.

MURPHY: *You told me after I interviewed you for* The Choice *that you were finished writing novels, then* The Indictment *came out.*

REED: Right. Steve, you know when the bug bites you, you never really quit. You never really quit the law business either. I think they'll drag me out of this business.

LISA SCOTTOLINE

Former Philadelphia lawyer Lisa Scottoline left law the hard way. After the birth of her daughter, her marriage fell apart. She became a single mother and turned to writing, becoming a quick success. Her first novel, *Everywhere That Mary Went,* was nominated for the prestigious Edgar Award. Her second novel, *Final Appeal,* won an Edgar the very next year. She continued writing bestselling legal thrillers, and her books have been translated into over twenty languages.

Scottoline graduated magna cum laude from the University of Pennsylvania, where she studied under National Book Award winner Philip Roth. After earning her law degree from the University of Pennsylvania Law School in 1981, she clerked for a state appellate judge in Pennsylvania. When her clerkship ended, she became a litigator with the prestigious law firm of Dechert, Price, and Rhoads in Philadelphia.

This interview took place in 1999.

FICTION: *Everywhere That Mary Went* (1994) ▪ *Final Appeal* (1995) ▪ *Running from the Law* (1996) ▪ *Legal Tender* (1997) ▪ *Rough Justice* (1998) ▪ *Mistaken Identity* (1999) ▪ *Moment of Truth* (2000) ▪ *The Vendetta Defense* (2001)

MURPHY: *Your new novel,* Mistaken Identity, *features a defendant who is alleged to be the twin of the defense lawyer. There have been a number of novels featuring an evil twin. In fact, I just read about one recently by Joyce Carol Oates. What distinguishes* Mistaken Identity?

SCOTTOLINE: We're not sure at the outset whether this person who comes along and claims to be the lawyer's twin is in fact the lawyer's twin. Since something like that had happened to me in my personal life; I wanted to use it. I also wanted to write a thriller in which there would be a question not only "Is this person the twin?" but also, "Is this person a murderer?" Instead of the usual thriller when you're thinking about who-done-it or why-done-it, you think about the implications for family and identity as well. So it lends a richness to the thriller that it wouldn't have ordinarily.

MURPHY: *And it also has an unusual defense. At least, the defense lawyer, Bennie Rosato, starts out thinking she'd like to try a twin defense—dressing up like the defendant and actually playing off the twin feature. But then she backs down. Why does she back down?*

SCOTTOLINE: As she investigates the crime, she starts to feel at some level that her client really may be her twin. At the same time she's starting to feel that this woman is probably a bad actor. Then she reaches the conclusion that although this woman may have committed murders, she probably did not commit the murder for which she's been charged. And so the question becomes, to me anyway, a central question of justice. In such a circumstance, is it justice if the woman goes free or justice if the woman goes to prison? I suppose you could reduce it to the evil twin concept. But sometimes things like that happen. It happened to me. I found out that there was this sister I didn't know I had, who looked a lot like me and talked a lot like me and felt very twinny when we first met. You can call it corny and hokey all you want. But when it happens to you, it really is a very startling thing and profound on a couple of levels. If you're a writer and it happens, you're going to use it!

MURPHY: *I imagine that was quite a shock. How old were you when that happened?*

SCOTTOLINE: It was just a few years ago, and I'm forty-three now. I always wanted a sister and a pony, so I got one of them. Initially it was a very strange thing. It wasn't welcome.

MURPHY: *You had no idea that there was somebody out there?*

SCOTTOLINE: No! I believed that I was the oldest daughter in the family and had a younger brother, and it turns out there was a half-sister who is older than I am.

MURPHY: *What did your parents say about this?*

SCOTTOLINE: They said, "We probably should have told you." And I said, "Yeah, that really would have been a good idea." Because I really do believe in all this family stuff, and I really did in a way always want a sister. So when she appeared and couldn't be denied, I was interested in her. And my only thought in terms of resentment was, "Why didn't you tell me?" Now we're great friends. And the book is dedicated to her.

MURPHY: *In the book Bennie Rosato really can't ask her mother because her mother is mentally ill and eventually dies. So that maintains the mystery throughout.*

SCOTTOLINE: Yeah. And luckily in real life I had a way of establishing that this person was who she said she was. But I could have easily been in a contrary position and a lot of people who get "found" probably are, and as Bennie said, it's very different to be found when you didn't know you were lost. That is a completely different thing than the adopted child who's doing the finding. They have all the cards, in a way. They know when they're going to contact someone. But for me it was a complete reconfiguring of my family constellation.

MURPHY: *In* Mistaken Identity *it seems that family is very important to the characters: Bennie Rosato's grief over her mother's death, her search for her father, even one of her associates has some family issues. Is this subject of particular interest to you, that is, exploring the family lives of your characters?*

SCOTTOLINE: Your observations are very accurate and thank you for them. What's really of interest to me is characterization. At bottom I want to write a really terrific thriller. That's my job. And I like that job. To do that I have to have really believable characters. *Publishers Weekly* said that my book will change the way people think about lawyers. And I really like that. I don't think I have a secret mission, but it pleases me no end to write a fully fleshed-out character who happens to be a lawyer and have people like him or her. That's good stuff. So family is apropos only because it fleshes out character. If you take some person out of the ozone and don't tell anything else about him, you're just being a bad novelist. That sounds kind of cranky, but it's true.

MURPHY: *You've been called "the female John Grisham." But where Grisham's lawyers are generally bad people, your lawyers—though sometimes flawed—seem to be well-meaning. Have you purposely tried to portray your lawyer characters in a more positive light?*

SCOTTOLINE: *People* magazine made the comparison and I took it as a compliment, an honor. To talk about Grisham's work for a minute: some of his lawyers are heroes, like the guy in *The Firm*. Grisham generally will do a kind of underdog lawyer who fights his way through to the truth.

MURPHY: *His good lawyers generally are either just out of law school or in law school.*

SCOTTOLINE: They haven't had enough time to be tainted by the practice yet, huh? Or educated, let's say, more neutrally. I don't write with reference to Grisham. I'm a fan of his, but I don't think you can read a page of Grisham and a page of mine and mistake the two. I think what *People* magazine meant was we write fast-moving stories about lawyers and we're both former lawyers. So that's where it ends.

MURPHY: *Let me ask you about the structure of the book. The first several hundred pages, of course, deal with pretrial proceedings. The information the reader has about Alice Connolly's guilt really comes down to two things: one, she was found running from the scene and from the police, and two, she was carrying some bloody clothes. Then at trial we learn for the first time—when the policeman testifies—that she allegedly confessed. Is it fair to the reader to withhold this kind of information for several hundred pages?*

SCOTTOLINE: Sure, it's fair. I withhold from the reader what would be withheld from the defense. The defense doesn't know everything the police are going to come out with. As the book moves on, the conspirators get a little desperate and so they start to embellish. So if it wasn't foreseeable, I don't have a problem not revealing it to the reader. In fact, I write these books as I go along, and I don't have an outline. I don't know how it's going to end, and I actually don't even know what will happen at trial. I just tell the story from the outset, with each chapter saying what would happen next. I started to realize that as Bennie got closer to this conspiracy it would begin to react in some rational and some irrational ways, and even some lethal ways. So, don't think I'm holding cards. I think I play fair, and I know that because I get fooled, too.

MURPHY: *I'm not a criminal lawyer, I'm a civil lawyer. But it seemed to me that the defense lawyers should know that kind of information before the trial.* **SCOTTOLINE:** It's hazy about what gets divulged and what doesn't. In civil practice—which is what I practiced as well—there's a great temptation not to reveal things if you don't have to. Criminal practice is no different from civil litigation that way, except that there are some things you are required to divulge. But I felt pretty confident that the prosecution wouldn't have been required to divulge these things to Alice Connolly's defense lawyer.

MURPHY: *Bennie is a senior partner in an all-woman law firm. Was this an effort on your part to appeal to female readers particularly?* **SCOTTOLINE:** No. Women buy eighty percent of the fiction anyway so if you write a female main character, you probably will have a woman picking up your book. You give me far too much credit. I'm completely disorganized. At the time I started writing I think I was the only woman lawyer doing this. And now I'm one of only a handful. I want to explore some gender issues. People started asking me, people like you, good, hard questions, saying, "Do you write a book differently because you're a woman lawyer as opposed to a male lawyer?" And I don't know the answer to that yet, after six books. So I just said, "Let's just drive headlong into that wall. Let's take on gender and law and fiction and the practice all rolled into one. So let's make it an all-woman law firm and see what happens." That's the kind of career planning I do. Are you impressed yet?

MURPHY: *Yeah, that's good.*

SCOTTOLINE: Like soup, you know. Carrots would be nice, let's throw some in. And then mix it all up and see how they relate. I may be coming to the not-all-surprising conclusion that I'm not sure that men lawyers are different from women lawyers. I'm not sure that male writers are different from female writers. That's a tentative conclusion, but it's sure something I'm finding out. In the end they're all characters. There's men and women in the book and, as it happens, men are half my readership. I try to treat both as fully fleshed-out, fully realized characters. Because that's the core thing; it goes back to writing a good novel.

MURPHY: *Even with Bennie being a female lawyer, she still gets involved in some rough-and-tumble scenes, so that didn't inhibit you at all.*

SCOTTOLINE: No, it doesn't. You have to be realistic about it, though. She tends to be an athletic woman. I actually am, too, but I'm not half as tall as I am in fiction. I have other women characters who are not so brave. In *Mistaken Identity* I have Judy taking boxing lessons. I took boxing lessons to write that.

MURPHY: *I was going to ask you that.*

SCOTTOLINE: Oh, it was really fun. It was also completely different from anything I've done, except litigation maybe. To physically throw a punch in somebody's face is not something I was socialized to do. So for a character to do that, I had to write that as a girl learning to box. I don't want to have women who act like men. Women are not socialized to throw punches. I don't want to have the "tougher than thou" street-fighter girl because it's completely unbelievable. And so even though Bennie can handle herself physically, she still can't do a lot of things that some men can do.

MURPHY: *It adds a lot of flavor to the book having one of the characters be a boxer.*

SCOTTOLINE: Thank you for saying that. That was harder to write. I've always liked boxing, I always watch it on TV, and so I had to write a woman taking boxing lessons, which in a way was easy because I was. But I had to write a credible boxer and to do that I had to hang out with a lot of boxers, which was really fun and terrific and interesting.

MURPHY: *You're in a good city for boxing, too.*
SCOTTOLINE: I'm in *the* city for boxing, sir.

MURPHY: *One question on some of the trial scenes. Bennie gets into the case a week before trial and asks for a continuance. Even though this is a capital murder case; the judge refuses to give her a continuance. Did you intend that as a red flag that there's something crooked about the judge, or is that realistic?*
SCOTTOLINE: I think the answer is both. There'd been a number of continuances in the case—I think I had seven or something—and so there was arguably some basis for this judge to deny the continuance. Also I wanted to suggest that, Gee, that's kind of a fishy decision. I mean it's really hardball and so the answer is both. I feel confident that it's realistic. The judges here can be pretty tough.

MURPHY: *One of the problems with legal thrillers is having your lawyer protagonist sometimes act as an investigator. You have Bennie go and rent the apartment that was shared by the defendant and her victim and, of course, that leads to a great discovery. Do you find a tension in sometimes having lawyers act out of role?*
SCOTTOLINE: That's the perfect way to put it because really that's the whole problem in this book. As soon as she decides to represent her twin, she almost instantly acts out of role and goes so far as to take the apartment. I'm aware of this as an issue—that's why I have her lover ask her if she's crazy. At some point her identity is merging, graphically, in one of the chapters. The fact she does that tells you something about her: she is loyal, she's sometimes emotional, she's impulsive. Essentially, what's happening in this book is this lawyer is examining her own identity at age forty-something and that takes guts. I know a lot of people who don't do that even at fifty. So I give

her credit even though she is treading a line between what's prudent and what's not. Who wants to read a book about a really prudent person? That's Casper Milquetoast, isn't it? What a bore.

MURPHY: *You've met with a lot of success—you're an Edgar nominee, and an Edgar winner for one book. Even though there are a lot of lawyers writing novels out there, not many of them have won Edgars. What do you think makes your writing distinguishable?*

SCOTTOLINE: I try to make my books really entertaining, to move along quickly, to deal with some central ethical or legal or moral question, but ultimately to be fun. It's got to be a really good novel—period. No matter whether you call it a legal thriller or what. And that's what I aim for every time. This book has done really very well. I made seventeenth on the *Times* list. That's terrific. And I think it's just because it's a really good book. And I don't mean to sound vain, but that's the goal every time. Just write a really good book.

MURPHY: *Unlike some people, you did not leave law to write. You left for your daughter's birth. Where did the writing bug come from?*

SCOTTOLINE: I think I secretly always had it. I was an English major. I majored at Penn in the contemporary American novel. But you know what I think honestly, Steve, and maybe this is something that your readers would be interested in. I think I actually learned to write in law school. I learned to write what I write exactly in legal writing. And this is after six books of me teaching myself. What I've come to learn is that in the first novel I kind of massaged a sentence a lot. I spent a lot of time on a sentence, thinking that the way to make the novel better was to improve the sentences at some micro level. Although all the sentences have to be as terrific as you can make them, what really matters is which sentences are there. With a thriller you want to keep the pace moving. That's really important to me, that the book moves along. I don't want to bore anybody: at lunch, on the phone, in a book. I just don't want to do that. I think that's self-indulgent. So in legal writing, what lawyers do every day is take a set of facts, highlight the relevant facts, and throw out the irrelevant facts without a second thought. Then the facts—in a way—persuade. I did that as a lawyer every day. As a law clerk I thought the most effective briefs were the people who just told the facts and put them in a certain perspective, the perspective that that advocate was trying to encourage. That's what I do as a writer, too.

For example, you called and I was in the middle of a chapter. Right then, I was writing in a certain person's point of view. I was throwing out the facts that would slow up the narrative, I was making sure that the ones that mattered were in there, and I essentially argued it. That may be why a lot of good legal thrillers are written by lawyers. We think analytically better and we pitch things better and we write well. The best lawyers have to make the best novelists.

MURPHY: *You've got your own website, where you started online editing of your first chapter. How did that come about?*

SCOTTOLINE: Actually the website was my wedding present from my husband, who does advertising. We had been talking about writers like Kurt Vonnegut, who used to go around the country, on college campuses, and read a work in progress just to hear people's reactions. It struck me that you could do that with a computer, since I don't have time to go running around to college campuses. Just put a real draft up there, advertise it, and let people come to the site and edit it. And they actually edited it. I got thousands of responses—I read them all and replied to them. Unlike my old job, where I went out and saw actual people, now I sit in this room all day and I don't really get the interaction that I like. I like people and I'm in a one-lady job and so it enabled me to see which sentences were working and which sentences weren't working in the most important chapter of the book. I changed things based on it. It was really enlightening and fun. I got a lot of lawyers writing me. It was just a great experiment all around, and I'm going to do it for the next book, too.

GRIF STOCKLEY

Grif Stockley's first novel, *Expert Testimony,* introduced Gideon Page, a humble deputy public defender from Blackwell County, Arkansas, who struggles to maintain a balanced family life and career. *Expert Testimony* received critical praise for its sensitive portrayal of Page's defense of an insane man accused of murdering a prominent local politician.

In Stockley's second novel, *Probable Cause,* Page confronts racial tension in his defense of a black psychologist accused of murdering a mentally retarded white girl during the administration of an unusual form of shock therapy (with a cattle prod).

For over two decades, Grif Stockley practiced as a legal services attorney and worked as director of litigation of the Central Arkansas Legal Services Program in Little Rock. His practice included representing battered women, tenants threatened with eviction, and poor people seeking to obtain food stamps. He was also involved in a class action with the National Center for Youth Law in San Francisco against Governor Clinton and others to obtain more services for children in foster care or in danger of coming into foster care.

Stockley has served as an adjunct professor at the University of Arkansas at Little Rock, teaching a legal clinic. He is a graduate of Rhodes College in Memphis and the University of Arkansas Law School.

This interview took place in 1993.

FICTION: Gideon Page novels: *Expert Testimony* (1991) ▪ *Probable Cause* (1992) ▪ *Religious Conviction* (1994) ▪ *Illegal Motion* (1995) ▪ *Self-Incrimination* (1997) ▪ *Blind Judgment* (1999)

Non-Page novel: *Salted with Fire* (2002)

NONFICTION: *Blood in Their Eyes: The Elaine Race Massacres of 1919* (2001)

———————————

MURPHY: *In* Expert Testimony, *you introduce Gideon Page, a fortyish, balding, self-effacing public defender. Not your typical protagonist. Why did you choose to write about this kind of a character?*
STOCKLEY: Gideon Page is a lot like me. I kind of fit the profile except that I'm a legal services attorney and not a public defender. Gideon Page evolved from some discussions with my agent, a woman named Charlotte Gordon in New York. It seemed easier to try to make him more like me than not like me. She liked it and sent it off to Simon and Schuster, where the editor suggested we try to make it a series.

MURPHY: *There are some references in both* Expert Testimony *and* Probable Cause *to Page using the bathroom, including one where he times his urination. How do these descriptions add to the exposition of his character?*
STOCKLEY: That's a good question. He is sort of idiosyncratic in some ways. I don't know that they are going to provide the reader with a flash of illumination. But I'd never seen that done in a novel before, where somebody timed his urination. In that scene, he was painfully aware that there were other people who probably were listening to him. The walls of the house he was in were pretty thin and he was kind of embarrassed about the whole thing. That's the way he is, painfully self-conscious about the impression he's making on other people. But that's a good question, nobody's asked me that. I don't have a wonderful answer for it.

MURPHY: *Page's client in* Expert Testimony, *Perry Sarver, is charged with murdering State Senator Hart Anderson. There are a lot of questions about Sarver's insanity and whether he is faking or not. What issues relating to the insanity defense were you interested in discussing in this book?*
STOCKLEY: I didn't really look at it from the standpoint of trying to preach a sermon. I had heard for years psychiatrists talk about

whether or not somebody was faking. I know the issue of whether people can fake insanity has always been discussed at the state hospital. Of course the psychiatrists always say they can tell. I really wasn't trying to come up with anything that I could look back on in twenty years and say, Well, I wrote something that elucidated a real problem in the field. It was more in the service of the plot than anything else.

Some of the things in the book actually happened to me, not so much with regard to Perry Sarver, but in reference to people who are mentally ill and want to get out of the state hospital. At one point Gideon is called by a woman in the middle of the night and she said, "You're responsible for the death of my son." That actually happened to me. We represented individuals for years in civil commitment proceedings so I feel a lot closer to the issue of predicting dangerousness. I've represented a bunch of people who wanted out of the state hospital, where I had to deal with that whole ethical question of what the lawyer's duty was. I have felt fairly ambivalent about those kinds of things.

MURPHY: *The title of the book, of course, is* **Expert Testimony** *and the experts include the victim's wife, Caroline Anderson, who is also a psychiatrist and coincidentally treating Perry Sarver. And Jerry Kerner, who is charged with hiring Sarver to kill Anderson. He's a coke addict and a psychiatrist who has sex with his patients. Was there something about these experts that intrigued you?*
STOCKLEY: It's the whole notion of expertise in this field. Over and over again you read that psychiatrists can't predict dangerousness, and yet that's what they're called upon to do. The whole area I think is problematic at best. I wasn't really trying to preach a sermon or make a point, just to show how it plays out in a lawyer's everyday life.

MURPHY: *Gideon Page's domestic life plays a large part in both novels. His teenage daughter, Sarah, is starting to date and there are many references to Gideon's deceased wife, Rosa. And of course, the dog, Woogie, is always running around.*
STOCKLEY: Woogie was a real dog. Woogie played himself. And Sarah is based on my relationship with my daughter, who is now a junior at Harvard.

MURPHY: *A lot of reviewers have commented on the descriptions of Gideon Page's family life as sort of setting apart your novels from typical legal thrillers. Did you consciously insert the family scenes for that reason?*

STOCKLEY: It's something that I found meaningful to write. And enjoyable to write. And I had a certain amount of interest in doing that. Like Gideon, I was in the Peace Corps in Colombia for two years and actually had a Colombian girlfriend, who wasn't quite as good looking as Rosa, but she was all right. I just didn't bring her back to Arkansas to get married. But I wanted to give Gideon a love life to make him more interesting as a character.

MURPHY: *Toward the end of* **Expert Testimony** *an issue arises about gays, and particularly about AIDS. In some respects, it seemed like the AIDS issue was kind of an afterthought. Was this something you had planned or something you just decided to put in toward the end?*

STOCKLEY: That was part of the plot from the beginning. I don't think it was an afterthought.

MURPHY: *Were you trying to make any points about gay rights by including that issue in your novel?*

STOCKLEY: No, other than the fact that in a place like Arkansas there's still so much hostility toward gays. I don't think it's localized to Arkansas by any stretch of the imagination but that is a problem in Arkansas and other states that are not as liberal, say, as California. There's a lot of discrimination. It's something that we've never faced here in Arkansas very much. But I don't know that I consciously was trying to make points about that; it just kind of came out in the context of writing the book. Maybe those things are more important to me than I consciously realize and I don't give enough credit to the unconscious mind.

MURPHY: *Did you get any kind of a reaction from the Arkansas reviewers on the gay issue?*

STOCKLEY: That's a good point. Literally nobody has said one word about that whole issue in the book.

MURPHY: *That might be telling in itself.*

STOCKLEY: Yeah. Arkansas really is the South; a lot of people don't realize that. We are very polite, in the sense that we don't confront things quite as directly as a lot of people do. Whatever people felt, they certainly didn't have anything to say either in print or to my face in commenting on the book. As you pointed out, most people focused on Gideon, especially women who have read the book. What seems to be attractive to them is Gideon's relationship with Sarah and his relationship with Rainey and other kinds of domestic issues. That's the most reaction I get from people; that's what they say they like best.

MURPHY: *Your next book,* Probable Cause, *deals in many respects with race relations. A black psychologist, Andrew Chapman, is charged with manslaughter and murder for the electroshock treatment of one of his patients, Pam LeMaster. And at the same time he's having an affair with her mother, Olivia, who is white.*

STOCKLEY: Let me comment on something you just said. You picked up on something. When I wrote the first book, *Expert Testimony,* my editor noticed how much I had really written about race relations, though it was peripheral. And in talking about the second book, he suggested that I write a modern *To Kill a Mockingbird.* Anyway, I had written a play called *The Metaphysical Beast* that was pretty much about the same thing except that the psychologist was white. So I made him black in this book and I had an opportunity to explore that. The issue of race and how we deal with it in Arkansas is something a lot closer to my own concerns than the issue of gays. I'm from eastern Arkansas, which is very different from the rest of the state. It's like living in Mississippi—we're just on the other side of the Mississippi River. We still have the Little Rock desegregation case; it's still going strong. Lots of issues involving racism. It's something that's never far from our minds in Arkansas, especially if you live in central or eastern Arkansas. It's just part of the culture, and a problem that we've never dealt with successfully.

MURPHY: *You mentioned that you didn't get any reaction in Arkansas about the gay issue in* Expert Testimony. *Did you get any reaction about the issue of a black man and a white woman having sex together?*

STOCKLEY: Not one single word. Once again, I have to attribute that to the way we deal with each other. If there were people who were offended by it, they were too polite to say so. But that's a natural way we relate to each other here. If you're offended by something, you just don't deal with it unless you're dealing with a real event. Those things just are not mentioned. I actually was invited back to Marianna, a town of about five thousand where I'm from, that has more blacks than whites. I was invited to speak at a literary club, average age about sixty. They were so polite and so pleased that somebody in Marianna had published a novel, that they were generally complimentary. We just really don't talk about things publicly that upset us and we don't really confront each other much here.

MURPHY: *In* Probable Cause *Dr. Chapman gives Pam the electroshock treatment because he wants to make her life better. He's motivated by love and professional duty, just as her mother, Olivia, is motivated by love. Yet, the DA doesn't see it that way. She sees it as grossly negligent and child abuse in a sense. Does that kind of tension exist in your practice?*

STOCKLEY: That tension, I think, is real. There are some people who would swear by electric shock as kind of a last resort, though there's still a lot of controversy about using electric shock for behavior modification. I did the research and the first time it was ever done the guy actually used a cattle prod. It has become a lot safer since then, but it was a big controversy. When I wrote the play I tried real hard to focus on the ethics of using that kind of aversive stimuli for behavior modification. It's something I've been interested in for years without really ever having resolved it in my own mind.

MURPHY: *I was curious as to whether President Clinton's election has done your book sales any good by focusing attention on Arkansas.*

STOCKLEY: We'll see. Simon and Schuster's going to fly me to Washington in January for a book signing at Mystery Books. They're going to invite Arkansans who are living in Washington, and maybe there will be some kind of boosterism. I've met both Bill and Hillary and, as a matter of fact, Hillary Clinton started the legal clinic up at Fayetteville and was chairperson of the legal services board. She's always been interested in legal services and has helped us raise money for Central Arkansas Legal Services. It'd be nice to have them help sell the books.

MURPHY: *What got you started writing in the first place?*

STOCKLEY: I'm not totally sure. They let me write a sports column for my hometown of Marianna. After I got out of law school I tried to write a book about race relations in Arkansas. Then I wrote a coming-of-age novel that was set in eastern Arkansas. A friend of mine who read it said, "You should have called it *Growing Up Bald in Marianna.*" I never took a writing course. I just kept on writing and kept getting rejected. Finally I got an agent who was willing to work with a manuscript. She did a lot of hands-on editing and got me to rewrite *Expert Testimony* a number of times before she was satisfied with it. Otherwise it never would have been published.

ROBERT K. TANENBAUM

Robert Tanenbaum began his career as a prosecutor in New York City, working under famed district attorney Frank Hogan. He worked his way up to homicide bureau chief and retired without losing a felony case. Currently in private practice, he has served two terms as mayor of Beverly Hills as well as eight years on the city council.

His novel *Act of Revenge* features the husband-and-wife team of Butch Karp, chief assistant district attorney in Manhattan, and Marlene Ciampi, also an attorney but now working as a private investigator for battered women. The novel begins with the assassination of two Hong Kong nationals at the Asia Mall. Witnessing the shooting from the store's loft is Lucy Karp, twelve-year-old daughter of Butch and Marlene. No ordinary child witness, Lucy is a prodigy with fluency in several languages. While Lucy is stalked and eventually kidnapped, her father has his hands full investigating a Mob murder while her mother investigates the decades-old apparent suicide of Mob lawyer Jerry Fine.

These diverse plot lines take numerous twists and turns as first Lucy then Marlene face threats on their lives. Tanenbaum keeps momentum going with such diverse elements as Chinese Tongs, Vietnamese hit men, and Mafia turf wars, until the final explosive finish.

Tanenbaum received his B.A. degree from the University of California at Berkeley in 1965 and his J.D. from Boalt Hall in 1968. He is a member of the California, New York, and Pennsylvania bars.

This interview took place in 1999.

FICTION: *No Lesser Plea* (1987) ▪ *Depraved Indifference* (1989) ▪ *Immoral Certainty* (1991) ▪ *Reversible Error* (1992) ▪ *Material Witness* (1993) ▪ *Justice*

Denied (1994) ▪ *Corruption of Blood* (1994) ▪ *Falsely Accused* (1996) ▪ *Irresistible Impulse* (1997) ▪ *Reckless Endangerment* (1998) ▪ *Act of Revenge* (1999) ▪ *True Justice* (2000) ▪ *Enemy Within* (2001)

NONFICTION: *Badge of the Assassin* (1979) ▪ *The Piano Teacher: The True Story of a Psychotic Killer* (1987)

MURPHY: *Act of Revenge is your eleventh novel featuring Butch Karp and Marlene Ciampi. Do you ever get bored writing about the same characters?*

TANENBAUM: No, because I'm writing about the values in the criminal justice system, and how in my opinion the criminal justice system ought to operate. Nothing gets boring to me. It's something I care about. It affects our quality of life so much, and is such an integral part and reflection of what we are as people. Criminal justice is one indicia of the kind of civilization one lives in. If it's guided by due process and is effective and fair and compassionate and sensitive, then you have a system you can be proud of from a humanitarian point of view. I care that people in officialdom—prosecutors and police— behave professionally and effectively and don't abuse their authority.

MURPHY: *Some people write character-driven novels, others plot-driven. It sounds like your books—and my reading of* Act of Revenge *would indicate this—are theme-driven in terms of showing the intricacies of the criminal justice system.*

TANENBAUM: They're driven from the point of view of story to the extent that each of the books deals with different kinds of interactions between defense bar and prosecution, courts, victims, and witnesses. I hope to entertain and enlighten the reader with respect to what goes on in the criminal justice system in the way it operates and the way it ought to operate.

MURPHY: *I've heard some writers say that once they've written one book about a character they've pretty much said everything they want to say about that character. But you seem to come up with new things to say about your characters, Butch Karp and Marlene Ciampi.*

TANENBAUM: It's been a growth process. In *No Lesser Plea,* they get together for the first time, though they've known each other as assistant DAs. And they grow, as we all do in the system. I've been practicing now for thirty-one years; I graduated from Boalt in sixty-eight, and my class started in the DAs office on August 5, 1968. So in thirty-one years I'd like to believe that I've grown, matured, and have a healthier perspective than I did when I first started. And that's how these characters are.

MURPHY: *These characters are quite unusual, particularly Marlene Ciampi, who's a very aggressive, tough woman, but also can be a tender wife and mother. Why did you choose to characterize her in this way?*

TANENBAUM: She represents in large measure a conflicting point of view with her husband, Roger Butch Karp. Karp is very much procedural oriented. That is to say, notwithstanding his personal feelings about a case, the case has to be dealt with professionally. Is there factual guilt to determine the defendant's guilt? If you're convinced a thousand percent there's factual guilt, then you make the second determination: Is there legally sufficient evidence to convict beyond a reasonable doubt to a moral certainty? If there is, then you try the case. If you don't win the case, you don't go out and try and execute the defendant. The system has gone its course; you go to the next case. So, regardless of outcome, assuming due process has been respected and fairness assured, you let the system run its course.

Marlene Ciampi brings in a Sicilian form of justice with respect to how she believes the system should work. That is to say, she will get protective orders in her capacity as a lawyer representing her clients as a private investigator. But if the courts don't protect her client and the ex-husband or existing boyfriend or ex-boyfriend or ex-lover or present lover—however that individual is described—nevertheless comes back and inflicts pain and suffering on her client, she is prepared to go out and administer self-help, which is her violent behavior. That's not something her husband believes in, so there is that tension that exists between the two of them.

MURPHY: *She is more willing to cross the line than he is.*

TANENBAUM: Yeah. He is not someone who is going to cross the line. He's someone who is going to do everything he can legally: work twenty-four hours a day, seven days a week on a case, and do it legally and professionally to be effective. On the other hand, she will work hard, but if it doesn't work out within the parameters of the system, she'll go out and mete out justice in a very violent way. She hates violence. She has a violent reaction physically after she does it and recognizes she shouldn't. But that's part of her makeup and her flaw as a human being.

MURPHY: *Usually the gender roles are reversed; that is, the man tends to be the more violent one.*

TANENBAUM: This is the nineties, you know. We have a recognition that women are quite capable of doing everything that some people thought only men could do. And frankly they probably do it better. So why not involve Marlene as a nineties woman who is quite capable professionally in being an effective prosecutor and defense attorney, as well as a private investigator. As private investigators are likely to do, and/or people generally if they're not disciplined enough to restrain their violent compulsions, she engages in them. So that's one of the reasons why she's an attractive character.

MURPHY: *She's certainly a breath of fresh air. It occurred to me, reading the book, that at various points the witty repartee between Marlene and Butch seemed to have a precedent in Nick and Nora Charles of* The Thin Man *fame. Were you modeling your characters after other characters such as those?*

TANENBAUM: No. Actually the characters came to mind mostly from my readings of Agatha Christie. I find her to be incredibly informed about the intricacies of the criminal justice system and I commend her for it. She also has a series of Tommy and Tuppence Barresford, a married couple, wherein Tuppence Barresford would be solving a military intrigue breaking the German Nazi code during World War II—while the two of them were on a cruise, for example. Her husband was simply reading the *London Times* and doing the crossword puzzle while unbeknownst to him she got involved fortuitously in attempting to break the code. The Nazis on the ship, who were dressed as waiters in the dining room, were in hot pursuit of her. That type of situation was presented in a very entertaining way by Agatha Christie. It was in that regard that I thought to have a heroine in my stories.

MURPHY: *You bring together divergent elements in* Act of Revenge: *Vietnamese and Chinese gangs along with the Mafia. A lot of legal thrillers feature the Mafia, to the point where I think the Mafia is overplayed. Do you agree with that?*

TANENBAUM: I think the Mafia is overplayed as stereotypes. They're always the bad guys to the extent that the characters are based loosely now on what most writers have seen in the *Godfather* series and other movies that depict organized crime people. When I write about them I do a reverse role. They're not in the fashion that generally we have come to know them. In the series they've been helpful more often than not with respect to solving crime. So I try to avoid the stereotype of the Mob boss and his underlings that we know so well now from our culture.

MURPHY: *I was particularly impressed with your references to Asian literature and customs. Did you acquire that knowledge from working as a DA in New York?*

TANENBAUM: I had a major case into one of the Asian gangs, the Tongs, that was involved in a series of homicides, similar to what happened in *Depraved Indifference,* the second novel. It dealt with a group of Croatians who skyjacked a plane from LaGuardia. This was in 1976, before the whole Croatian issue became very popular. I had to learn a great deal about what was involved in order to prosecute the case and understand what was happening. So, similarly, I was able to get a treasure of knowledge with respect to these issues when I was investigating the crimes of this particular gang, and even the so-called Italian organized crime because the Tongs were encroaching upon their territory.

That's a whole phenomenon in New York right now. The Red Chinese are ransoming off families from the China mainland to families in American cities, particularly New York, who are paying ransom dollars to get their families out. And so you have a tremendous influx of émigrés from the China mainland into New York. That's why Chinatown today is bursting into different neighborhoods.

MURPHY: *In* Act of Revenge *you have a couple of different plotlines going. One is the assassination of two Hong Kong visitors; second, Marlene meets the wife of a Mafia don in a woman's shelter and goes on to investigate her father's suicide many years earlier. Obviously, these plotlines have to intersect at some point, which they do. In writing a book like this, do you have any concern that these disparate plotlines intersecting would be viewed as a coincidence?*

TANENBAUM: In storytelling, I think it's important to avoid the notion that characters just exist in novels for plot purposes. And I hope I avoid it to the extent that so much of what I'm writing about is really true. Nevertheless, sometimes the phantasmagorical truth appears to be over the line, over-the-top fiction. And I hope to avoid that because they in fact come together in life. Sometimes when art follows life, which it should, people don't believe it. They think it's made up.

MURPHY: *Right. I don't mean to imply it doesn't work in your book. . . .*
TANENBAUM: It's a very valid point; believe me, it's something I'm very concerned about in storytelling. I don't want it to be too complicated and I don't want it to appear—oh, lo and behold, now out of the clear blue or the ether comes floating through a resolution of various plot lines that exist. That is a concern of mine from inception. I hope to deal with it in a fashion that makes sense logically.

MURPHY: *You go back in the book to the alleged suicide of Jerry Fine from the Empire State Building. That takes you on a whole new course of investigating his partners and bringing in a lot of other issues that really have nothing to do with the Chinese, except at the end when it comes together.*

TANENBAUM: Exactly, sort of a surprise ending. I thought it would make it more interesting and entertaining.

MURPHY: *I got the sense that that jump from the Empire State Building was a true event.*

TANENBAUM: That case of Jerry Fine is a very real case and deals with a lawyer who in fact was disbarred and should not have been.

MURPHY: *You've written a couple of true crime books as well as the fiction and you've indicated that the fiction is based in large part on your own experiences. When you look at a case that you've prosecuted or investigated, how do you, as a writer, turn the actual events into compelling fiction as opposed to true crime stories?*

TANENBAUM: The two nonfiction books I did are *Badge of the Assassin* and *The Piano Teacher*, which is about a psychosexual killer in Manhattan. I knew after finishing *The Piano Teacher* that I was going to novelize these stories because I really didn't want to get involved in details, reportage, about people I had worked with. I just didn't want to reveal the innermost secrets based upon my own observations of everybody. And so then I decided it would be good to create an environment based upon my own experiences which is based upon the whole New York City district attorney scene, and create characters and story lines that would clearly reflect reality, but the reality within which had been created. So it's sort of like an enigma wrapped in a puzzle in the old Churchill description. And it makes it relatively easy. That is to say, I don't have to do very much research in order to create the world of the novels.

The difference between the novel and nonfiction is in the novel you create your own world. And your own reality. The continuing nature of the character permits the growth to take place and the transformations to occur nicely and, hopefully, a little more neatly perhaps than in ordinary life. Certainly more rapidly because you're in control of it. With nonfiction, of course, you tell it like it is, based upon what happened. That may or may not be exciting, stimulating, or titillating. But it's what happened. To do that, you have to reveal your observations, some of which occurred in confidence and in privacy. I didn't want to tell these stories by treading upon that privacy line. That is to say: if I had dinner or lunch or a private meeting with people, I didn't want to have to report that in order to be accurate. But with the novels I could still make the compelling points, I felt, and still entertain the reader. At the same time, hopefully, the reader will be that much more apprised of the criminal justice system and issues that I care about. And I wouldn't have to invade the privacy of people with whom I had worked.

MURPHY: *You've got a character in the book, Tran, who seems to me to be the archetypical wise man. I don't know if you're familiar with Jim Frey's theory that all stories derive from myths and there's always one character who's the wise old one. Did you intend Tran to be this kind of character: the voice of wisdom, but also the protector of Lucy?*

TANENBAUM: Of course, that's what he does. But he's also a character against type. He's a former Viet Cong fighter. At the end of the war, he's not Red enough for the regime that takes over after America leaves. Then his family winds up getting killed, he becomes imprisoned and escapes. So he has no great love for the Communists who were in power in Vietnam. And he's a former schoolteacher. He comes to a tragic position in Manhattan when his restaurant gets firebombed by a gang of kids with whom he had had an encounter. That's in a prior novel. He gets befriended by two of his patrons, who happen to be Marlene and Lucy, heroine and daughter. So Marlene does a Good Samaritan act by inviting him to work for her in her agency. But again that fits type because most of the people working for her in some fashion are misfits. So it's very much a misfit organization working together, not only helping others but trying to help themselves get their own life straightened out. And of course he brings with him his vast knowledge as a teacher and one who has experienced incredible sorrow and hardship and engaged in warlike behavior.

MURPHY: *You seem to be able to write books fairly quickly. I think I read somewhere you're doing one a year now.*

TANENBAUM: Right. In the nineties I did one a year.

MURPHY: *That's quite a prodigious output, even for somebody writing full-time, and I know you're still practicing somewhat. How important is it, in writing your novels, to emphasize style over the themes that we talked about earlier and the criminal justice system itself?*

TANENBAUM: My focus is clearly on making the compelling points about the stories that I'm telling, which are stories mostly that I lived through. I can let readers know that this is the way the criminal justice system should operate—not what you read about and what you're told by politicians. This is the way it can work and be effective, and yet at the same time be compassionate and sensitive. Then that's a system that we have to strive to keep in place. And when we deviate from that, when it becomes too autocratic or too neanderthalish in its administration, then we know that we've gone too far in one direction. So that to me is the major focus. That's the sole, total reason that I do these books.

MURPHY: *I get the sense that you're not the kind of writer who agonizes over every sentence.*

TANENBAUM: No. This notion of writer's cramp or being in a slump, I can understand. I don't belittle the notion that that's a potential, but the issue here is I'm compelled to tell these stories that are very important to me personally. I hope that the reader will share that point of view in recognizing what the issues are. The criminal justice system has such an important impact and plays such an important role in the quality of our lives. Both from the point of view of making sure that as victims those people who commit violent crimes are brought to justice, and at the same time that it's done pursuant to law. And I don't want to hear from people in the system that so-called technicalities are letting people off the hook, when that's not the case. These technicalities, by the way, equate to the Bill of Rights, so they're far from technicalities. The Fourth, Fifth, and Sixth Amendments are not technicalities. Ever since 1791 they were important enough to fight a major war about and they're to be cherished. So that's an important consideration with respect to everything that I'm doing in these books.

MURPHY: *You've still got a lot of writing years left and I'm wondering if you thought ahead to maybe running out of material from your cases for future novels. Do you think that will happen?*

TANENBAUM: No. It's sort of like, will the news still be reporting the inevitable car chase, and the murder du jour on the five or six o'clock news. There's too much involved in the interpersonal relations of people for me to feel as though I have in some fashion completed my task in trying to apprise everybody about what is so important about this system and the way it ought to work compared to the way it does. And how people use it for political reasons and charge people with capital punishment, for example, when they don't have the evidence to do it. And they run around with pretrial press conferences despoiling potential jury pools. These issues are so real and they happen so frequently that I feel that the vehicle I've been given to tell these stories is very, very fortunate and something that I respect greatly. I don't know how much time I've got left, but for the time I have I still have all the stories to tell.

MURPHY: *Have you thought of writing a novel not involving Butch Karp and Marlene Ciampi?*

TANENBAUM: No, not at all.

MURPHY: *You're going to stick with them.*

TANENBAUM: There may be some nonfiction I'll get into. But I certainly will stick with them in the novel form.

MURPHY: *You seem the quintessential prosecutor. Did you have any difficulty switching to the defense side?*

TANENBAUM: No. I never really got involved in much street crime because of that. I've been blessed with the good fortune of never

having to make an insincere argument to a jury, so I don't really handle that much street crime because generally in street crime if you go
by the statistics clearly most of the people arrested are guilty. You
know, you don't have the good fortune of always getting the unjustly
accused. That was the case with my defense of Amy Grossberg, the
girl accused of capital murder in Delaware for killing her newborn
baby. So I really don't handle that much street crime.

SCOTT TUROW

Scott Turow achieved literary fame in 1977 with the publication of his book *One L: An Inside Account of Life in the First Year at Harvard Law School*. Before attending Harvard, he earned a master's degree in creative writing at Stanford University. After spending several years at the U.S. Attorney's Office in Chicago, Mr. Turow entered private practice with the Chicago law firm of Sonnenschein, Nath, and Rosenthal.

His first novel, *Presumed Innocent,* became an international bestseller and is often credited with creating popular demand for legal thrillers. The book was made into a hit movie starring Harrison Ford as prosecutor Rusty Sabich. Narrated by Sabich, *Presumed Innocent* explores the tensions Sabich experiences after he is charged with murdering his colleague and former lover, Caroline Polhemus. Turow skillfully plants clues while taking the reader on a tour of the seamy side of Kindle County's criminal justice system. Until the pieces come together at the end, the reader continually wonders whether the seemingly honorable prosecutor really did kill Polhemus.

This interview took place in 1988.

FICTION: *Presumed Innocent* (1987) ▪ *Burden of Proof* (1990) ▪ *Pleading Guilty* (1993) ▪ *Laws of Our Fathers* (1996) ▪ *Personal Injuries* (1999)

NONFICTION: *One L: An Inside Account of Life in the First Year at Harvard Law School* (1977)

MURPHY: *Before you went to law school, I understand you had a manuscript that was unpublished. Can you tell me what that was about?*

TUROW: This was a book called *The Way Things Are* and it was about a rent strike on the north side of Chicago. It was not a bad book. It was not unpublishable, but it went unpublished. It was a sort of disappointing, disconcerting experience.

MURPHY: *Was it a novel?*

TUROW: Yes, it was a novel. It was about a young man who had been a draft resister and fled to Canada. When his number came up in the lottery a safe distance from eligibility, he returned to the United States. As the novel opens, his girlfriend's left him and he's literally asleep and screams in the dark. It's about his coming back to life in all kinds of different ways. To describe it, it doesn't sound like it would be that bad or that good. It was overwritten, and the biggest problem with the book was I finished it in 1974 and the market for sixties novels had sort of passed by. I've been asked why I don't publish it now and the answer is it would have been a decent book for somebody who was twenty-five years old to publish but not somebody who's forty. So it's consigned to history. I thought it was unfair when it wasn't published, but it's not a book without evident flaws.

MURPHY: *You have no plans to try to get it published now?*

TUROW: I am not unaware of the symbolism, but it sits under my computer now. I use it to prop up my monitor and that's where *The Way Things Are* resides.

MURPHY: *Did your inability to get that manuscript published lead to your going to Harvard Law School?*

TUROW: I often say that, and my frustrations with that book certainly reinforced that decision. But I had actually decided to go to law school before I sent the book to New York. I finished it in the spring of 1974 and sent it to my then agent. It was at that point in time, as I was finishing that book, that I had begun thinking seriously of going to law school. I made that decision ultimately in the spring of 1974.

I decided that if the book is published, then it's published; if it's not, it's not.

MURPHY: *Where did the idea for* One L *come from?*

TUROW: The idea for *One L* came really backhandedly. When I made this decision to go to law school, I wrote to the agent who was then peddling *The Way Things Are* in the interval between the spring of 1974 and the spring of 1975. *The Way Things Are* had been turned down at somewhere between eighteen and twenty-three different publishers. I've never had the strength of heart to go back and count the rejections, but it was many. So I wrote to her, kind of apologetically, and said that I was going to law school, just really to advise her of that. I said, "By the way, if you know any writers, it would be a great idea to write a book about law school because there is really no good nonfiction treatment of what law school is like from the law student's perspective." There was no further discussion between us about this. One day I went to my mailbox. I was living over on Fair Oaks in the city near Dolores in the Mission. Lo and behold, there's a contract to write the book that became *One L*. She had taken my letter and shown it to an editor. As far as I can tell, they were both half smashed. And thus, there comes *One L*. When I finished the manuscript after my first year in law school the editor literally could not remember why he had bought the book. He had no idea. And he called me up and said, "Tell me, why was it that I wanted to publish this book?" And I had to sell him again on his own idea.

MURPHY: *When you wrote the book, you kept a journal while you were at law school. Did your fellow students know you were doing that?*

TUROW: They did not. My closest friends knew sometime during the year what I was doing. But, in general, most of my classmates did not. There were four or five people who knew what I was up to. Most of the people who are the basis of the central characters in *One L* knew that they were being observed in this fashion, although I am not sure any of them really ever believed it was going to be anything. They all read the manuscript before the book came out. But most of my class-mates didn't know.

MURPHY: *How did you ever find the time during the first year to write* One L?
TUROW: Like many lawyers, especially trial lawyers, I've had a lot of very trying periods while I have been in practice. But I really don't think I've ever in my life worked harder than I did during my first term in law school. Writing the book and being a very intense law student was very hard. It really was.

MURPHY: *Did you ever estimate how many hours you put into it?*
TUROW: I don't know. All I know is that I really feel sincerely that I worked from September through September without any real time to myself. There were no vacations. When I sent the manuscript of *One L* to New York, it was two days before classes were going to reopen. So I had one day off and then I took a tour around Boston Harbor. That was it. During that summer we went to visit with a friend of ours who had come to Connecticut to visit her family. We went down there and saw her. I brought my typewriter. My friend Marsha is the person who really named the book. She asked, "What are you writing about?" And I said, "It's just about what it's like to be a One L." She said, "What's a One L?" I told her and she said, "That would be a good title." But anyway, when we went down to see Marsha, I brought the typewriter and continued to work.

MURPHY: *After it was published, did you get any reaction from your fellow students?*
TUROW: Oh, yes. I like to say that the reaction from the students was in a direct relationship to the light in which they were portrayed. There are a lot of composites in *One L*. Both to protect people's privacy and simply for the sake of narrative economy, a lot of different people were combined in single characters. But people nonetheless decided, Well, I'm So-and-so. If they thought So-and-so was a positive character they tended to like the book a lot. And

if they had a dim opinion of it . . . And that ran to the faculty. That was just a uniform reaction, that people liked it or didn't like it depending on how they fared.

MURPHY: *Have you had any real strong reactions from anybody who disliked their portrayal in the book?*
TUROW: I have never gone on record anywhere saying, This is So-and-so and that's So-and-so. One of my friends who is now a law professor herself runs around and tells her students, "Well, I'm Gina." Arthur Miller has always claimed that he was Perini, and I have never commented on that.

MURPHY: *And you don't want to comment on that now?*
TUROW: And I won't comment on that now. All I can tell you is that he gave an exam in his copyright course at the end of my first term which had a question that said, "You are an associate in a law firm. The senior partner introduces you to his client, Rudolph Perini. Professor Perini has undergone the indignity of having a student write a book about him. Please advise Professor Perini as to what causes of action he has against the student," who is referred to as Ray Ripoff.

MURPHY: *After law school, you went to Chicago and worked as a prosecutor in the U.S. Attorney's Office. What made you want to work as a prosecutor?*
TUROW: I was looking for an alternative to corporate practice. It was too long a distance to travel and too short a period of time to come from the Stanford English Department, where a legitimate communist by the name of Bruce Franklin had been a member of the faculty when I got there, to becoming a part of a corporate law firm. No human being is quite so malleable, I think, as to be able to traverse that kind of ground in so short a period of time. I certainly wasn't, so government seemed to me to be a reasonable alternative. I had a good sense of what some of the hazards of ACLU, Nadar-type work might have been, although it was intriguing to me. I became per-

suaded by a couple of friends of mine, principally one who is up in Seattle, that there is actually a lot of good to be done by being a prosecutor, because of the amount of discretion that you have. I had been exposed to similar arguments when I was in college by a guy named David Dick who was, at that time, a sergeant in the New York Police Department and was trying to recruit people to become cops out of college. I was kind of enticed by the argument then, and I was enticed by it when I was in law school.

I had a very good friend who was at the U.S. Attorney's Office in Chicago and I met the U.S. attorney through him during the summer I was writing *One L.* He offered me a job for the next summer and I took it. I really liked the U.S. Attorney's Office and that certainly reinforced my belief that this was really a useful thing to do as a lawyer. So when I saw that I was going to be lucky enough to get one of those jobs, I couldn't think of turning it down. Ironically, though, the thing I focused on the least was the fact that I was going to be a trial lawyer. I viewed myself as a kind of policy maker in individual cases, if not on a broad-scale basis. When I took the job I suddenly realized, Now you're going to have to try lawsuits. You don't know anything about them. I didn't think of myself as a public speaker, and so it was quite an education to become a trial lawyer.

MURPHY: *During law school, hadn't you actually prosecuted a case?*
TUROW: I did. After my summer at the U.S. Attorney's Office I enrolled in the clinical program at Harvard, which is a NITA program for the first three weeks and then a clinical component. My placement was at the Suffolk County DA's office. I ended up trying my first jury case there, which was a so-called barking dog case. But it really was about a guy who had eight dogs in a city which says that you can only have three.

MURPHY: *We call other kinds of cases "barking dogs."*
TUROW: This is literally a barking dog case. The guy who was my supervisor there, a guy named Tim O'Neill, became in some very

abstract ways some of the inspiration for Rusty Sabich. Tim said to me, "Twenty years from now you are still going to be talking about this barking dog case," and he was right! I talk about it all the time. The defendant was a man named Charlie McCarthy, of all things. Charlie's neighbors despised him. He had these eight dogs and they barked all the time and he had been tried and acquitted. He had been tried again, because of course each day was a new offense. He had the eight dogs on such and such a day and he was acquitted of that, so they took it and charged him with having eight dogs a month later and tried him again. We tried him at Christmas and of course it mistried. So he had been acquitted and mistried and no other assistant in the office would go near the case. It was then left to me to try Charlie.

MURPHY: *So did you get poor Charlie convicted?*

TUROW: Yeah, poor Charlie was convicted, although you have to bear in mind that this was the third jury trial that Charlie had had in a six-month period in the Boston Municipal Court, which was just an amazingly overburdened court. The chief judge of the court tried the case. My closing argument lasted thirty minutes. The charge to the jury took forty-five. I mean, you never heard a simple ordinance explained more painstakingly and the jury's obligation to follow the law more carefully. Charlie was convicted.

MURPHY: *You mention that one of the inspirations for Rusty Sabich came out of your experiences in the Suffolk County DA's Office. When did you actually start writing* Presumed Innocent?

TUROW: I began *Presumed Innocent* as near as I can recall sometime in 1979 and I really didn't know where I was going with it. I just wanted to write something that was in my own voice, that wasn't going to be terribly self-consciously literal and was going to be about the criminal justice system because I was already feeling very animated about it and that provided the initial inspiration for *Presumed Innocent*. But I really began writing just about characters and settings. I had this idea at the outset about—as Lipranzer said—this naked dead lady, but that was about it. The voice for Rusty—I didn't know who or what Rusty was, I knew that I wanted to do a narrative voice that was a little bit different than the traditional kind of hard-boiled American detective novel. But I had no idea where I was going with it. I just wrote every morning on the commuter train as I was on my way to work to be a prosecutor.

MURPHY: *And you did that from 1979 until when?*

TUROW: I did that from 1979 through about 1982 and I got to a point where there is a scene where Raymond Horgan hands Rusty Sabich the "B" file. I wrote it when the train was then pulling into the station downtown and I was sitting there looking at the thing thinking, "What in the hell is this? Where am I going with this?" I had no idea. I had a murder. I didn't know who had committed it. I had this election. I didn't know how it was going to turn out. Now I had this file. I had one more subplot and I didn't know what that meant. I put it aside for a couple of years and I meditated. I'd garden on Saturdays and I'd think about *Presumed Innocent* and what the plot would be, re-stucco the house and think about the plot, and after a couple of years in which I was really working on something else and thinking a lot about *Presumed Innocent*, I figured it out and then went back to it and wrote the end and then went back into the very beginning and wrote through it again.

MURPHY: *So you actually had written the book for about three years without knowing what the ending would be.*

TUROW: Oh, yes. It was 1984 before I knew what the end of *Presumed Innocent* was. It was about five years.

MURPHY: *Is there any part of Scott Turow in Rusty Sabich?*

TUROW: Oh, I am sure there's some part of Scott Turow in Rusty Sabich. I am not as quiet as he is. I am not as depressed. I am not as lonely. But there's certainly a lot of a similar worldview. There is no question about that. I am not as deprived as Rusty.

MURPHY: *Did you base the plot on any actual case?*

TUROW: I really didn't. Some of the inspiration for it, for the crime, came from cases that I saw. But those were authentic rape/murders, the cases that I saw in Boston. There was very much a question of having a finite starting point and just letting your imagination expand on it in an almost abstract fashion to see what a murder is.

MURPHY: *It is interesting that the crime in* Presumed Innocent *was different from any of the trials you had as a prosecutor. Did you find that difficult in the evidentiary part of it?*

TUROW: I didn't find it particularly difficult although I was very worried that I wasn't accurate. I think that if *Presumed Innocent* came out any later it might not have been. I think that there have been significant advances made in sperm typing and things like that that didn't exist and still really weren't perfected by 1987 when the book came out. I think any year now *Presumed Innocent* is going to be outdated in terms of its forensic evidence; I did check and make sure I was accurate then. I mean, I had seen murder cases tried while I was in Boston but I hadn't actually done one as a prosecutor.

MURPHY: *There is a reference in the book to Nico Della Guardia and a case he had prosecuted involving a black physician charged with manslaughter for an abortion. I know there was such a case in Boston in the late 1970s.*

TUROW: There sure was. The background of *Presumed Innocent*, as I said, the initial working points of *Presumed Innocent*, drew heavily from the experiences that I had in the Suffolk County DA's office. At the time that I was there, Garrett Byrne, who was an eighty-year-old man, was running against Newman Flanagan. Flanagan had come out of Byrne's own office just in the same fashion that Nico comes out of Horgan's. The case that Flanagan had used to propel himself into notoriety was the Edelin murder/manslaughter case. A horrible, demagogic prosecution of this black physician who performed an abortion in a Catholic hospital. It excited all of the ugly passions of the folks in Boston with which you are undoubtedly well acquainted. Now, in the initial drafts of *Presumed Innocent* there were reams about this and it all ended shrunk down to a couple of lines. But it certainly provided a kind of Mecca. I never met Newman Flanagan and I have no idea whether Nico has any resemblance at all to Newman, because I just don't know him.

MURPHY: *Do you know if Ray Horgan has a resemblance to Garrett Byrne?*
TUROW: Well, I can say categorically he doesn't. I met Mr. Byrne and he was eighty years old when I worked there. I think he was eighty-four, as a matter of fact. Raymond, as the plot necessitates, is a somewhat more virile character.

MURPHY: *Did you have any of the same difficulty getting* Presumed Innocent *published as you had with your first novel?*
TUROW: No, *Presumed Innocent* had all of the good fortune that my earlier efforts had lacked and there were multiple bidders for *Presumed Innocent*. It's one of those books—and in some ways I stand apart from it; I stand apart from the phenomenon—that, for whatever reasons, seemed to excite people as soon as they read it. There were a number of editors throwing huge amounts of money at the manuscript. It was very exciting, a dizzying, amazing kind of experience.

MURPHY: *Were you surprised at the response?*
TUROW: No, I was shocked at the response. My hope had been that *Presumed Innocent* would be published. When I sent it to New York I had entertained doubts about that. I really sat around and had discussions with my wife, Annette, about where I would go. "If this book isn't published, I'm just gonna give up. I'm not gonna keep doing it." And she'd say, "You don't mean that." "Yeah, I mean it. If this book isn't published, this is really not fair. This book's got a lot of commercial potential, you know, this book ought to be published." And she'd say, "It'll be published. Don't talk like that." But that's where my head was at.

MURPHY: *Any idea how many copies of* Presumed Innocent *have sold to date?*
TUROW: Well, let's see. *Presumed Innocent* sold in hardcover about

700,000 copies through Farrar, Straus. Three hundred thousand or 400,000 copies were sold by the Book Club, and Warner Books has now sold about 3.8, 3.9 million paperbacks, so we're talking somewhere in the neighborhood of five million copies and that's in the United States and Canada. There are about sixteen foreign editions so there are a lot of copies of *Presumed Innocent* out there.

MURPHY: *With all those sales, there must be some plans for a movie.*
TUROW: Yeah, the movie rights were bought before publication by Sydney Pollack. He is the producer. A guy named Alan Pakula, who made *Sophie's Choice* and *Parallax View* and *All the President's Men* is going to direct it. They're casting about now trying to get a screenplay that everybody is satisfied with.

MURPHY: *Who would you like to see play Rusty Sabich?*
TUROW: I don't have a clear preference. There are lots of late 30-ish, early 40-ish–type guys in Hollywood who I think do a really good job. I mean, everybody would do something different with the character. Kevin Kline, William Hurt, Richard Dreyfuss, Harrison Ford, there are all kinds of different names that I have heard mentioned . . . Kevin Costner. Rusty's kind of an everyman in certain ways. I think the more interesting question is who plays Carolyn and that's a tough call. Were it my movie to cast I would start there. That is not the kind of thing that movie makers everywhere will do because they start with the box office. These days the male stars tend to be bigger stars than the female stars and that's where they are going to start. They want to secure their box office.

MURPHY: *Do you have any preferences for who would play Carolyn?*
TUROW: I don't. I'm not sure that I'm familiar with all of the actresses in Hollywood that might be available. I have heard somebody say Jane Fonda at one point and I thought that was kind of an interesting suggestion. Kathleen Turner is the most commonly suggested. A lot of people mention Glenn Close, after *Fatal Attraction*. There have got to be other women who would be good but I think the point is that

you have to start with her because the man has got to play off her. She's an elusive, difficult, interesting character. As Sydney Pollock said to me at one point, "Every man who walks into that theater is going to have his own fantasy of who Carolyn Polhemus is while I gotta pick one woman to play that part."

MURPHY: *Were you influenced in your writing by any particular author?*

TUROW: The influences on me are odd ones. The writers who I admired enormously were Saul Bellow, John Updike, Bernard Malamud, whose influence I think is probably invisible in *Presumed Innocent*. I think maybe a scholar would point out that Updike is an exponent of the present tense. I'm sure that's one of the places where I got that. Then, more in the adventure genre, there were people like Conrad and Graham Greene, whose books I admired enormously, and le Carré. That's my constellation, and that looks all the way across the night sky. I consider those people to be different kinds of writers although they are all realists of one kind or another.

MURPHY: *Were you ever influenced by the mystery writers like Hammett, Chandler?*

TUROW: The answer is no and I suppose that's surprising. I am not well read in Hammett. I've been through lots of Chandler and I like it. I admire it. But if you and I were to sit down with a Chandler novel, I would go through it page by page and point out to you things that I just don't like. I don't like the hard–boiled, unresponsive central figures of those books so they really didn't engage me like all of these other kind of very internal books that I was talking about before did.

MURPHY: *Last month you published an article in the* **New York Times Magazine** *called "Law School versus Reality," in which you criticized the Socratic method used in law schools.*

TUROW: Well, the criticism of the Socratic method is old and it really goes back to *One L*. I don't feel, based on my observations of law schools, that the Socratic method has anywhere near the kind of choke hold on legal education that it did even ten or twelve years ago when I started. But I do feel that the methodology and the curriculum are in dire need of revision. There has been a lot of controversy that surrounded the publication of that article. I had all kinds of mail on it, particularly from law school teachers, some of whom think that I had absolutely no right, as somebody who is not a law school teacher, to comment on this. The theory being that since I'm not on the law school campus every day I must not know what I'm talking about. Other people think it's great. But I thought about this subject for many, many years because *One L* has made people sort of turn to me with their own law school experiences. And I feel strongly that the law schools, whatever their many virtues in teaching certain kinds of intellectual skills, fall down in training lawyers in the sense of instilling any kind of professional values. And by that I mean that they have really steered clear of a deep, complex contemplation of what it means to be an attorney. There's lots of thought about the law but very little thought about the profession. I really think that's something that is severely lacking in the law school curriculum and it's something that ought to be, in and of itself, an area for examination.

MURPHY: *If you were the dean of a law school, what changes in the curriculum would you make?*

TUROW: I think the most significant change I would make is that I would move courses in professional responsibility into the first year. There are about ten or twelve law schools around the United States that do that. But certainly the first revision I would make is to move professional responsibility into the first-year curriculum and to begin at the threshold asking students what it means to be a lawyer. And the only way you answer that question, I think, is by defining the duties and responsibilities of an attorney. It just seems to me, as I said in that article, that's what you really want somebody to start thinking about the day they come through the door. Do you really want them to think about personal jurisdiction or do you want to say to them, "You've got a client. He's on trial for his life. He comes to you and says that he's gonna lie about what happened or he tells you a story that contradicts what happened before or he tells you a story that's somewhat inconsistent or he tells you a story that's slightly inconsistent." And to take people through to find for themselves what the responsibilities are.

The reason I think that's important is there are so many lawyers who come out of law schools who are not equipped by the law schools to even confront what they end up dealing with in practice. I'm not talking about skills. The best way to learn to draft a contract is to draft a contract. That's not what I'm talking about; I'm talking about an intellectual framework that will let people think in advance about what they're going to be about as lawyers. And there is very little of that in law schools, at least to my observation.

I refuse to defer to the law school faculty members who want to say that because I'm not on a law school campus every day I don't know what I'm talking about. I talk to plenty of law students; I hear about plenty of curricula, and I still think virtually all of them fall short of what I had in mind.

ALFREDO VÉA

San Francisco criminal defense attorney Alfredo Véa's second novel, *The Silver Cloud Café,* was released to excellent reviews. On the surface a murder mystery, the book turns out to be much more, taking the reader on a wild magical ride through different worlds, both ethereal and earthly. When a drifter confesses to a brutal murder in San Francisco, the case appears to the police to be open and shut. As Véa retraces the pasts of the accused and the victim—to the migrant worker community in Stockton in the late 1950s and a children's Passion Play competition in the Philippines—the reader begins to question reality. Véa's cast of characters—angels, disgraced priests, a prostitute whose mother was a nun, hunchbacked dwarfs, and a cross-dressing bouncer—both enthrall and challenge the reader. Even the lawyer has an unusual background, having been raised among migrant workers where he witnessed a killing that relates in disturbing ways to the present murder. As Véa blends the past with the present, the spiritual world with the earthly world, he creates a marvelous tapestry unlike any other fiction produced by today's bestselling lawyer-authors.

Véa earned his undergraduate and law degrees from the University of California, Berkeley. Raised in the migrant worker camps of the San Joaquin Valley, he was drafted into the army at the age of seventeen, spending nearly a year and a half in Vietnam during the time of the Tet Offensive. He has devoted his legal career to criminal defense, first as a public defender, now in private practice.

This interview took place in 1997.

FICTION: *La Miravilla* (1993) ▪ *The Silver Cloud Café* (1996) ▪ *Gods Go Begging* (1999)

MURPHY: The Silver Cloud Café *starts with a murder, but it's not a typical murder mystery by any means. One thing you do is interpose time. You flip back and forth between the late 1950s and the early 1990s, but also within those time periods. Did you use this technique for any particular effect?*

VÉA: I learned something about this effect from listening to Indian storytellers—American Indian and East Indian. They have storytellers that would tell a story for twenty-four to twenty-five hours in a row. They build these repetitive signposts that tell them, "I'm here now, here is a digression, let me get back to the main story." Digressions are the things that the Javanese and the East Indians hunger to hear. The same is true with visual art. If you study visual art, you see digressions from the initial sight.

I'm repulsed by the ideas of American history and what we consider a history to be. Because it's so much more organic and human than that. There isn't a human being out there on Montgomery Street right now that you couldn't pull aside and with a few questions get an incredible history going. And that history, each thing, would remind the teller of something else. You would have these digressions that change the color, change the hue of that moment. That's the way I like to hear a story. I hate chronological order. It's boring to me, but I really like to flesh out the story and give people enough ammunition so that later on they're well loaded and they can see what it is I'm saying to them at the end.

MURPHY: *Rather than surprise them?*

VÉA: Hopefully they'll be surprised, too. But then they have to ask questions about that surprise. What do you really mean by the surprise? Is the surprise really happening in actual life? Did this guy really jump off the roof over here? Why is he making this analogy with Simon Magus? Why does this woman have a mirror in her left hand? Why are these things happening? They need to know that the writer is serious about these kinds of questions, rather than just mistakes that the professors pull out of a work.

MURPHY: *There's a reference in the book to the linear way of thinking of western people. This book clearly is not a linear book. Is there something about the Hispanic culture that lends itself to a nonlinear way of thinking about the world around us?*

VÉA: There is. In *La Miravilla*, my first book, there is a discussion of linguistics because my grandfather spoke Yaqui and Gaelic. He had some Irish friends, but he didn't like to speak Spanish because he hated the Spanish. My grandmother is a Spanish Catholic. The conflict between the two was a model of the conflict in Mexico between the Spanish Catholics and the indigenous people. In this instance, I was the battleground. My grandmother baptized me forty, fifty times against my grandfather's wishes. He was a very kind man and he really didn't care what my grandmother did.

That book is written so that someone who has never spoken a word of Spanish in their lives can feel what it's like to speak Spanish. It takes twenty percent more words to say a sentence in Spanish than English. I tried not to do that too much. Some of the Yaqui and Aztec wordings are not iambic. They are dactylic, so I change the stresses on a lot of these chapters when there is the Yaqui presence. And I removed a lot of European archetypes in the book and just filled it with native American Irish and African archetypes to create this whole world that works just fine.

Also, in the Mexican Indian world, the spirit life is more alive at night than daytime, whereas in our lives here we think of nighttime as empty. That's not true for Indians. That's not true for West Africans. And probably not even for Irish. So the books are written that way to try to fill the nighttime and remind people who they really are. They're not television people and they're not Internet beings—that doesn't define us. There are a lot of things that define us which require a little bit of looking and some appreciation.

MURPHY: *There's also a strong element of the supernatural or spiritual world in* The Silver Cloud Café. *The reader's never sure whether something is actually happening or if it's in another dimension. What role does that play in your writing?*

VÉA: I got that from my grandparents, too. There is a different kind of spiritualism in the second book than the first one, because I've put in Cabala, Gnosticism, and others. But I wanted people to see the other worlds within our world. That's why the specifics about San Francisco. They're walking up the street looking at specific things in San Francisco but other things are happening that are not normally seen. Mulciber, the architect, is mentioned in there. He is the architect of Hell.

One of the frameworks of this book is Dante's *Inferno*. San Francisco obviously is the inferno. That's why the Tongan transvestite is named Beatrice. And I wanted people to take a close look at what we've become. And there are so many people here and so many things to value. Again, the worlds within worlds. And that is why the Cabala is there, the seven earths and seven heavens, which describes things in terms of different worlds. It would be nice if our model was that way. We could accept the worlds within us, other than needing this neon myth floating above our heads about who we should be and who we shouldn't be.

MURPHY: *I got the impression that the different worlds were not just the seven worlds but the different worlds inhabited by the Mexican Americans, Filipinos, Hindus, the gay people. These are all different worlds, and their experiences are so much different.*

VÉA: It would be nice if "different" in our culture didn't have a negative connotation. I listen to Japanese Americans talking about their experiences and they say, "I don't understand what happened. I felt white." Why should they even have to feel that in order to be accepted? What really bothers me is that there is no such thing as positive race. There is racism, there's some sort of nihilism in between, and nothing after that. People who believe that they are the most beneficent about race say, "I don't see color." That's the best they can do. Well, I have a color. That's one of the things that I'm talking about in this book. There are positive aspects of race and I want them out here. They are why we are who we are. People come to San Francisco not to see the Anglo-Saxons, but the Russians, the

Mexicans, and the Guatemalans in the Mission. They want to go to Chinatown, see the Irish out there on Irving Street.

Why isn't it an institutionalized part of our psyche that this difference is great? Maybe because we have such a savage, savage sorrow in our conscience for the number of people who have died in order for us to put up the American dream over their tombstones. We have these reservations filled with sad people, and the amazing thing about Vietnam is the highest number of draftees put into the infantry were American Indians, the absolute highest. Right in the infantry. A draftee takes an exam at boot camp. If he has a pulse, he passes the exam, and doesn't go into the infantry. I'm serious. It's an idiotic exam. For example, "What would you rather do? Fondle a woman's breast, go to a movie theater, or lead a team into combat?" Okay, tough. This is really tough. I was insulted by the stupid test. But every Indian I ever saw in Vietnam was in the infantry. This book I had that has a lot of the actuarials on that bears it out. These guys got savaged. Some reservations lost three hundred young men. And they went after Chicanos. There was something about East Los Angeles that changes nice young Mexican kids into savages so a lot of those guys were in the infantry. I hear it every day when I go to talk to college classes. There is no positive aspect to race. That's absolutely wrong, and I want to do something about that, and I want other people to do something about that.

MURPHY: *Do you think there is a tendency in this country to whitewash everybody, sort of pretend there are no differences out there?*
VÉA: You see it now. On the Internet. On the commercials on TV: no gender, no race. Why is that positive? What's going to happen to us? Sometimes I wonder whether or not it used to be just a puritanical land grab. Think about it. All the real estate agencies in Hawaii are owned by churches. All of them. Puritanical land grab. They are doing it in Samoa now.

MURPHY: *I understand that you did a lot of research for* The Silver Cloud Café. *What sorts of books did you look at?*

VÉA: I read a lot of history of the Philippines, migrant workers in the Philippines, and the history of migrant labor in California, the laws of the State of California, especially in Stockton, the antimiscegenation laws. I read a lot of Cabala, which is tough reading. A lot about the Gnostics. Because this was an alternate world. The gnostic world could have been our religious world but it was stomped out. It was a feminist world that could have existed until the Council of Nicaea in 327 when everything that smacked of feminism was removed from the Bible. The only thing left was the Song of Songs. All these alternate worlds I had to study. Books about the Magus heresies, about saints, histories of saints, lives of saints. The women in the taxi dance club were all built around the idea of sainthood. All to get across the idea. These Filipinos—every Friday night—would go into Stockton to dance in these clubs. If they wanted romance, they would go to the taxi dance clubs. These women there were sanctified to them. As a little boy this is how I saw it. These saintly women. And these brown men, these Mexicans, these Filipinos, were my angels. They took care of me. They made sure that I was taken care of, that I learned how to read. They taught me math out there. I was so scared when I finally went to school. I'd never been really socialized in school, but I was so ahead of everybody.

MURPHY: *That was a great story about Father's Day at school, when the boy was embarrassed because he didn't have a father, and all the migrant workers showed up.*

VÉA: True, absolutely true. It still kills me. It took me years to really appreciate the thing that happened with those migrant workers. I wanted to build a story dedicated to these men who cared about me. I thought about them being my angels, my guardians, my protectors, and so I started learning about angels. Why not? Why can't angels be brown, and hunchbacked midgets and homosexuals? These are all real people. So I learned something and I learned it a lot. And then I used part of it in the book. It makes me feel like I'm in control of what I'm writing.

MURPHY: The Silver Cloud Café *intersperses Filipino people with Mexican, Hindu, and others. Intersperses their languages, too, which really made it compelling.*

VÉA: I love to do that. I love to hear it, it's a reality. Language is like the crucible of the culture, the most important one. If you go to Woodland now there are two restaurants in Woodland where you can get carnita curry. I have a friend named Jorge Sing, I have a friend named Mohindru Gomez. There is the confluence of culture right here and they are trilingual. They speak Hindi, Spanish, and English. And some of the phrases they come up with are absolutely poetic. And the food is amazing.

MURPHY: *The book emphasizes Catholicism, with the workers from the Philippines and the Passion Play, and the Mexicans with the Christero Wars. The Catholic Church doesn't come off too well in the book.*

VÉA: Well, that's true. Especially my feeling about the Church in Mexico. It abandoned the people in the Christero Wars. I think in the Passion Plays it abandoned the people in the Philippines, too. Their expectations are so high and their returns are so small and the Church makes a lot of money. But it's an irony in the book: I've never seen people more religious than these migrant workers.

MURPHY: *The Church looks terrible yet it motivates people to continue living.*

VÉA: That's right. It was the thing they brought with them. It was the thing that held them up. They had altars at each end of the Quonset huts. They were amazingly moral people. They'd get in fights because they were tribes of men. Sometimes somebody would get cut, but generally that was being dealt with because there were no police; we never called the police in the fields. You had no recourse in court; things were being dealt with one person to one person. But generally the level of morality was enormous, and I was always being told things in those terms. My memory of that time is such a tapestry of religious myth of those angels, those crazy angels floating around. Plastic angels at the top of the Quonset are huge symbols in my memories and my dreams.

And one of the things I try to do when I write these books—I don't know if it's egotism—is to make a tapestry that matches my memory of these people. It is one of the ironies of our lives that our childhood lasts such a short time. As children we're disabled by lack of experience, then enabled by an incredible imagination. And as adults we would, hopefully, have a fully empowered mind, we keep probing that disabled, enabled past. We can't really do it; there isn't a match that allows us to really do it; but we come as close as we can. And in some of us it causes great pain to do that. Things were huge to us then.

MURPHY: *You use a lot of real San Francisco judges and lawyers in the book. Did you actually get permission to do that?*
VÉA: Yes, I got permission from them. Every writer I know does it, they use their friends in these things. Why make up a name? Nobody outside of San Francisco is going to know them. Plus it recognizes them. It's better than a Hallmark card.

MURPHY: The Silver Cloud Café *seemed to me, in many ways, to be a combination of Gabriel García Márquez and John Steinbeck. Were those people influences in your life, in your writing?*
VÉA: Oh, yeah. John Steinbeck very early. I like some of his stories better, though, than *The Grapes of Wrath*, which bordered on absolute socialism and scared a lot of people. Yeah, it did. And so did Márquez. I love Márquez, I think there's a lot of freedom about his books. I worry sometimes about magical realism becoming formula, though I don't think I've done that. I've tried hard to make sure that that doesn't happen. That there's a reason for everything, rather than just trying to sell a magical realism book.

The Grapes of Wrath was the first time I'd read anything that related to my life experience; I had a lot of friends who were Okies in the fields. Except for one or two times, I never had a real experience with racism. Because I was so far out there in these fields. I did have a sense, however—and this is where *Silver Cloud Café* started—that these migrant workers felt they were living an imitation of life, not a real life. Most people out there were living real lives, you know . . .

MURPHY: *They were on the edges.*

VÉA: Yeah. They were just on the edges, faking it. And they were right. That's how they were being treated, and still are. Some of the guys that were evicted from the International Hotel were guys I knew as a kid, in the fields of Stockton, and in the Central Valley and Imperial Valley. I was out there with them. I came out here and there they were, in the last days of their lives, being evicted from their homes. What a miserable thing to do. They had to use that property.

It's still a hole. It was mean spirited and ridiculous. And a perfectly nice application of thinking without real regard to history. Which is why I write about it all the time. I try to tell the reader—this is here, let's see where it is historically. There's an organic life behind all of this. There are lives behind all of this.

MURPHY: *As a writer, do you see one of your roles to correct the inaccuracies and the mythology in America?*

VÉA: Oh, yeah. That's my crusade. One of my crusades. Another one of my crusades is to get Chicano kids and Indian kids and black kids to look around and raise the bar in their writing. You know, one of the things that happens is that Chicano American writing is in its own little category; it's like an affirmative action category. A lot of people just slide off into it. But it's the poor Irish in this country that made American literature for two centuries. Without regard to their Irishness, really, even though it was always there.

We need to do the same thing, too. There's an intellectual tradition in Africa; there's one in Mexico. What happens to it when it crosses these borders? I want to point that out. I want kids who are suffering from biculturalism to look at it in a heightened state, rather than from some folk-art state that doesn't exist here. I want people to read Brendan Behan and Márquez. Right now, so many kids I talk to in universities, especially Chicano kids, ask me, "Why should I read Japanese literature?" They have that same myopia now that the larger culture around them has. That's my other big crusade aside from wanting to write.

MURPHY: *You see a lot of books that are categorized as Asian American, Mexican American, black, lesbian writers. It seems that the publishers, at least, are trying to categorize writers by ethnic identity. Do you think this does more of a disservice to the writers than otherwise?*

VÉA: I can see the reason in the beginning. They see a cognizable market out there for this particular writer. But I think it eventually does a disservice because you tend to have co-opted the moment. You read one lesbian writer you don't need to read another one. It denies the person and the art after a while. This issue has been gone over, it's tired. Yeah, I think the writers also have a responsibility to be more universalist and say, "I don't want to be categorized this way, I want to be categorized this way secondly. I want to be an American writer first; these other categories might have some bearing on what I do, but the issue should be whether or not the words I put together add up to art." That should be the issue.

MURPHY: *You've obviously got a love of writing. What do you think a similar love of writing or reading would do for minority kids generally?*

VÉA: I deal with a lot of minority people as a criminal defense lawyer. I'm not a linguist, I'm not a psychologist or a sociologist, but I do know that given a wider vocabulary, whether that vocabulary be literal in terms of the number of words in one's mind, or a vocabulary of poems, or a vocabulary of writers, your personal expectations are expanded. Your own thoughts get larger. I think that words are the pockets that ideas go into. I talk to kids all the time charged with murder who never read a novel. They endure. They endure and exist on five hundred words.

MURPHY: *You're kidding!*

VÉA: No. Absolutely. They've never heard Mozart. There are so many "nevers" in their lives. Most of my clients have never even had an alarm clock to set because they have nowhere to go. They have tiny,

tiny little lives. So when you have a tiny life, that's your expectation of the person next to you and there's nothing stopping you from hurting him. You don't develop morality. I think that the more you read, the more ideas you're exposed to, the more you realize that you are alive, and that's what all those books on your shelf say—we're all alive together right now.

MURPHY: *I know you're working on a third book and it will draw on your experiences in Vietnam.*

VÉA: Yeah. Less about Vietnam than about its impact on people. It's hard for people to understand how it is that this load is different than the Korean War load, or Desert Storm load, or World War II. Why is it that these guys are living under bridges, begging on street corners, having a difficult time dealing with that war? There was something very different about that war. It was a hands-on war. It was also a minority war. It was happening at the same time the Civil Rights movement was going on. Weird things happened. The soldiers weren't told. The black soldiers. No one was told Martin Luther King had been killed until five days later because Washington was afraid the African American soldiers would stop fighting. So on April fourth, when Martin Luther King was killed, no one knew. April eighth they knew and they only knew because Hanoi Radio broadcasted it. So here are these guys fighting Vietnam and America at the same time and had the conundrum of the U.S. Army being the only place you could sit down and eat with white guys.

One thing that happens in the third book is something that we used to do in Vietnam. We used to call it "supposing." Just to get our brains right after something really terrible happened. I couldn't sit around and cuss all day long—you become really a vile human being, and your language deteriorates, everything deteriorates, an insect. But I started this thing of "supposing" and we would all sit around and "suppose" a scenario. Suppose there had never been slavery in America. That was one of the favorite scenarios for the black soldiers. They would talk about that. Suppose the slaves hadn't been brought here, if they'd gone somewhere else. And we'd develop this huge thing. We would ache to get to it and I feel that same ache now in writing. We develop the scenario where Africans went to Spain and France, and blues and rock and roll started there, not here. Jazz would start in northern France. As a result, in the entire world the predominant language would be French, not English. What that says in a backward way about the contribution of African Americans as a result of their music, which many linguists agree with now, is that the predominant language of the world is English because of the slaves.

It's these confluences of cultures that generate the real culture in America. It wasn't the English. It was the Irish who were being oppressed by Cromwell, by the famine, who came here, and the Scotch Irish who generated culture. The collision between the Irish and the blacks changed music forever here. The collision between Irish, Welsh, and Mexicans developed country and western music. That's what happened here. Not some exalted English model. Unfortunately, minorities in America always have to assail the canon. The canon is, "Columbus was a great guy." We have to assail that with realities of Columbus, and we have to do it every year. We don't have a mechanism here for incorporating these other true facts into our canon. We love the mythology. Our racism was based on that.

One of the supposings—it was my favorite, it's in this third book—is what would have happened if Cortez had landed at Plymouth Rock and the Pilgrims had landed in the Yucatán. One of the primary things is that Mexico's mestizo culture, they intermixed. The Spanish sent letters home: My God, they're all naked. You know, there are breasts everywhere, I'm in heaven. The Puritans sent letters home: They're all naked. There are breasts everywhere, it's an abomination in the eyes of God. Where was the difference?

MURPHY: *Do you plan on writing about the actual experiences of Vietnam?*
VÉA: Only one actual experience. I think that's been done. And people have seen explosions, even though it's never real until you hold

somebody's arm when it goes limp. It's never real, you can't even come close here. So I want to do it a different way to try to get to the experience and how it makes guys I know feel, how it makes me feel now. So it's an unusual format. Hopefully, it won't be characterized as a Vietnam War book.

WALTER WALKER

San Francisco personal injury lawyer Walter "Skip" Walker published five novels from 1983 to 1992. Although his novels met with positive reviews, sales were spotty. Since 1992 he has written two novels and published none. Despite this setback, Skip keeps writing, hopeful that his talents will once again be appreciated.

In *A Dime to Dance By,* former high school football star, and now second-rate attorney, Chuckie Bishop whiles away his time sharing stories at the local bar with his drinking buddies. Forced by his boss to undertake the defense of an old high school friend who shot a man in the line of duty as a police officer, Chuckie suddenly finds himself in the middle of a political scandal that will rock not only the foundations of his town, but everything he knows about himself. The book won the Commonwealth Club Award as best first novel.

Skip has enjoyed considerable success as a plaintiff's lawyer. He has tried or argued nearly one hundred cases in various forums, including thirty jury trials, six of which have resulted in seven-figure verdicts. His successful representation of plaintiffs in difficult legal situations once caused him to be featured in a supermarket tabloid under the heading, "The Lawyer Who Makes Crime Pay."

He is a graduate of the University of Pennsylvania, where he studied creative writing under Philip Roth, and Hastings College of the Law.

This interview took place in 1989.

FICTION: *A Dime to Dance By* (1983) ▪ *The Two Dude Defense* (1985) ▪ *Rules of the Knife Fight* (1986) ▪ *The Immediate Prospect of Being Hanged* (1989) ▪ *The Appearance of Impropriety* (1992)

MURPHY: *You've now published four novels, most of them with pretty good reviews. Why haven't you achieved the notoriety of other lawyer-authors, such as Scott Turow?*

WALKER: That's something that's puzzled me, I suppose, as much as anybody else. The process of publishing a book is something that really takes quite a long time. I first started writing when I was in law school at Hastings, and about the time I graduated in 1974, I finished my first novel. I was working for Phil Burton, who was the congressman from San Francisco, and I asked his press agent if he knew any literary agents. And he said he had a great one for me. I contacted that one and that person claimed to be delighted to be representing me. Unfortunately, he was located in Milwaukee, which is no place to have a literary agent.

Through a long, involved process, by 1980 I finally had an agent in New York, which is where you have to have one. I wrote what at that point was my fourth book. It was called *A Dime to Dance By* and the first publisher to whom we took the book was Harper and Row and they agreed to publish it. At the time I was just so delighted with being published that I didn't care if they were going to pay me money or promote me or anything else. When the book came out it got a lot of good reviews, ranging from such publications as *The New Yorker* to *Penthouse*, and all the newspapers who picked it up liked it. So at that point I kind of thought I was off and running.

But after three books with Harper and Row I was still getting good reviews and only moderate sales. So I thought the same question that you've asked me: Why is it that I'm not getting more attention? I thought I could either assume it's because my books weren't deserving of more attention or I could assume that my publisher wasn't promoting me the way I would like to be promoted, the way other authors are being promoted. So I elected to switch publishers and go with Viking, and Viking just published my fourth book, *The Immediate Prospect of Being Hanged*. Again I've gotten tremendous reviews on this book from the *Wall Street Journal* and *USA Today*, among others. Still and all, despite the attention, my name doesn't seem to be sticking. So I can't answer beyond that.

MURPHY: *I've read in some of the reviews that you consider your books to be ones of moral ambiguity. What do you mean by that term?*

WALKER: I think that I pose questions in my books as to what is the right thing to do in a situation of stress. As a trial lawyer, I see people functioning in stress all the time and I also see that there are two sides to many stories. As a human being living at this point in time, I see that what is the right response for some people isn't necessarily the right response for others. A lot of times I have pursued the question of: Is the right response that which society tells you you should carry out, or that which you feel in your heart and your soul is the right thing to do? For example, in my book *Rules of the Knife Fight*, a lawyer is asked to defend a friend of his who has committed a murder and whom he knows has committed murder. The question is: Society would say that the right thing to do is not to provide this murderer every possible assistance; but as a matter of friendship, isn't that really the right thing to do, to do whatever you can for your friend? I don't give answers to these questions, but I certainly delve into the issues and try to present them in such a way that the reader might ask him- or herself the same. That's what I meant by moral ambiguity. In other words, there can be more than one moral response to a situation and it depends on whose morality is being applied.

MURPHY: *You mentioned that you started writing when you were in law school and I read that you did start writing after reading a Ross MacDonald novel. Is that true?*

WALKER: What happened was I had gone to undergraduate school at the University of Pennsylvania and had gotten interested in creative writing. I knew I could write well and kind of worked up my courage to the point where I took a creative writing class and I did well enough there. I was asked to be in a special seminar with Philip

Roth and Roth rather discouraged me in my writing. He said there wasn't enough sex or violence in what I was writing. At the time I thought that advice was a little peculiar coming from him. So I elected to go to law school rather than follow it.

But while I was in law school, I started reading a lot of mystery novels and in particular I became enamored of Ross MacDonald. I thought that the settings he was creating in his books were just fascinating. I couldn't put them down. But invariably I would get to the end and be disappointed because there was always some sort of mother fixation or Oedipal complex that was the key to solving his mysteries. After I read about seven or eight, I remember throwing one across the room and saying, "Jesus, I can do better than this," which wasn't really true. I don't think now I can do better than Ross MacDonald but I certainly would have more variety to my solutions. That was the basis that caused me to sit down and start writing a novel that ultimately was never published but was my beginning in the literary field.

MURPHY: *You actually wrote three novels before you first got published?*
WALKER: Yeah. I wrote a novel called *The Hot Dog Man* about a San Francisco private detective. I tried to incorporate all of the good things from Ross MacDonald novels and change what I thought was the bad thing about MacDonald novels. That was the one that my first agent thought was so great and he encouraged me to immediately write a sequel—which I did and which was no good whatsoever. Then, with a little more time and consideration, I wrote a third book involving the same character. That book was ultimately published as *The Two Dude Defense* and it's really the only detective mystery that I have written, but it was published after *A Dime to Dance By* came out and got good reviews. *A Dime to Dance By* was kind of a peculiar cross-genre book. It wasn't really a mystery at all, but reviewers, bookstore sellers, bookstore owners were not one hundred percent sure how to classify me. When *The Two Dude Defense* came out they said, "Ah-ha, I see he's a mystery writer after all." So my third book that was not published the first go-round,

ultimately was published after I had some success with another novel.

MURPHY: *It's interesting that Philip Roth encouraged you to have more sex and violence, because the novels you have published seem to have a lot of sex, particularly adultery. In* **The Immediate Prospect of Being Hanged** *there is adultery and in* **A Dime to Dance By** *there is adultery.*

WALKER: I guess that's true. I'm not sure if they have a lot of sex in terms of words per page or scenes in the book, but certainly there is sex in each of those novels. The issue of adultery does come up, I suppose as tangential to these questions of moral ambiguity that I at least think I'm posing. My characters are never perfect human beings.

MURPHY: *In* **The Immediate Prospect of Being Hanged** *your main character is not a detective or district attorney but a litigation assistant. Why did you make that choice?*

WALKER: That's a good question. Nobody's asked me that question yet. I did not want him to be a private detective although his role is as a detective employed by the district attorney's office. What I found fascinating about the character was he was quite clearly much smarter and more capable than his boss, who as a thirty-six-year-old district attorney had a very good position for his age and yet was constantly aspiring to something more, such as being congressman or governor or United States senator. I wanted to do something of a comparison between the capable, competent person who had apparently no ambition whatsoever and the person who was far less competent but was just consumed by ambition. Also, the position he was in allowed him to be something of a director of the events that were taking place and that would ultimately lead to the trial where everything was revealed; and, of course, he turns out to be a key player, not only in the investigation, but unwittingly in the solution of the case. So it just seemed that that was the ideal position for that particular character.

MURPHY: *Why have you chosen the first person for three of the four books that have been published?*

WALKER: I suppose because it gives me an opportunity to make cynical remarks out of the corner of my mouth while I'm writing and it allows me an opportunity to respond to certain situations without going into a great deal of explanation. In other words, the reader can follow what the first-person narrator is saying and disagree with him, rather than be spoon-fed what the reader's reaction should be. So I kind of enjoy writing in the first person. It's sometimes easier to get into the character, to sit down and immerse yourself in the character. Quite often you know which way the scenes are going to go, but you don't know the lines of dialogue until you get there. So as the first-person narrator, a lot of times you can respond as you, the individual writer, might do if you were placed in the situation in which your character is placed. Sometimes that can just be fun.

MURPHY: *The Immediate Prospect of Being Hanged has gotten very good reviews, but some of the critics have made points about certain aspects of the book I want to ask you about. One is, you've been criticized for the long historical opening about Woodedge. Why did you use that?*
WALKER: "Woodedge" is actually the name I gave to the town of Weston, Massachusetts, which last I saw had the highest per capita income in Massachusetts. It was the town in which my father grew up and my grandfather owned a fairly large piece of property there. My first book, *A Dime to Dance By*, and my third one, *Rules of the Knife Fight*, were set in the city of Quincy, which is the other side of Boston. That is where my mother's family came from and is a much more working-class city because there was a shipyard there. In growing up I heard a great many stories about my father's town and I had a certain perception that it was quite a bit different, obviously, from Quincy.

But what I did was I went to Weston. I went to the library. I went to city hall. I talked to some of the old town historians, people who were now in their eighties who have a good many memories of what the town was like when they were younger. I gathered up a lot of information before I ever sat down to put a plot to my novel. Much of that opening section, the historical part, is actually true. It comes from histories of the town of Weston. What I wanted to do was establish a certain atmosphere to explain to people, before they ever got involved with the characters or the plot, exactly what it was that made this particular town different. The town was founded in 1620 or 1640 and most people out in California, for example, would find that somewhat incomprehensible, since towns here have been founded primarily during the twentieth century. But that may be a legitimate criticism if it's too slow, as Pat Holt from the *Chronicle* said. Then, well, people are entitled to their opinions.

MURPHY: *There is also a scene in* The Immediate Prospect of Being Hanged *about a racquetball game between Patt Starbuck and a lawyer named Skip. Why did you include that scene?*

WALKER: Yeah, that was kind of a joke, because everybody knows me as Skip. I had written the book originally without including that scene and my editor at Viking thought that we needed one more scene of exposition of the character. We discussed this possibility and it just so happened that I was over at the Bay Club and this thought came to me while I was dressing that you see everybody wearing their gym gear and they all look alike. They could be from any background whatsoever. When they get to their lockers you see people putting on the different uniforms of their workday and all of a sudden the relationship can change between two people who might have been completely equal when they were both in their gym clothes, at least in terms of appearance. And so I added that scene. And just as kind of a little "in" joke, I threw myself into it as the racquetball opponent. Then I sat back and waited for everybody to comment on it and nobody commented until I picked up a copy of the *Recorder*. The reviewer there, whom I don't believe I know, focused on that particular point.

MURPHY: *In your first published novel,* A Dime to Dance By, *a lot of the scenes revolved around talk in a barroom with the main character, Chuckie Bishop, and his old friends. Is this an autobiographical novel?*

WALKER: No. It's really not. What happened was my family moved around a bit. I was going to a prep school, a boarding school in western Massachusetts, and I would spend my vacations with my cousin, who was my age, in the city of Quincy. He was kind enough always to include me in whatever things he was doing at night and on weekends and he would just sort of drag me along. So I would be on the periphery of his group of friends, who really didn't know me but would carry on their conversations. I spent an awful lot of time just listening to what people were saying, always feeling as though I was an outsider and never really included, but enjoying the opportunity more or less to eavesdrop on what other people were thinking, saying, and doing at that particular point in their lives. And much of what I was writing about in *A Dime to Dance By*, many of those dialogues and many of those scenes, are my memories of what I actually heard and what I actually experienced on the periphery of this group back in the mid 1960s.

I remember in particular there was one of this group of friends who did not seem to fit in with the rest. As it turned out, his life has been quite a bit different. He went to MIT and Harvard Law and now he is a lawyer in Boston. When he was around, he was always trying to fit in with the rest of them and be just as tough as they were. When he was away they would all talk about him behind his back because he really didn't fit in. Although he was a friend of theirs, he quite clearly was different from the time he was a young kid. So in some sense Chuckie Bishop came from him. I also remember playing American Legion baseball and there was a star on my team that all the coaches always catered to despite what the rest of us were doing. They were treating him as though he had a very special gift, although he never went beyond American Legion baseball as far as I know. But he did have some talent then and so I also wanted to incorporate his image. What happens to people when they peak at the age of seventeen? What happens to high school athletic heroes when that was the greatest thing that ever took place in their lives? So, Chuckie Bishop was, in many ways, a combination of that star on my baseball team and this other friend of mine who was always part of the group but never quite fit in with the rest.

It is not autobiographical because Chuckie just isn't me. I didn't marry a high school cheerleader or have to get married or become a father at seventeen as Chuckie did. However, some of Chuckie's reactions to situations, as I indicated before, would have been my reactions. Some of the things he said might have been the things that I said. So in that sense it's autobiographical, but the character in this situation was not. I never returned to my hometown, I never practiced in a small city like Chuckie did. And, if anything, I suppose I'm overambitious, whereas Chuckie clearly, like the character Patt Starbuck in *Immediate Prospect*, is underambitious, at least until a cathartic event comes along and propels him into some sort of action to make him make the most of his life. To take advantage of the opportunities and the talents that he has, instead of just wasting them or watching them go by or watching them dissipate.

MURPHY: *Chuckie has a mentor named Sid Silverman and he gives Chuckie a lot of advice on how to practice law, how to get clients. Is this Walter Walker speaking?*

WALKER: Yes, to some extent. I practiced with a firm in San Francisco called Handler, Baker, Green, and Taylor for a couple of years. That was the only time I ever had to bill by the hour. It was brought home to me by my mentors in that firm that a good portion of everything that we did as lawyers was business related. So some of the lessons that they attempted to teach me were lessons that Sid Silverman attempted to pass along to Chuckie Bishop.

MURPHY: *In* The Two Dude Defense *your main character is Hector Gronig. Wherever did you get that name?*

WALKER: This book was written at a different time in my life, back in the mid seventies. I kind of liked the character Hector in *The Iliad*. So that's where that came from and Gronig I tried to make ethnic without being any specific ethnic origin. And it just seemed to me that was the desirable thing to do back then, when I was writing that particular book. But to this date, people still complain about the name. Particularly they say, "I assumed he was an old man and it wasn't until about two-thirds of the way through the book I realized he was supposed to be pretty young."

MURPHY: *The book starts off as pretty much a straight mystery and then Hector gets involved in a lot of bizarre scenes. Were you considering this to be a parody at any point?*

WALKER: No. Somebody referred to it as a stylish mystery and I kind of felt pleased by that because it was meant to be a different kind of mystery detective novel. The mystery was never of primary importance to me. I was trying to write scenes that were entertaining and describe characters who were entertaining and who were based in part on people that I had known or come into contact with or heard about during my first years in San Francisco. There is no character in the book who is definitely somebody I knew, but there were scenes and events and characteristics that were convolutions of things that I had heard about or known of. So, it was supposed to be funny but not a parody.

MURPHY: *You had a scene in the book about a gay Italian gangster named Jimmy the Dog who is in a hot tub with Hector. Where did you get the information for that?*

WALKER: I don't know. Gosh, I just can't remember. I always remember that scene as being very, very funny, though. I thought it was funny while I was writing it. I don't know, I'll have to go back and read it and see if I still think it's funny. But I was really hoping people would read scenes like that and laugh out loud and yet not be lost to the fact that the character Hector Gronig was not a clown. He was a person who was of interest in and of himself, and yet had lessons to learn, and by learning some of those lessons he could improve his life. That's why his wife, from whom he was separated, was to me also an important character because she was the one who was constantly urging him on and trying to get him to learn lessons.

MURPHY: *You mentioned you did some research for* The Immediate Prospect *at the Weston Library and other places. Have you done research for your other novels, too?*

WALKER: Yeah. In fact, when I wrote *A Dime to Dance By*, I quit the firm I was with and decided that at that point—I was thirty years old,

I had been writing at night and on weekends for about six years, and I hadn't had anything published—that if I really wanted to be a novelist, I was going to have to concentrate on it. There had been a political scandal in the city of Quincy that involved a cemetery, where the superintendent of the cemetery, who was a political appointee, was simply digging up old graves and reselling the spaces to people who wanted to have their relatives buried. And it may not seem like too big a deal, but back there it was a very emotional issue because generations of families had lived there and now they were finding out that some of their relatives were simply being dug up and thrown into a dump. I knew about that firsthand because when I was a student I had received a political-appointee job working in the cemetery. I had participated in digging up some of those graves, not because it was my idea, but because somebody told me to go out and dig up a grave. We'd dig it up and would find bones and so forth and we'd say, What do we do with these? And all they told us was, Make sure you don't touch the bones with your hands because you'll get diseases. It wasn't until I read in the newspaper what was actually involved that the issue came home to me.

In any event, the political machine that was in power in Quincy was toppled by a reformist candidate, and I thought this was a quintessential story of small city, New England politics. I was able to bring in a lot of issues about the Irish and Italian conflicts among people who were working there. As I started writing the story, this political scandal got lost and the characters started to take over. But I spent most of the summer of 1980 researching that issue by digging up all the old newspaper accounts and talking to people involved, and again, once I had the framework for the story I sat down to write it and a whole different story came out. But I was comfortable because I knew the framework.

MURPHY: *You mentioned that you do writing on weekends and at nights. Do you do that all the time or do you go in spurts?*
WALKER: No. The only time I don't write on weekends and nights is if I'm involved in a trial or preparation for a trial. Then the writing gets pushed aside. Otherwise, I go home and write from about nine

o'clock to midnight every night, and as much as I can on Saturday or Sunday—usually it means I start at nine and write until about two. Sometimes we go away on vacations or we are invited to do something or I'll go skiing or something, and so it's not a matter of "No, I can't go anywhere or I can't do anything because I have to write," but I certainly try to use all the time that I have when I'm not practicing law or participating in something with my family to write.

MURPHY: *Aside from Ross MacDonald, were there any other authors who influenced your work?*

WALKER: Yes. George V. Higgins, a Boston lawyer-novelist whose books are almost entirely in dialogue. Also Harry Crews, who taught me the importance of making my characters interesting. Hemingway influenced my work. My favorite book ever was *Catch-22*. One thing I learned from Joseph Heller was to make your character likable; make your protagonist, your narrator, somebody that the other characters like as well. Obviously, I was influenced by Chandler, but there is kind of a trilogy of Dashiell Hammett to Raymond Chandler to Ross MacDonald that I think has influenced a lot of writers. Graham Greene is a writer whom I've read a lot, although in recent years I kind of steered away from him. One of my favorite books was Robert Penn Warren's *All the King's Men* and that probably had a great influence on the characters whom I use as my protagonists. Warren's protagonist was observing everything that was going on and didn't seem to be doing all of the things that he could be doing with his life, until finally some event occurs that propels him into action. I would have to say that that was one of the more influential books on my writing.

MURPHY: *One thing I noticed about the newspapers on both the East Coast and the West Coast is that they all comment on the titles of your books. How do you come up with the names for the titles?*

WALKER: The titles of my books are something in which I take a certain amount of pride. I know that as a reader I have always been attracted to certain books by titles so I give titles a great deal of thought and consideration. The first one, *A Dime to Dance By,* was just some phrase that had come to me that I had written down and kept in a drawer for many years. The title may even have come before the book and the two things just seemed to go together. *The Two Dude Defense* was a title that I got from a criminal lawyer who told me that he was in big trouble on a case and he was going to have to apply the old "Two Dude Defense," where his client says, "It wasn't me who did it, it was these two dudes." The lawyer noted that we are lucky that the Dude family is so ubiquitous in this area because they seem to be involved in so many crimes. The title *Rules of the Knife Fight* came from the statement in *Butch Cassidy and the Sundance Kid* when Paul Newman was about to get in a knife fight with a rival in his gang. He pulled a quick dirty trick to come out on top in that fight and admonished his rival by saying, "There are no rules in a knife fight." The title *The Immediate Prospect of Being Hanged*, of course, comes from a paraphrase of the old Dr. Johnson quotation. It goes something to the effect of, "Nothing quite so concentrates the mind as the immediate prospect of being hanged." In each case, these are matters to which I have attempted to give the title a great deal of thought in conjunction with the book that I was writing.

WILLIAM P. WOOD

William P. Wood's novel *Court of Honor* explores the emotional reaction of Judge Tim Nash to his decision to act as bait in a federal sting of his fellow judges. During the course of the sting, Nash learns some surprising things about his colleagues and eventually about his own father, a retired judge.

Wood describes Nash's reaction to these surprises:

> *Nash started driving, hands loose on the wheel. There was one nearly infallible, invariant rule he had learned as a prosecutor, then as a judge. When a file or police report came to him, he was certain of some wrongdoing, no matter how apparently pristine the person's life appeared at first glance. Run a deeper check. Spread the search and something would be hauled back. . . . There are no exemptions. There is no immunity for anyone. There is always something.*

A district attorney in Sacramento before he retired in the early 1980s to write full-time, Wood received a B.A. from Middlebury College in Vermont and a J.D. from the University of the Pacific, McGeorge School of Law.

This interview took place in 1992.

FICTION: *Rampage* (1985) ▪ *Gangland* (1988) ▪ *Fugitive City* (1990) ▪ *Court of Honor* (1991) [released in paperback as *Broken Trust* (1995)] ▪ *Stay of Execution* (1995) ▪ *Quicksand* (1998) ▪ *Law and Order* (2002)

NONFICTION: *The Bone Garden: The Sacramento Boardinghouse Murders* (1994)

—————

MURPHY: *Your novel* Court of Honor *involves a "sting" operation of Superior Court judges in Santa Maria. What inspired you to write about a sting of judges?*

WOOD: I suddenly realized, after having been a DA for five years and working at the California District Attorney Association, a lot of my friends, people I'd worked with or come into contact with, had gone on the bench. I couldn't recall reading an account of what it was like to be a judge: how they act, what they talk about, things that go on when the lawyers aren't around. And that interested me, just showing that world in itself. From a writer's standpoint, of course, it's not just enough to show a world; you have to show it doing something interesting. One of the ways you do that is to subject it to some kind of challenge or stress, or a problem. Frankly, the idea of a "sting" is in the news an awful lot these days and I think that the law enforcement technique of choice, certainly for white-collar and official corruption crimes, is definitely going to be the undercover operation. So the two ideas came together—to show how judges act, how they might react in an extreme sort of moral question, and talk a little bit about how undercover operations are going to become more of a major topic in the nineties.

MURPHY: *You've worked as a prosecutor in Sacramento, where the FBI ran a sting of state legislators. Were you involved in that sting at all as a prosecutor?*

WOOD: No. I'd known some of the people over in the U.S. Attorney's Office, but I didn't have anything to do with any of the capital undercover operations. I did watch some of the trial of one of the defendants, and I knew the judge in the case, so we had a chance to talk a little bit after that was over. I had a chance at that point to see how some of the federal courtroom procedures differed from those that I was used to in state court.

MURPHY: *The protagonist in* Court of Honor, *Judge Timothy Nash, is involved in acting as a bait of sorts for several judges. In the process of telling* *the story, you show a lot of empathy for the judge in terms of the loneliness he goes through, the breakup of his own marriage. Was it important to you, in writing this book, to give the more humane side of being a judge?*

WOOD: Sure. If you're on the other side of the bench and practicing, you tend to view judges as kind of Olympian figures. Even if they're ridiculous or silly or whatever, they're still "different" from everybody else. When you see judges on their own, talking about the problems that they've got—why, these are just people trying to do the best they can with an extremely difficult set of problems and challenges.

A lot of people I know who have become judges never anticipated how lonely it is. It isn't simply a question of not having friends; you can't really talk to them exactly the same way. The judges themselves don't talk among themselves all that often. They don't have the time generally, because they're in their own courtrooms and the day is very long. From the moment of going on the bench, a judge has to treat everybody else in a different way. There's always somebody who wants a favor, always somebody who has a problem, always somebody who's just trying to be ingratiating. The whole kind of normal social banter back and forth really changes utterly once you're on the bench. At least, that's what I observed and that's what these folks are telling me.

MURPHY: *Judge Tim Nash experiences all those problems but he also regrets, at the end, his decision to get involved in the sting and starts to feel sympathy for the judges whom he has enticed into taking bribes. Do you have a general reservation about sting operations?*

WOOD: Yeah. There are stings involving drug cases and then there are these official corruption cases. There may be a difference between the kinds of people you're going after. Certainly, in *Court of Honor*, I thought that—as I had one of the characters say right at the very beginning—these are judges and they have a conscience and a moral sense going in that a lot of other potential criminal defendants don't have. So that might make them "special cases" in a sense. Yeah, I think there is an ambivalence about stings. They really are indispensable in some kinds of cases. On the other hand, they do play an awful lot on temptation. One of the problems that everybody has—

judges, it doesn't matter who you are—is a limit to moral tolerance. You don't exactly know where your own limits are, and stings necessarily test that limit. And Nash, of course, comes up against people he thought would be easy catches in a sting operation and discovered they're not. He discovers people who he thought would be very resistant and they're not. So it was a way of throwing light on human nature. And for that reason, I think it's hard not to be a little torn about stings. They could have a very devastating effect not only on the people who get caught, but, as in Nash's case, the one having to be in the position of being bait like that. In his case it did involve people he had known, but I think it would probably be the same if it involved strangers, too.

MURPHY: *At the same time Nash is involved in the sting, you also have a sub-plot of a criminal murder trial that Nash is presiding over: defendant Evans Soika charged with the murder of a gas station attendant. What parallels between the sting operation and this murder trial interested you?*
WOOD: There were a couple things: The murder case is simply a murder trial. It's very straightforward in the sense that the offense took place, there is certain evidence, you put it on, and the jury makes a decision.

In the case of the sting that Nash is involved in at the same time, the question is: Has a crime even been committed? Are you participating in the creation of a crime? I wanted to draw a contrast between those two sorts of offenses. The murder, obviously, was the most extreme one to use as an example. The other thing, too, was that in the murder case, the killer Soika had taken the gas station attendant hostage and there had been some negotiations that went on about eight hours before things finally came to a head. I wanted to draw some parallels between the kind of useful lies that hostage negotiators tell in order to try to save an innocent person, and the kind of lies and half-truths or shades of truth that Nash uses in the course of the sting. Because, again, the purposes may be similar but the effects are quite different. They are all obviously law enforcement tools, but I am probably a little more ambivalent about that sort of dissembling, that sort of shading the truth in the course of an undercover operation, particularly in these official corruption cases. Unless there's just an absolutely clear-cut violation that's already on record, the possibilities for people to misinterpret actions, for actions to really be transformed under the pressure of money or favors being offered, is very great. I thought that was an interesting question to explore. Again, the whole book really is dealing with the question of how much would it take for you to do a corrupt act, to turn aside an oath, to betray a friendship. The real answer is nobody really knows until it actually happens.

MURPHY: *In the Soika murder trial, there was a lot of maneuvering back and forth, efforts by the defense attorney to get a mistrial. It occurred to me that you were trying to show how much goes into defending someone who seems quite obviously guilty versus the people Nash was enticing into the sting operation who were on the edge. Is that the kind of contrast you were trying to make there?*
WOOD: Exactly.

MURPHY: *There is also in the book a cross-sting, where Nash is tape-recorded by police officers who think he is taking bribes. He thinks they're the ones taking bribes, so we have the state attorney general going against the U.S. Attorney's Office. Why did you put the cross-sting into the novel?*
WOOD: That was to highlight a little bit of the peculiarity of undercover operations, especially in this area of official corruption, where the possibilities of misinterpretation and misperception are so great. In *Court of Honor* what happens, as you mention, is that the cops look at one thing and they assume that this judge is involved in an undercover operation. They mistake him for a truly corrupt judge, and mount their own operation to try and catch him with the help of the state attorney general. Meanwhile, he's working with the U.S. attorney, Department of Justice to try to catch corrupt judges. He, in turn—because of an informant who's participating in his operation—is looking at them as bad cops, as dirty cops.

And I was intrigued by the general possibilities for essentially a dog chasing its tail. That's pretty much what it comes down to—the things they're trying to grab onto. All of these people are so elusive to start with that you can make mistakes very quickly and very easily.

One of the hazards for people who are involved in undercover operations—that they're very aware of, and that happens fairly frequently
where competing agencies or individuals don't know who in fact
they're talking to, don't know what in fact is going on—you have
different agencies fiddling around with different agencies rather than
criminals.

MURPHY: *The sense of discovering secrets pervades* Court of Honor. *Tim
Nash, in the course of proceeding with Operation Broken Trust, finds out
about some past misdeeds of his own father, a former judge. Why did you
insert the past problems of Tim Nash's father into the plot?*
WOOD: One of the reasons was that Nash has led a very insulated life.
He kind of went onto the bench because of his father's intervention.
His father was a very respected member of the community and a
well-respected judge. So Nash's movement from being a lawyer and
then getting on the bench was kind of a royal prerogative; it was simply assumed it was going to happen.

One of the things that I was interested to do was stir things as far
as he was concerned: What happens to somebody who is at the center of community life, who has been subjected to pressure of not only
having to put friends in jeopardy, but also to the possibility that his
father has committed some wrong in the past, and thereby gotten
caught up in various kinds of things.

It was a way to highlight the character. I wanted to make sure that
one of the characters at least would say that part of the problem is
that everybody has secrets. Everybody's got something that they'd
just as soon not have public or not have talked about. What Nash by
accident comes across is a major offense his father committed years
before that has sorted itself out. But it's had reverberations in his own
life. But for this undercover operation, going after friends and people
he'd known, he never would have found out about it. It would have
passed entirely, life would have been very placid.

There's an example in the book of a tidepool, where the creatures
in the pool are in equilibrium and they're not aware of anything that
can threaten them. The undercover operation is a rock thrown into

this tidepool. Everything is upended. Everything is put in question. And for Nash what happened was he suddenly was faced with a very personal aspect of his own life that was going to be radically transformed because of this undercover operation.

MURPHY: *You portray the leader of Operation Broken Trust, Neil Roemer, the chief public integrity officer, as an ambitious, single-minded individual. Have you come across people like him who were involved in sting operations?*
WOOD: Yes. I had a federal judge who read the book tell me a little while ago that he had met a number of people who reminded him very strongly of the Roemer character. With the exception of Soika, there are no absolutely black-and-white characters in this story. Everybody pretty much operates from decent motives, or at least publicly acceptable motives. Soika's defense attorney, Escobar, for instance, is engaged in certainly a publicly lauded motive in trying to make a vigorous defense of his client. Nash is trying to root out corruption. Roemer is trying to clean up the judiciary or clean up law enforcement.

One of the things I was interested in doing was to have all of these good intentions produce very different consequences, which can happen fairly easily. And to see what happens when very good intentions backfire. How do people react in a situation like that? And in the book everybody has a different reaction. How they're constituted as people describes how they react to having what they thought were pretty good motives and pretty good reasons for doing things suddenly turn around and bite them.

MURPHY: *Roemer chooses Santa Maria as the site for his sting for a variety of reasons, including the size of the city and the type of people there. Why did you choose Santa Maria?*
WOOD: This is a fictional city. It is not the actual city of Santa Maria in California. It had characteristics like Sacramento, where I spent a lot of time. Yet it wasn't going to be Sacramento, but a northern California city of some size without being the state capital. That made it a more interesting area to look at, frankly, as opposed to setting it in a real city.

MURPHY: *I'm glad you explained that because I remember one passage in the book where it took somebody an hour to go from Santa Maria to Sacramento and I thought that didn't sound right.*

WOOD: I can believe it. Even worse, when my first book was made into a movie, *Rampage*—I have set three books in Santa Maria, this fictional city—the director sent two people down to the city of Santa Maria to scout locations there. They had to report back to him after they got there that this is a little dinky town. It doesn't look like anything, at least for their purposes in the movie. So at that point I had to tell them that it was not a real city, it was just a fictional city—completely.

MURPHY: Rampage *involves capital punishment?*
WOOD: Yes. It's about a serial killer and the insanity defense, a very down-to-earth, very tough look at what happens in a long trial of a serial killer. The director is William Friedkin, who did *The French Connection, The Exorcist, To Live and Die in L.A.* He has a very powerful way of getting authenticity to a scene and to action. It's a courtroom story, but there's a fair amount of action in the story as well. So I think it's a very strong picture.

MURPHY: Rampage *came out in 1985. Did you base the serial killer on any true crime?*
WOOD: It has a lot of things in it. It has a number of serial killer cases that had popped up about that time. It's based a lot on things that I did in the courtroom. In the book, for instance—this is not in the movie but in the book—there's a county grand jury scene. I had taken cases to the grand jury, but I never read about a grand jury proceeding being accurately shown. I thought, just from that standpoint, it would be kind of fun to do a scene showing how a grand jury actually operated. So the book has a lot of things in there that I did or saw or heard about when I was a prosecutor, and draws on a lot of anecdotal things that happened to me when I was trying cases.

MURPHY: *With so many legal thrillers being written these days, and many of them becoming bestsellers, what makes your books distinctive?*

WOOD: I think because the situations are more unusual than most of the courtroom or legal thrillers that I've seen. I'm far more interested, I think, in the human aspect of what happens to these people. In *Rampage*, for instance, it's not only a story about how the legal system operates, but what happens to survivors, and what happens to people in law enforcement: In a sense, almost, the courtroom, the occupations, just provide a backdrop because, as in *Court of Honor*, the interesting things frankly are who these people are and what's happening to them. The courtroom and the law provide a very interesting backdrop, both because it's an area that people find intriguing on its own and because it does have a moral underpinning. But I'm more interested, frankly, in what happens to the people.

MURPHY: *There are a few well-known mystery writers in the Sacramento area: Karen Kijewski and John Lescroart, for example. Do you consider yourself to be writing in the mystery genre?*

WOOD: No. As you saw in *Court of Honor*, there really aren't any mysteries in a sense. I haven't written any mysteries. In *Rampage* there's no mystery of who's committing the crimes and no mystery of whether he's going to get caught. There's no mystery frankly in that sense at all. The "whodunit" story: Can we stop him before he does whatever he's going to do again? That story interests me as much as "What do we do next?" All of the books I've written explore that question from different angles more than anything else. It's the more human question of "What do we do now?" We have a judicial system, we have to judge, we have to do all kinds of difficult things, and how do we do it?

MURPHY: *Other than the novels, have you done other writing—short stories, that sort of thing?*

WOOD: I'm doing a nonfiction book on the Dorothea Puente trial. When I was a prosecutor I sent her to prison for five years for doping and stealing and forging and I think there was one other crime she pled guilty to. Now, however, she's charged with nine counts of first-degree murder.

MURPHY: *Had you sent her to prison before she committed those murders?*
WOOD: I sent her to prison in 1982. She got out after three and one-half years in 1985 and committed what's now charged against her as her second murder later in 1985, almost as soon as she got out of prison. I went down with two deputy DAs in 1988, while they were still digging bodies up at F Street. So I've been involved in the case obviously for a very long time as it turns out. It's one of the most bizarre experiences, frankly, to pick up a newspaper in 1988 and see a familiar case come back into the public eye in such a terrible way.

MURPHY: *Did you have any indication when you prosecuted her that she was capable of such heinous crimes?*
WOOD: Yes. Unfortunately, the Sacramento Police Department had some suspicions, and right after she was sentenced on the case I had in 1982, I was approached on the phone by a family who said that they had suspicions she had killed their mother. That was in 1982. It has turned out that that particular murder is now charged against her as the first count.